"This is a treasure that every therapist shoul[d] read, with many clinical illustrations, and [re?] who have complex PTSD or a dissociative disorder. The authors never lose sight of the client as a human being and not a disorder, and they provide maps to navigate relational challenges, self-harm and suicidality (including how to navigate the pain of losing a client to suicide), flashbacks, difficulties with memory work, and more."

Kathy Steele, MN, CS, *author and international presenter on complex trauma and dissociation, ISSTD past president and Lifetime Achievement Award winner*

"Lynette Danylchuk and Kevin Connors have produced a book that lives up to its name. It is highly practical and instructive but also highly sophisticated in its presentation of the needs and the treatment of the complex trauma and dissociative client. This book is a guide to both the novice and the more advanced therapist. It offers constant reminders that these clients were extensively damaged by what happened to them and benefit from knowledgeable and relationally responsive and compassionate care in order to heal. I highly recommend this text."

Christine A. Courtois, PhD, ABPP, *coauthor of* Treating Complex Trauma: A Sequenced, Relationship-based Approach *and coeditor of* Treating Complex Traumatic Stress Disorders in Adults *(both with Julian Ford)*

"The second edition of *Treating Complex Trauma and Dissociation* is even more comprehensive and informative than the first and holds a wealth of academic and practical material. This is a book which not only belongs on your bookshelf but is one to be pulled out often for consultation or just to savor and absorb a section. Kudos to the authors for this gift."

Joan A. Turkus, MD, *medical director, Complex Trauma Disorders Program, Dominion/HCA Hospital Falls Church, Virginia; ISSTD past president and Lifetime Achievement Award winner*

Treating Complex Trauma and Dissociation

Treating Complex Trauma and Dissociation is the ideal guide for the front-line clinician whose clients come in with histories of trauma, abuse, self-injury, flashbacks, suicidal behavior, and more. The second edition includes the latest research and developments in treatment for trauma and dissociative disorders. The book is written with the knowledge that survivors may read it, and the authors have consciously maintained the dignity of the survivors throughout. Clinicians will find that the chapters help them develop their own responses and practical solutions to common questions, including "How do I handle this?" "What do I say?" and "What can I do?" *Treating Complex Trauma and Dissociation* is the book clinicians will want to pick up when they're stuck and is a handy reference that provides the tools needed to deal with difficult issues in therapy. It is supportive and respectful of both therapist and client, and, most of all, useful in the office.

Lynette S. Danylchuk, PhD, is a fellow, past president, and Lifetime Achievement Award winner of the ISSTD (International Society for the Study of Trauma and Dissociation). She has been a therapist in private practice, a supervisor, a consultant, and has presented internationally.

Kevin J. Connors, MS, MFT, is a fellow and past president of the ISSTD (International Society for the Study of Trauma and Dissociation), served on the board of directors for the National Partnership to End Interpersonal Violence Across the Lifespan, and also on the advisory board for the Hecht Trauma Institute.

Treating Complex Trauma and Dissociation

A Practical Guide to Navigating Therapeutic Challenges

Second edition

Lynette S. Danylchuk and Kevin J. Connors

Routledge
Taylor & Francis Group

NEW YORK AND LONDON

Designed cover image: © iStock Photo

Second edition published 2024
by Routledge
605 Third Avenue, New York, NY 10158

and by Routledge
4 Park Square, Milton Park, Abingdon, Oxon OX14 4RN

Routledge is an imprint of the Taylor & Francis Group, an informa business

© 2024 Lynette S. Danylchuk and Kevin J. Connors

First edition published by Routledge 2016

Library of Congress Cataloging-in-Publication Data
A catalog record has been requested for this book

ISBN: 978-1-032-10873-5 (hbk)
ISBN: 978-1-032-10871-1 (pbk)
ISBN: 978-1-003-21754-1 (ebk)

DOI: 10.4324/9781003217541

Typeset in Baskerville
by Taylor & Francis Books

Contents

Illustrations

Figures

Tables

Preface

"Oh, ____! What do I do now?"

We've all had those moments—realizing we don't know what's going on, or see what's happening and have no idea what to do to help. Trauma overwhelms people, and renders them momentarily helpless. In working with traumatized people, it is not uncommon for those experiences of overwhelm and helplessness to show up in therapy. Understanding what's going on is one part of the picture. Having some idea of how to work with these experiences is the critical second part that is often missing in training programs.

As the world becomes more trauma-informed, there's been a welcomed humane, and compassionate shift from, 'what's wrong with you', to 'what happened to you?' This has been an opening for genuine healing for the people who are struggling with the impact of being traumatized. When we learn what has happened to them, we see their courage and strength in being alive and available for help. Some come willingly, even desperately, and some who have no choice still manage to authentically show up when they perceive that there may be a better way to live, a healthier, more satisfying life for them.

Every clinician has at least one, the client who lives in chaos, complicating treatment with frequent calls, constant crisis, unremitting self-mutilation, or repeated threats of suicide. They may also come labeled as problematic, oppositional, manipulative, or worse. They present with a confusing history of diagnoses including depression, bipolar disorder, generalized anxiety disorder, borderline, schizoaffective disorder, eating disorders, as well as multiple addictions. With such a complex array of emotional and behavioral difficulties, there are no simple solutions, only a maelstrom of intrapsychic dynamics, overwhelming emotions, and distorted beliefs generating internal storms and external anguish. Difficult therapy is often attributed to the "difficult client", a label that can distance the therapist and result in therapy becoming even harder. The client labeled "difficult" is almost always the person who has survived the most difficult experiences. Survived, but at a cost.

This book synthesizes knowledge about complex post-traumatic stress disorder, attachment theory, and dissociative defenses as well as often overlooked but equally critical issues of power, control and shame. Empathic attunement to this complex interplay empowers therapists to formulate effective and nuanced treatment plans. Client reactions are reframed, shifting from oppositional or manipulative to an appreciation of the nature of their defenses, the history of their abuse, and the direction of their healing.

This is a practical book, emphasizing skills, techniques, and perspectives that help the therapist connect with the client and help the client move beyond therapeutic impasses and acting out behaviors.

We will also address the common reactions of therapists in situations where the client's behavior leaves the therapist feeling lost, frustrated, and confused—some of those "Oh,____!" moments.

The therapist is challenged to identify the trauma in a way that advances the therapy by exploring what is being expressed through the therapeutic relationship. The therapist is challenged to be empathically engaged and sensitive to the dynamics within the client and within the transference. The therapist is challenged to communicate in ways and on levels where language often fails. The therapist is challenged to guide the client through new ways of thinking and perceiving.

Acknowledgements

Over the years, we've all had those unsettling moments—sitting in our consult rooms, looking into the eyes of a person in great distress (pain, fear, anger, shame) and not knowing what to do or say. Some of us are fortunate enough to have had friends and colleagues to turn to for advice, suggestions, and support. Some of us have been able to reflect on lessons taught by other clients. Some of us have stumbled along.

One of the benefits of being able to write this book is to share what we've learned over decades of working with people dealing with complex trauma and dissociation. We've learned from them, and from our colleagues, and it's gratifying to begin to see a lot of what we've learned come out in print, and in presentations. This book is our contribution to knowing what to do to help people recovering from trauma. It's meant to help with those OSM moments (oh, shit! moments) when the therapist needs to say or do something, and has no idea where to start to respond. We've all had those moments, and they have often proven to be transformative, taking us out of preconceived ways of being and into genuine relationships with people we truly care about.

Lynette—

I would like to thank all my friends and colleagues at ISSTD, especially my study group (we've been meeting for over 25 years), Steve Frankel (our great leader), Andrea Rectin, Janice Foss, Kimberly Porter, Kelly Couacaud, and Elizabeth Schenk. For all of my clients—thank you for sharing your journey with me. I learned so much from witnessing your honesty and courage. I also want to thank my husband, Pete, my daughter Lisa, and my son Mike, wonderful, loving, and brilliant people; and Matt, loved forever.

Kevin—

I want to first and foremost thank the brave and amazing people who have allowed me to walk with them on their pathways to recovery and growth. I deeply value and am inspired again and again by what you have shared and taught me. I recognize and honor your courage and fortitude to face the world each day, to risk reaching out.

I wish to thank colleagues who have inspired and educated me -members of the ISSTD, thought leaders from the Institute on Violence Abuse and Trauma, my teammates at the Hecht Trauma Institute—your support, encouragement and wide reaching mentorship has expanded my understanding, and hopefully is reflected and passed on here.

I need to thank the fairest in the land, my wife Susan, who believes in me when I am lost and confused. To my family; Maggie and Nico, Andrew and Kelsey, and to grandchildren; Ash and River who remind me to love and laugh.

An individual having unusual difficulties in coping with his environment struggles and kicks up the dust, as it were. I have used the figure of a fish caught on a hook: his gyrations must look peculiar to other fish that don't understand the circumstances; but his splashes are not his affliction, they are his effort to get rid of his affliction and as every fisherman knows these efforts may succeed.

Karl A. Menninger (1972), Fish Pamphlet. Great Britain, Mental
Patient's Union

Part I

Understanding Trauma and Dissociation

1 Understanding Trauma and Dissociation

The Meaning and Impact of Complex Interpersonal Trauma

They come for help appearing anxious, in pain, angry, or seemingly fine. You may see what they carry in their eyes and in the way they move. Your heart goes out to them and you know you'll do everything you can to help. However, helping is not that easy. There's more to this person than you can possibly see at the first meeting, or in the several that follow.

When a person who has multiple traumas comes in for help, or is sent in for help, there is always more than meets the eye. Trauma layered upon trauma creates a burden that can make it hard to live, hard to work, and hard to trust. That internal burden is expressed externally and indirectly through behaviors often labeled as manipulative and attention seeking. Therapy, built upon a foundation of trust and emotionally intimate dialogue can become stymied in a swamp of mistrust, undermining and challenging your clinical acumen, your intellect and compassion, and the very fabric of the therapeutic relationship. Still, somewhere inside there's a spark of life and hope that has this person seeking something better, trying to heal. They have shown the strength to come in for help, or they've found themselves in a position that requires help.

In order to help traumatized people heal, the clinician needs to learn about trauma and about the individual who has come for help. That sounds obvious, but it's not unusual for treatment to start with no sense of the client's history, or of what happened to this person. More and more, people are learning to wonder what happened to a person rather than immediately judging what is wrong with that person. The recent movement to trauma-informed care has been very helpful in creating an environment of respect for the client and an assumption that behavior may be more of a reflection of the person's trauma history than any kind of flawed personality. The shift in perspective is a breath of fresh air in this field, felt by clients and all those who help them.

This is a significant and critical shift in how the therapist views the client and their behavior. It has been said, "Hate the sin, not the sinner." The person's behavior reflects the complicated context of what that person has had to live through, what they have been forced to survive, the tortured and tortuous relationships they have existed within.

DOI: 10.4324/9781003217541-2

The behavior does not define the person. However the behavior often expresses what the person feels but cannot say. When language is insufficient or unsafe, their actions tell us what hardships they wrestle with, what crosses they bear.

Every client comes from a context, a family, life situation, and culture. People naturally adapt to the situation into which they are born in order to survive. If it's a good situation, healthy and safe, the person can focus on growth and actualization. If the situation is negative, for any reason, the person will need to adapt, using their energy to survive, developing coping mechanisms and missing out partially or completely on developmental stages. It takes a lot to live through traumatizing experiences, and the time and energy devoted to working with trauma diverts that person from working in many other areas of life. There's often little or no time to play, to develop social skills based on trust, and to feel free to explore the world. Most of the person's focus is on survival.

In therapy, behavioral problems emerge. It's inevitable, because the person has been traumatized, and if that trauma has gone on for a long time, that person has not had the opportunity to learn healthy emotional regulation and social exchange. Their patterns and defenses are strong because they've needed to be strong. Changing those patterns is possible, but difficult, like rebuilding the foundation of a house while still living in it.

Add to this, the reality of the social environment that may continue to impact the person negatively through lack of support—physically, emotionally, and economically. Adaptations that have emerged out of the need to deal with trauma in an unsupportive environment are still necessary. Those adaptations can contribute to the person having difficulty accessing whatever support may be available. Their learned distrust of others, their conditioned inability to articulate what they need and, consequently, to be able to identify and accept real help contribute to the challenge of recovery.

At this point in history, the impact of the social environment has become a focus of attention. We use the word "intersectionality" for all the many ways in which a person is impacted by negative social interactions. Kimberlé Crenshaw defines intersectionality as

> a lens, a prism, for seeing the way in which various forms of inequality often operate together and exacerbate each other. We tend to talk about race inequality as separate from inequality based on gender, class, sexuality or immigrant status. What's often missing is how some people are subject to all of these, and the experience is not just the sum of its parts.
>
> (Crenshaw, 2018)

Too often, instead of being understood, the client's behavior becomes a negative label, the person is identified as the label, and treatment becomes focused on managing their behaviors by controlling superficial symptoms. Because the behavior can be chaotic or dangerous, this approach is understandable, and the client may welcome the attempts to control symptoms. However, if symptom management is all that is being done in therapy, true healing may never happen. People with identity problems will often take on the label—it will stick.

For example, a client came in with the diagnosis of Obsessive Compulsive Disorder. She got that label because of her need to check and re-check the locks on her doors and windows before going to sleep at night. No one had asked her about her life history. If they had, they would have discovered she'd been kidnapped from her home and severely abused for years before escaping. No wonder she checked the locks on her doors and windows. It was immediately obvious that this behavior was motivated by trauma, by the desire to stay safe, and not by an Obsessive Compulsive Disorder.

Another client presented with a history of treatment failures marked by her case file being three 3-inch thick binders documenting her struggles in every imaginable kind of group therapy process. Typical of cases like this, she had multiple diagnoses including Major Depression, Bi-Polar Disorder, Schizoaffective Disorder, and Oppositional and Defiant. Throughout her long and storied career with the treating organization, no one had bothered to ask about her history. No one had explored the conflicts and betrayals she had experienced in all major relationships prior to entering therapy.

Complicating the therapeutic relationship were her dissociative defenses—dissociative amnesia, depersonalization, derealization, and dissociative trance states that were the hallmark of her coping with intense affect or conflict. As she withdrew into herself in the face of triggering group content, she became quietly less and less responsive. When the group facilitator would then call on her or ask her to leave at the end of the session, she was so removed emotionally and cognitively from the experience as to be wholly unavailable. The resulting ire of the group leader when faced with her "blatant disregard of the boundaries of the group setting" only served to drive her into further dissociative withdrawal. The therapist perceived her as a problem client, unwilling to accept the structure and rules of the group. She saw the therapist as another in a long line of disappointed and angry authority figures. Worse still, these dysfunctional interactions confirmed, for her, her identity as a failure.

If we view the above dynamic with the understanding of the centrality of the treatment relationship to therapeutic growth, we can easily understand why her treatment failed.

Behaviors do not emerge from a vacuum. They almost always represent a person's attempt to deal with their environment. Human beings naturally adapt to their environment—it's the best way for them to survive. The adaptations are a reflection of the environment in which they were learned. For example, people learn to be manipulative if asking for what they want or need results in deprivation or abuse. Having learned that the direct path leads to failure, they learn to use an indirect path. Another example is the tendency to escalate into crisis. Having learned that the only way out of a crisis is to go through it, people may actually push for a crisis in order to be done with it. That looks counterproductive to many people on the outside, but makes perfect sense in the context of the person's life. That's the point, the behavior does make sense in the context of the person's life, so asking about a client's history, their experiences at home, school, and other places, helps the therapist understand how the behavior may have functioned to help the person sometime in the past.

If the client has been severely traumatized or hurt fairly consistently over a long period of time, asking about their history may not immediately provide much information. The client may not remember or be able to share what is remembered. There may be disruptions in memory, amnesia, and/or avoidance because the trauma is too painful to face. That does not mean the client is "resisting", but means that the client's defenses are protecting them against overwhelming emotions. Nor does it mean that the client won't trust the therapist. The client has no reason to trust the therapist until trust has been developed between them. With betrayal being such a common experience for trauma survivors, that trust may take a very long time to grow.

At the beginning of therapy, both the therapist and client are negotiating a relationship that each hopes will be helpful. Normally, each person is trying their best to show up for the other. Old traumas, especially relational traumas, impact the client's ability to trust the therapist, and the therapist is often challenged by their own comfort level with the intensity of traumatic material.

It is not uncommon for people with multiple traumas to have dissociative issues of varying kinds. Dissociation may serve as a circuit breaker for emotions that are too intense to feel, or it may have evolved into a way of being in the world, or both. Over the course of work with a client, you may see patterns of conflicting and confusing behaviors, a client who may shift from angry and shaming, to shame-filled and despondent, to frightened and frozen, alternately erudite and intellectually challenging, then stuck, quiet, and seemingly able to understand only the most concrete language. Multiple symptoms may include eating disorders, substance abuse, domestic violence, and self-harming behaviors. All of these things may have dissociative elements that will need to be addressed.

Most mental health practitioners are not trained to identify complex trauma and dissociation in their clients. If they know about PTSD, it's mainly in relation to military trauma. If they do know about dissociation, they may only think of the most extreme form of that, Dissociative Identity Disorder, perceive it to be rare, and miss the signs of that and milder forms of dissociation in the clients they see. When the clinician has a comprehensive understanding of trauma based disorders and dissociative defenses, the potential outcome of therapy improves, and more clients get better.

For example, one client came in with very different clothing, spoke with different voices, and behaved very differently in sessions. For a clinician who was experienced with working with dissociative clients, this client was clearly dissociative. His psychiatrist labeled him "psychotic". What helped in that situation was to ask the psychiatrist what he saw in his office, and share with him what was seen in the therapy office. The client may have had psychotic episodes in the psychiatrist's office, and not in therapy, but that was not the case. The psychiatrist was seeing the same behavior and hadn't considered that it could be dissociative. The result of that conversation was that he began to see the client as more dissociative than psychotic, which impacted the medications he prescribed.

The awareness that trauma impacts people has been around for a long time. Back in 1916, Freud described psychic trauma as

> An experience which within a short period of time presents the mind with an increase of stimulus too powerful to be dealt with or worked off in the normal way, and thus must result in permanent disturbances of the manner in which energy operates.
>
> (Freud, 1916)

More recently, the impact of major stressors in a person's life through the Adverse Childhood Experiences Study, has added to our understanding of the consequences of serious stress and trauma on health and behavior (Felitti et al., 1998).

Trauma comes from the Greek word for wound. It may be helpful to reconceptualize Post-Traumatic Stress Disorder as Post-Traumatic Stress Injury. Dissociative Identity Disorder may be more accurate if relabeled Dissociative Identity Adaptation. The important shift is in recognizing that the person's reactions and responses are not because something is wrong or disordered about the person; but reflect the person's attempts to cope with what was done to them.

PTSD and Complex PTSD

A single trauma can have a devastating effect on a child, or an adult. However, with single trauma, there's a sense of "before" and "after", and the shift from pre-trauma to post-trauma is often recognizable to all. Acute Stress Disorder (American Psychiatric Association, 2022) symptomatology is a relatively normal and understandable response to a traumatic experience. If the symptoms persist past one month and certainly if they persist past six months, the person is said to be suffering from PTSD.

In PTSD, the client's phenomenological presentation shows them alternating between a state of extreme arousal marked by hyper-vigilance, irritability, and pronounced startle reactions and a state of withdrawal and numbing marked by flat or blunted affect, social isolation, and constricted behaviors. These alternating defensive behaviors are often exacerbated by intrusive "flashbacks" or profound invasive episodes where past memories are recalled with such cognitive, emotional, and sensory strength as to challenge current reality testing and leave the client unsure and unsettled as to where and when is "here and now". The physiological, neurological, endocrinological, and psychological elements of this disorder make an uncontrollable and unbearable impact on our client's lives, relationships and sense of self.

With the accumulation of traumas, however, the impact becomes complex, and there may not be a "before" sense of self that can be identified. Consider what happens when the trauma is on-going, multiple times per week across 15–20 years. Imagine the abuse starting when the child is most vulnerable and just entering into the crucial period in psychosocial development. Consider what happens when the perpetrator is someone within a close personal, emotionally intimate relationship with our client. Suppose there are no or very limited resources to help the developing child make sense of the daily experience of abuse and neglect.

How does this impact the child's emerging sense of self? How might this inform the child as to the nature and meaning of interpersonal relationships, the value of engaging in emotionally open, vulnerable, and trusting relationships? What intrapsychic defenses might be needed to cope with the sense of overwhelm? Without a stable, nurturing presence, how will the child come to balance conflicting demands?

The resultant cacophony of discordant emotions, intense, unmitigated emotional responses, covert manipulative behaviors, combined with a pervasive sense of mistrust, shame, and powerlessness is the hallmark presentation of the survivor of complex trauma disorders.

A series of traumatic incidents results in complex trauma, but the symptoms of complex trauma can also develop from an insufficient environment coupled with a single trauma. An insufficient environment may mean an inadequate attachment, an unsafe environment such as a dangerous neighborhood or proximity to war, or a background of relatively mild abuse prior to a major trauma. In these cases, the person is already on shaky ground emotionally, and a single trauma can be far too much to handle, causing the person to collapse.

What happens to people during trauma? What Freud describes as "stimulus too powerful to be dealt with" translates into what Daniel Siegel describes as being outside the person's "Window of Tolerance", beyond the person's emotional ability to manage or tolerate, (Siegel, 2020). The window of tolerance represents the levels of intensity, high and low, that can be tolerated by a person, levels within which the person feels able to respond and be in control of himself or herself. People learn their limits, and they will stay within them if at all possible. When the person goes out of their Window of Tolerance, they become non-functional, moving into states of rigidity or chaos.

Trauma either sends a person over the line into chaos, out of control, or below the line, into rigidity. The traumatized person may swing between extremes, going through waves of chaos and rigidity, which gradually decrease over time. While in this traumatized place, the person becomes less able to tolerate new incoming stimuli. Already overwhelmed, not much more can be taken in or dealt with adequately. Simple, ordinary frustrations or difficulties

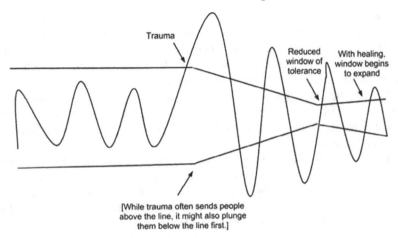

Figure 1.1 Window of Tolerance
Note: Based on Daniel Siegel's concept of the "Window of Tolerance" (Siegel (2020).
Source: Lynette Danylchuk, Ph.D. copyright 2012.

feel like overwhelming crises, and the person can't handle them in normal ways. As the person heals, the waves of emotion subside, and, the ability to self-regulate and function increases. Post traumatic growth is possible, with greater ability to tolerate higher and lower levels of emotional intensity and stay conscious and present. Without healing, however, the Window of Tolerance may remain small, resulting in an inability to deal with intense emotions that come after the trauma.

Developmental Trauma

"Permanent disturbances in the manner in which energy operates" (Freud, 1916) can be another way of describing developmental trauma. The normal development of a child is disrupted because of the overwhelming energy of trauma and the need to survive in hostile environments.

Still another way to think of the impact of trauma is to notice its effect on the cognitive-behavioral developmental concepts of assimilation and accommodation (Piaget, 1952). Piaget describes how infants and children develop from innate reflexes to intentional actions. When all goes well, the child moves from simple instinctual or random experiences into sequenced patterns of behavior aimed at getting needs met.

A key element of Jean Piaget's theory of the cognitive development of the child is the focus on the child's endeavor to understand and master the world around them. The child's developing sense of understanding can be expressed as an increasingly complex series of rules, operations and schemata. Schemas are the building blocks of knowledge. The child may create a schema that is "dog" when first encountering a dog and being told what it is. Assimilation allows the child to see different dogs and recognize them as variations of "dog". Accommodation occurs when a new animal is discovered, perhaps similar to a dog but not a dog, like a pony, for example. If this process goes smoothly the child's equilibrium is maintained. When too much is experienced and cannot be processed, the child's equilibrium is thrown off and that makes learning difficult. Through the processes of assimilation, accommodation, and equilibrium, the child improves and enhances his/her/their means of making sense and operating in the world.

Assimilation refers to the process of integrating new information, new behaviors, and new understandings into the existing ideas, behaviors, and coping strategies while reinforcing current cognitive schema. For example, little Kevin learns to open the door to his bedroom by twisting a knob. He recognizes the door by the outline of the frame and the position of the round knob. Later he goes to his friend Lynette's house for a playdate and is told Lynette's in her room and to go play there. Lynette's bedroom door looks somewhat the same, with an outlining frame and hinges along one side, but instead of a round knob, there is a lever. After a moment's reflection, little Kevin tries twisting the lever as if it were a round knob. Success! Mastery! The door opens. He has accommodated to the difference in door handles and assimilated new material, doors can be opened by knobs or levers.

Accommodation identifies the process when the new information absorbed is sufficiently different to cause a shift in the existing cognitive schema. The next time little Kevin goes to visit Lynette, he is told she is outside in the backyard. Alas, the sliding glass door looks nothing like the door in Kevin's cognitive schema, no outlining frame, no hinges, no round knob or lever. He stands stumped and stymied.

Assume for a moment, Kevin's mother, spotting his confusion, demonstrates how to open the sliding glass door. With a newfound sense of wonder and awe, he plays with the door for a few moments sliding it open and closed before going out to join his friend. His concept of what doors are and how they work grows in a wholly new and different direction. Again there is a growing sense of mastery.

When a sufficient level of cognitive understanding and growth occurs, the child moves onto the next stage in learning how to organize and process the world and relationships. As the child successfully navigates this convoluted and complicated course, the emerging sense of self is one of mastery, adaptability and adjustment. The child is an active participant in the search for meaning and understanding. The parent and other adult caregivers play key parts in empowering and facilitating the child's search for meaning.

In the above examples, we cannot exclude other important developmental dynamics. First, consider when our hero is successful at opening the door with the lever or learning to operate a sliding glass door. Little Kevin has added to a developing sense of mastery and autonomy (Erikson, 1959). His developing sense of self grows in a positive and integrated fashion.

The second dynamic to consider is the quality of the relationship between little Kevin and his mother. We assumed she was a "good enough caregiver", empathically attuned to discern his distress and supportive enough to provide information and encouragement to help him master the sliding door. However, what if she fails in that role? Imagine that she and Lynette's parent arrange the playdate as an excuse to drink. In her frustration and anger at being interrupted by a disappointed and tearful child, she yells and smacks him. Little Kevin not only fails in that opportunity to learn how to manage the door; he is overwhelmed with a sense of shame. The breakdown in the processes of learning (assimilation, accommodation, and equilibrium) causes conflict and confusion in the developing sense of self.

When the shame, the hurt, the confusion, and/or the conflict become too much to manage, the disruption to the sense of self is too much to be integrated into a comprehensive whole. The process of dividing and compartmentalizing the disparate ways of being, of unmanageable and conflicting cognitive schema begins to involve dissociation.

As children grow and develop these cognitive maps, there is a balance of how much and how fast the new information can be absorbed. Piaget termed this process "equilibrium". When the child has too much coming at him, there is not enough time to assimilate new material and equilibrium will not be reached. Blocking out material or dissociation is not a choice at that point, but a response to an inability to take in too much emotional information.

Children are taught to identify and manage their emotions through interactions with their parents. When the parent is healthy, the effect on the child is obvious, emotions are acknowledged and correctly identified, and the parent continues to be with the child and guide the child through intense emotions with equilibrium, teaching by example that emotions can be expressed through words, heard, and dealt with to the point of calming down and returning to a place of stability. The following is a real story, something observed on a very busy day out shopping.

The Mother at the Mall

At a large shopping mall, shortly before Christmas, a mother was coming out headed for the parking lot. She was pushing a baby stroller covered with packages and bags from different stores. There was an infant in the stroller and by her side, holding onto one hand, was a small boy, perhaps three or four years old.

The boy was screaming and crying, "I want the 'Captain Red Rocket' toy!" The mother was calmly trying to tell him that Christmas was coming and that perhaps Santa would bring him the toy. The little boy would have none of it and kept crying for the toy. When tears and pleading didn't work, he screamed in frustration and with all the rage that a youngster can muster, "I HATE YOU!"

Gently his mother replied, "I know you're disappointed, but just wait and Santa will bring you the toy."

Having none of this, he continued to rage and the mother responded to each volley with continued and unwavering patience, re-framing his anger as disappointment. When his anger failed to deliver the goods, the little boy brought forth the big guns. "I don't love you! I only love Daddy!"

Nonplussed, the mom came back with, "I'm glad you love Daddy."

Not ready to give up, the boy changed tactics. "I don't want to hold your hand."

As they were approaching the busy parking lot, the mom explained he needed to hold on for safety's sake. Then she offered him the choice of holding her other hand. Able at last to exercise some power and some control in the situation, he elected to hold her other hand. She carefully guided him behind her back and around to her other side where he took the proffered hand. Off they went to the family car.

This story highlights the role of the "good enough caregiver" in teaching affect modulation, in developing affective awareness and in introducing an effective emotional vocabulary. In this story, the mother practices and models affect modulation both through her mannerisms and behaviors, by not reacting with anger and escalating rage at the small child's demands. She also identifies and re-frames the child's anger as disappointment. The mother's use of the word "disappointed" helps the youngster to recognize nuances and feelings beyond simple rage and gives him new words to better express himself. The maintaining of safe boundaries ("You have to hold my hand in the parking lot.") is balanced by the development of the appropriate levels of power and control ("Which hand would like to hold?").

Considering both the discussion of Piaget's theory of cognitive development and the example above, we look at the emergence of the child's sense of self as growing out of this complex interaction between the child's internal search for understanding, the successful navigation of the obstacle course comprised of countless developmental tasks, and the supportive input and guidance from "good enough" caregivers. When all works well, such a child grows into a healthy, mentally and emotionally flexible adult.

A strong sense of self emerges out of this kind of environment, where a young child can express emotions and have a parent help both accurately identify them, stay lovingly connected to the child, and keep the child safe. The energy of the child can then go into integrating new experiences and knowledge within a stable environment. Like a young plant with adequate soil, water, and sunlight, the child can grow strong, able to withstand future storms. In traumatic situations, the child is like a seedling inadequately planted, struggling to survive, and easily uprooted. That's not the child's fault. In many situations, it's not the parent's fault either, but the reality of an unfair, problematic, or dangerous environment.

These key developmental tasks are often not adequately addressed when a child grows up in an abusive home. In dysfunctional families, the child's attempts to protest or complain are seen as threats to the parents' control and power. Labeled as misbehaving, rude, insolent, pushing back, or worse, the child is often subjected to reprisals and further maltreatment. Abusive parents do not help the child to develop a sense of authority, power, and control. Nor do they help the child to develop the linguistic skills necessary to identify the abuses occurring or to detail the impact of those abuses.

The enabling parent, silent partner to the abuser, is usually reluctant to acknowledge the abuse and avoids their own feelings as well as any feelings toward and awareness of the child. To maintain the homeostatic fiction that abuse is not occurring, dysfunctional parents in turn teach their children to ignore their feelings and thoughts. The dysfunctional parent further denies the child's experience and/or distorts and warps what the child reports. Thus the child grows up without a healthy, comprehensive, affective vocabulary and without the ability to identify and understand their feelings.

Correspondingly, our clients have significant difficulties expressing themselves. They have difficulty identifying their emotions and any concomitant physical sensations. They may lack all but the most rudimentary words for their emotional experiences. They fluctuate between fearing any expression of displeasure to bouts of uncontrolled rage. The thought of saying "No" can strike terror in their hearts.

Human beings take a long time to mature. Our brains don't fully develop until our mid-20s. So, for a few decades, we are actively developing our brains, learning about who we are, who others are, how the world works, what's expected of us, what the rules are, and what happens when those rules are broken. Our identity comes from all of our experiences, a collective sense of who we are that is felt within ourselves and validated by others. When the environment is unstable, people will automatically do whatever works to survive. Survival takes priority over development. The more often a child has to focus on survival, the more that child will have skipped healthy developmental experiences.

Development of the Self

Object Relations, Erikson's psychosocial developmental model, and Attachment theory posit that the self evolves through interactions with others (Erikson, 1950; Klein, 1935, as cited in Svrakic & Zorumski, 2021). Judith Herman suggests that the breakdown in the ability to be in relationship with one's self and others is a central element of psychological trauma (Herman, 1997, as cited in Parish-Plass, 2020).

Survivors repeatedly re-invent themselves, attempting to conform to demands of intended partners. Narcissistic demands and attachment wounds created within dysfunctional families disrupt normal developmental processes (Sar & Öztürk, 2007). Attempts at adapting to perpetrators' shifting ultimatums and abuses leads to the creation of inauthentic self-states (Atwood & Stolorow, 2016; Schimmenti, 2017). An overwhelming sense of shame may lead to the child hiding from themselves as well as others by creating a "false self" (Parish-Plass, 2020).

Multiple psychological theories posit that the Self develops in relationship with others. Erikson (1950) suggests the Self evolves and grows as the person attempts to resolve different developmental crises across the lifespan. These crises involve cognitive, affective, and relational challenges. The resolution, or failure to resolve, of each individual crisis lies in the interaction between the person and significant others in the person's life at that time. It is important to note the shift from parents to peers to partners as the person matures (Gerson, 2014).

Attachment Theory describes the four fundamental modes of attachment, secure, insecure-avoidant, insecure-ambivalent, and disorganized, arising from the dynamic, dyadic interplay between child and caregiver. The empathic and attuned interchanges, non-verbal and preverbal, lead to the child's subjective sense of being safe and secure, valued and valuable.

Erikson's stages of psychosocial development track the development of a person's "ego identity". Identity is the fundamental organizing principle involving experiences, relationships, feelings, beliefs, values that coalesce into a gestalt of our subjective sense of self. This conscious sense of self is constantly evolving, and grows more stable and enduring over time. The challenges and conflicts that Erikson posed correlate to and help inform our understanding of attachment styles and how they manifest in a person's sense of identity.

Stage 1: Trust vs Mistrust (0–18 Months)

Is the world a relatively safe and welcoming place; or is it rejecting, cold, uncaring?

Consistently good enough parents attend to the infant's physical and emotional needs. Those care-givers who engage in empathically attuned interactions with the infant create secure attachment. Failure on the part of the parent or care-giver to emotionally bond with the infant sets the stage for insecure attachment styles. The lack of secure attachment translates into the infant's sense of mistrust (Sege & Harper Browne, 2017).

Stage 2: Autonomy vs Shame and Doubt (18 Months to 3 Years)

The child is beginning to develop, assert, and master basic tasks and functions (food preferences, feeding themselves, toilet training, choosing toys or clothes they like).

Parents allowing, supporting, and reassuring their child's attempts at independence, who provide safe spaces and guidance for their child to play independently, who supportively, not punitively, encourage toilet training, help the child develop a secure attachment base. Anger and criticism can foster insecure-avoidant attachment while inconsistent criticism and praise may contribute to insecure ambivalent attachment (Howard, 1991).

Stage 3: Initiative vs Guilt (3–5 Years)

The child begins to assert a broader range of control and power over external events—playmates, toys, and tasks. Freedom to make their own choices must be balanced with safe boundaries and encouragement to make good choices.

Parents help create a secure base by providing guidance and structure, while allowing their child safe space and freedom to assert their own wishes and wants. They support the child in making their own plans, acknowledging and accepting their child's different tastes, preferences, and inclinations. Ridiculing, dismissing, or over-controlling the child may cause the child to feel ashamed and result in the child becoming overly dependent, leading to an insecure-ambivalent attachment style.

Stage 4: Industry vs Inferiority (5–12 Years)

Although the parents are still the primary attachment figures and source of validation, shifts now occur, and teachers, friends, and schoolmates grow in degrees of influence.

Academic and recreational activities help develop a sense of competence. Parents need to support their child's engagement in multiple areas, and respect the child's feelings, likes and dislikes. Continuing to define likes and dislikes leads to a stronger self -concept. Encouragement and approval generate competence and self-esteem. Acceptance and love should remain unconditional and not based on performance. Encourage effort and curiosity rather than strictly focusing on performance outcomes (Malik & Marwaha, 2022).

Stage 5: Identity vs Identity Confusion (12–18 Years)

This stage in psychosocial development centers on realizing a personal identity or sense of self. Adolescents test out new and different identities, separate from those based primarily on their relationship with their parents. Successfully completing this challenge leads to a stronger sense of self. Not succeeding results in role confusion, wherein the person lacks a clear sense of who they are, where and how they fit into a job or a relationship.

Parents of adolescents can support their child by providing physical and emotional space to explore their feelings, beliefs, and values while maintaining healthy boundaries that provide some structure and a safety net. From an attachment perspective, successfully navigating this stage results in a more stable and secure sense of the individual as themselves. Parental anger, criticism, and rejection contributes to the reification of an avoidant, insecure personality. Inconsistent engagement, infrequent interactions contribute to and reinforce an insecure, ambivalent attachment style (Arnold, 2017).

Stage 6: Intimacy vs Isolation (18–40 Years)

The challenge of this stage lies in being able to risk being true to oneself (as that self has emerged over the past 20 years) while entering into emotionally close relationships with other people. As the sense of self is becoming clearer and more stabilized, the ability to enter into a deeper, more emotionally vulnerable, and ultimately more intimate relationship with another person grows. When the sense of self is more secure, the other can be seen as a unique and wholly separate person. From an attachment perspective, the person is capable of entering into an empathically attuned relationship as an equal, able to see the other as a person in their own right and able to care for them. Failure to develop a secure sense of self leads to greater sense of isolation and depression (Mushtaq et.al., 2014).

Stage 7: Generativity vs Stagnation (40–65)

The challenge of this stage is to make a contribution to something greater than one's self. From an attachment perspective, this extends beyond parenting to contributing in the lives of others; in extended families, with friends, and even into one's community and beyond.

The ability to successfully navigate this stage reflects challenges of earlier stages. Being happy with and proud of what one has done reflects the stage of autonomy vs shame. Being connected with others and feeling included is a necessary and essential element of being able to contribute and make a difference, reflecting the stage of trust vs. mistrust. Feeling that one's contributions are meaningful reflects the stages involving initiative vs guilt and industry vs inferiority (Newton, Chauhan, & Pates, 2020).

Stage 8: Integrity vs Despair (65 +)

In this stage the person asks themselves if they have lived a good life, a meaningful life. Can they look back with a sense of accomplishment and fulfillment? Or, do they feel bitter, depressed, and regretful that they were unproductive and that their time was wasted?

From an attachment perspective, successful resolution of this eighth stage reflects a secure and stable sense of attachment and the ability to, in turn, be a secure attachment figure for others (Westerhof, Bohlmeijer, & McAdams, 2017).

As the child grows, with secure attachment figures supporting and encouraging the child to successfully resolve the psychosocial crises posited by Erikson, their subjective sense of who they are grows. The child is free to explore and define for themselves their wants, wishes, and dreams. Over time, an authentic sense of self emerges, coalescing and expanding throughout the person's lifespan.

If the child is raised without the secure attachment base, without support for meeting these key developmental challenges, the child flounders and struggles. Combined with incomplete information or distorted directives meant to promote and protect the parents' need, the growth of the child's sense of Self is distorted and derailed. Seeking attachment and approval, children adjust themselves to meet parental expectations. The absent, uninvolved parent fails to provide a rich and stimulating dynamic field to foster the child's growth and to support the child's exploration. The more controlling and critical the parent, the less secure the child becomes in respect to their own sense of Self. The more disorganized and narcissistically oriented the parental expectations, the more the child invests in trying to meet external demands and pressures (Liotti, 1992).

Rather than explore different ways of being until the child finds authentic modes of expressing themselves, the abused child stifles dreams, subverts wants and wishes, and adopts false "faces" to minimize insult and isolation. As the success of these measures is dependent on the whims of the parent and not the efficacy of the child, the resulting rewards of connection and closeness are spotty and variable at best. Given the randomness and the variability of the reward ratio, the child tries harder and harder at becoming compliant with ill-defined, ambiguous, or non-existent directives. Worse, the child moves further and further away from developing an authentic sense of self.

This dynamic is apparent in the abused child's sense of being externally controlled. The abused child grows up being made to do things and engage in behaviors they fear and/or abhor. Too often the perpetrator offsets their own guilt and shame, by displacing responsibility with phrases like, "Look what you made me do." or "You made me do this to you.". The resultant organizing relational paradigm implies a world of externally controlled people; I make you do things to me and you make me do things to you. Further, if I could just find the right thing to do, the right way to be, I could make you stop hurting me. Again, the abused child seeks to define themselves by externally oriented measures.

This dynamic extends to and complicates treatment, diminishing our client's opportunities for recovery. The strategy of seeking to comply with and meet the needs of the important Other is employed inside the therapeutic setting. The unaware, uninformed therapist may mistake their client's compliance for therapeutic progress. Real growth requires empowering the client to navigate a difficult path fraught with conflicts, disappointments and illuminated by small victories, moments of wonder and appreciation. The therapist navigates an equally arduous path balancing support and encouragement with questions, challenges and curiosity.

When the person has no opportunity to heal, life can become emotionally narrow. The trauma remains, frequently causing intrusive flashbacks, persistent negative cognitions, upsetting thoughts, and shame (especially with victims of sexual assault). With unresolved trauma, people spend a lot of energy staying away from the extremes of emotional intensity that feel threatening to their ability to control. Life becomes focused on staying safe and maintaining the feeling of being in charge of one's self. The inability to face normal distress tends to add to the person's feeling of overwhelm. Avoidance and acting out become very familiar strategies, through emotionally shutting down, backing away, or through the use of sex, drugs, disordered eating, violence, or other ways the person has found to escape or express what feels unmanageable. The strategies reflect the person going outside their window of tolerance, and their attempts to get back in it.

In addition, what works for normal stress relief may exacerbate symptoms, at least initially. Meditation is an excellent skill to learn for trauma survivors. However, meditation involves being present. If the client is facing too much emotional or relational material, meditation may trigger another wave of overwhelm.

Learning to use skills like this from someone who is trauma-informed makes a big difference in the person being able to succeed. For instance, meditation for some traumatized people, works best at first if they leave their eyes slightly open. For all trauma survivors, if they can close their eyes and focus on a picture of their own creation, seen as if on a screen just inside their head, between the eyes and up about an inch, makes the effectiveness of meditation a lot better. Focusing on that area tends to calm the mind (Forner, 2016).

> Mindfulness is about awareness; dissociation is about un-awareness. These brain activities are rival brain activities, and it is even fair to say that the dissociative mind is phobic of mindfulness. Knowledge or awareness of anything that is trying to be or successfully being dissociated, is counter-intuitive. Knowing and awareness is tantamount to death, when your body/survival system is dissociating (not know, not aware). It's like your system says "scatter information, do not connect the dots, we can't know how bad it is, we cannot be aware"… Knowledge/awareness when you're trapped or have nowhere to run to will kill you quicker. Knowledge or awareness will result in action, action is not good when you need to freeze and play dead. Not knowing, being numb, unaware may save your life. Mindfulness again, is knowing and awareness. As with all strong interventions, there can be a strong reaction. Mindfulness is a very strong intervention that opens up what is there. This forced attempt at knowing and awareness puts a dissociative system on super high alert. When faced with further threat, what does a dissociative system do? It tends to dissociate more, it works harder at not knowing or becoming aware, to save you.
>
> (Forner, 2015)

Yoga is another practice that is often recommended to trauma survivors for good reason. It involves connecting the mind and body, and most trauma survivors have disconnected inside to some extent. It can be an enormously helpful part of a person's healing. However, there are hundreds of kinds of yoga, and countless numbers of yoga teachers. Matching the type of yoga with the survivor is essential. In addition, it's helpful for survivors to meet the instructor before the class, get a sense of how the class is run, locate the exits, and let the instructor know that he, she, or they may leave early if necessary. Encourage the client to find a yoga class and teacher that supports feelings of secure attachment, to feel seen, safe, soothed, and secure. (Danylchuk, 2015).

People dealing with complex trauma are caught in the middle. They can do a lot of the things that will help, but many of those need to be modified for them. They often are aware of their trauma, which is both good news and bad. It's helpful to know what has caused their distress, and it's very difficult to hold that knowledge and seldom, if ever, have a chance to share it with someone who can hear, and help.

2 Complex Trauma and Dissociation

There is a pain—so utter—
It swallows substance up—
Then covers the Abyss with Trance—
So Memory can step
Around—across—upon it—
As one within a Swoon—
Goes safely—where an open eye—
Would drop Him—Bone by Bone.
                                                Emily Dickinson

Complex Trauma and Dissociation

Complex trauma, repeated trauma without the chance for recovery in between, affects all aspects of life. The body and mind do not have sufficient time to recover, and the impact of stress accumulates. Multiple traumas impact relationships with self and others, increase the need for defenses of all kinds, and take time away from non-traumatic life experiences. Complex trauma includes the experience of repeated traumas, sometimes going back to childhood and continuing from that time. Those experiences may take many forms, including abuse, betrayal, abandonment, exploitation, antipathy, and rejection.

(Courtois & Ford, 2013)

Trauma that occurs repeatedly over time impacts that person's psychological development. Critical stages of development may be skipped, damaged, or incomplete, leaving the person having to address those areas in therapy along with the traumatic events. Developmental Trauma occurs when the person is young, repeatedly abused, and lacks nurturing and healing responses from caregivers, resulting in deficits and distortions in psychosocial development.

When trauma or traumas happen in the context of a relationship, the impact is worse. In general, it is more difficult to heal from a relational trauma than a natural disaster. Natural disasters, earthquakes, storms, fires, etc., usually happen to many people, are publicly known, and help and

DOI: 10.4324/9781003217541-3

support are normally sent as soon as possible. In contrast, relational trauma involves harm from another person, the closer that person, the worse the impact. Relational trauma is often secret or disbelieved, involves betrayal and a loss of trust, with little or no support. Thus, the effects are far worse than trauma from natural disasters (Freyd, Klest, & Allard, 2005).

Complex trauma results in a variety of reactions, generally divided between attempts to avoid the trauma or reminders of it and indirect attempts to confront it. The goal of the behavior, whatever form it takes, is to deal with intolerable events while simultaneously staying apart from full knowledge of the trauma. People are trying to stay within their window of tolerance.

Veterans may go camping to take themselves far away from fireworks on the 4th of July. Well aware that they would be triggered, they avoid that painful and embarrassing incident by leaving and giving themselves a different experience. They are motivated by their trauma and are deliberately avoiding what they feel is intolerable. That is an attempt to self-regulate, and an appropriate act of self-care.

People also use self-harm, problematic relationships, drugs, and alcohol in attempts to self-regulate and manage their moods, while awareness of their trauma history remains blocked partially or completely. The underlying dynamic is a combination of trying to stay safe, and managing emotions, while staying within the person's window of tolerance.

The more severe and long-standing the trauma, the more maladaptive behaviors may be used in the attempt to stay sane and stable. Some of these behaviors are learned, things observed or experienced within the family, community, or culture. They are passed down as ways to deal with overwhelm. They may be the only ways known to the person to deal with overwhelming distress.

Often the maladaptive coping responses can become contradictory and confusing. Sexual abuse survivors may avoid sexual situations, find themselves partially dissociated during sex, take part in promiscuous and dangerous sexual encounters, or engage in varying combinations of these activities. These perplexing and seemingly paradoxical responses often become habitualized behaviors and part of their identity.

Within the dysfunctional war zone of the original abuse, these strategies may work. In the short run, as a means to manage and avoid feelings, they may help. However, in reasonably healthy, good enough relationships, these behaviors are glaringly and woefully inadequate and ineffective. In therapy, people learn new ways to manage emotions, but the new ways tend to take longer, at first, and it takes patience to learn and use these non-harmful techniques before they become quickly effective.

For example, a client became extremely distressed in session, and in her distress, begged the therapist to hit her. The therapist refused, and talked with the client until she calmed down. When the client was back to a calm state, she told the therapist that when she was a child and became upset, her dad would hit her, and she would become calm instantly. Actually, the slap took her from hyperarousal directly into hypo-arousal, but her experience was that all the distressing feelings went away. In talking, she could see that the therapist had calmed her down in a way that allowed her to stay present and feel real, and that felt better to her than how she would have felt if slapped. She'd never been taught how to become calm without violence, and actually didn't know what "calm" meant. To her, it was the same as "numb". The experience with the therapist gave her a new way to understand "calm", and a realization that her past experience did not help her get there at all. It was a faster shift out of overwhelm, but it had simply taken her from above the line to below the line, and hadn't helped her come back to herself.

In working with war veterans, one of the coping patterns that would often show up would be to move from that numb place by getting in situations that evoked the same adrenaline rush as was felt in the war, such as becoming an emergency medical technician, or other emergency-related job, returning to crisis situations in an empowered way. Less adaptive were the high-speed car or motorcycle driving, swimming in dangerous waters, gambling, and walking in areas where they were likely to be attacked. For many of these people, those were the only situations that managed to pull them up from below the line of the window of tolerance. They accomplished that by throwing themselves over the line, a place that felt familiar and alive, but once again in danger.

Whereas the first client needed to learn what "calm" felt like and find healthy ways to get to that state, the veterans throwing themselves above the line in dangerous situations needed to learn what being normally alert meant and awaken themselves in safe ways to that state.

In some cases, where trauma occurs repeatedly and the person is denied the time or support to heal, the extremes of emotion or conflicts may be dissociated. In these situations, the person attempts to stay in the window of tolerance by separating from the trauma, splitting off from it as if it happened to another person. Imagine the child who fears being close to a molesting father at night, who then has to approach the same parent in the morning to receive lunch money for school. Imagine a child being hit by her mother, who needs the mother's comfort, but she is the one who is hurting her. Neither child can run away from the parents, each is wholly dependent on them for physical survival. Nor can either remain in close emotional connection with such terrifying figures.

To further complicate the situation, children have no one to turn to to help them make sense of this overwhelming conflict, to identify the mutually exclusive aspects of the paradox internally or externally. Gregory Bateson was close when he described the classic "double-bind". (Bateson et al., 1956) The result is not schizophrenia, but a dissociative disorder. A common strategy in these cases is to have two ways of being, one that is connected to the abuse and one that is not. This is adaptive to the situation. The intolerable is put aside in the psyche, keeping the child able to survive and take in as many of the positive aspects of life as possible. This "putting aside" may be a split in consciousness, such as Marilyn Van Derbur's "day child" and "night child"; her conscious living during daytime as a happy, healthy child, and her experiences of incest by her father at night. Those two on-going types of experiences were incompatible and remained separate in her psyche for decades, first allowing her to become Miss America, and then leading to a collapse and flooding of memories in middle age (Van Derbur, 2003).

This dissociation or compartmentalization can be adaptive while in the trauma, but it is frequently maladaptive in non-traumatic situations. On-going trauma in early life that results in a dissociative disorder will result in the person being unable to integrate traumatic events into on-going consciousness. Just as Marilyn blocked out her night-time trauma, others may need to block out repeated abusive events, unable to integrate them into the rest of their life. The more time and events are left unintegrated, the more the person leads a compromised conscious life. When the blocked events are brought to light, many people may be able to acknowledge them, knowing them to be true. Others, those who have dissociative disorders, may know the truth in some parts of their mind, but genuinely not know it in others and can, therefore, deny the truth when it emerges, truly unable to feel like that experience happened to them.

Dissociative disorders result in a disruption of self-awareness, and relatedness. The feeling of self can be affected through derealization, depersonalization, fugue states, and gradations of Dissociative Identity Disorder. In derealization, the external world feels unreal. In depersonalization, the people feel removed from themselves, as if watching themselves from another place. Fugue states involve amnesia for personal identity, are generally short-lived, and reversible. Whenever dissociative symptoms are present, the client may know or not know what happened, sometimes within the same session as aspects of the self connect with the truth and then disconnect because that truth can't be tolerated.

Complex trauma can involve some or all of these dissociative defenses, but the person still manages to develop a coherent sense of personal history and self that serves as home base, a place inside that remains consistent over time. The personality does not feel split, and the person's history is known, even if at a distance. The emotional impact of the traumas is what the person needs to address, learning to tolerate what was originally overwhelming, and coming to a place in which the body and mind can be conscious and relaxed.

When the situation is severe enough to cause the person to become unable to remain present, the result can be a dissociative disorder. As was said, with depersonalization, the person will feel removed from the self, an experience of feeling unreal. With derealization, the person feels removed from the rest of reality, as if reality weren't real. Somatic dissociation can also occur, with conversion disorders and other disruptions of the integrity of consciousness and the body. With Dissociative Identity Disorder, the most complex dissociative adaptation, the person will not have a solid sense of self within, but will have developed many different ways to be so they can respond to conflicting demands from others, and the need to know and not-know their own history.

What do we mean by "dissociation"? As Paul Dell explains, dissociation (noun) is generally used by clinicians in a way similar to other diagnoses, as in referring to dissociation in the same way one would refer to depression, or anxiety. Dissociative (adjective) refers to symptoms, also a use similar to other diagnoses, such as saying a client is dissociative, or anxious, or phobic. When used as a verb, however, "dissociate" can lead to some confusion, because it infers a conscious effort, describing the client as doing something. Saying, "the client dissociated", sounds like they did something, as does saying, "the client dissociated the memory". Therapists don't use other diagnostic words in the same way. The client doesn't "depress", or "bi-polar", that doesn't make sense because it implies an act that includes volition of some kind. And yet, people say, "she dissociated", and that can give people the impression that the client chose to dissociate rather than has shown a dissociative symptom (Dell & O'Neill, 2009). When people use the word "dissociative" in either of these last two ways, it can feel as if the client is being held responsible for something they cannot control, and that often increases the feelings of shame and powerlessness too familiar to these people.

What happens in therapy when the client is unable to stay conscious in a consistent way, when important or critical issues are not within conscious reach or the person's presentation shifts so completely that the experience is of dealing with another person? Most therapy relies on the client being able to have consistent and intentional consciousness. People with dissociative issues, from relatively mild forms of dissociation to Dissociative Identity Disorder, lack that ability to varying degrees. Undiagnosed, unrecognized dissociative processes are a significant confounding factor in the treatment of complex trauma clients.

Generally, interventions that are primarily cognitive in nature do not work as well with dissociative clients as they usually do with others. While those cognitive skills have an important place in treatment, they are not as effective with dissociative clients because when the person is in a dissociative state, that cognitive skill is not available, and so, it can't help. In some cases, the focus on cognition may result in people who are dissociative feeling worse about themselves; because they can't use it at will, and can't do what they witness others doing, and that feels like another failure.

Another example of how cognitive work may not be enough for dissociative clients is having some part of the person knowing that what happens in a flashback is not currently happening and still not be able to stop the flashback. Over time, it does help the person develop a "split screen", becoming partially aware of current reality while in a flashback, but it seldom stops one in its midst. The flashback doesn't come from the frontal cortex, the seat of reason, and it typically overwhelms rational capacity. Similarly, when a person is dealing with Dissociative Identity Disorder, one aspect of the person may have great cognitive abilities, and be so completely blocked from other aspects of the self, that the knowledge doesn't get through at all, leaving part of the person caught in outdated ways of thinking. In some cases, there will be part of the person's mind that functions as an inner observer, watching the self be caught in past trauma, completely unable to help, which can reinforce a sense of helplessness and powerlessness felt originally in the trauma itself, an internal re-enactment.

Dissociative defenses and Dissociative Identity Disorder involve consciousness tied to survival, physical and emotional, with the ability in DID to be in alternative, frequently non-compatible, self-states according to the person's need to respond to a situation or to block consciousness from trauma. Pierre Janet, describing dissociative defenses, said,

> they embody painful experiences, but become autonomous by virtue of their segregation from the mainstream of consciousness... ... (they) did not belong to the personal consciousness, were not connected to the personal perception, and lacked the personality's sense of self...
>
> (Janet, 1907)

The person with DID is one person who experiences life as if many people, many "me's" and "not me's", and some people with DID call themselves "plural". Although adaptive in traumatic situations, dissociation can make non-traumatic life extremely difficult.

In Dissociative Identity Disorder, the experience of the person while in the window of tolerance appears normal, and in the Structural model of dissociation is called the Apparently Normal Personality (ANP). Meanwhile, the person's other emotional states may be above or below the line, and are called Emotional Personalities (EPs). For dissociative people, the ANP, while seemingly normal, has a much narrower range of emotional tolerance. In some cases, there is little or no emotional connection for the aspect of the person seen as the ANP. When emotion does enter the scene, even a little can be experienced as too much, and the person will slip into an emotional aspect that carries a different sense of self, an EP. The more severe and long-standing the trauma has been, the more ANPs and EPs may be present in the person's internal psychological system.

With treatment, the person with DID learns to tolerate and integrate greater amounts of emotional material, and the Window of Tolerance grows larger, incorporating the history and experiences that had been separated in the Emotional Personalities, resulting in an integrated person.

In dissociative clients, different aspects of the self often form patterns that attempt to move the person back into their window of tolerance. Since that window is narrow, the person is often triggered into other self- states. Those states may or may not have their own names. The differentiation between parts of the self varies with each client, a reflection of the client's needs and capabilities. Highly anxious parts may signal the emergence of parts with little or no emotional valence. Very depressed parts may activate energized parts which become upset or bored with the lack of energy in the person's

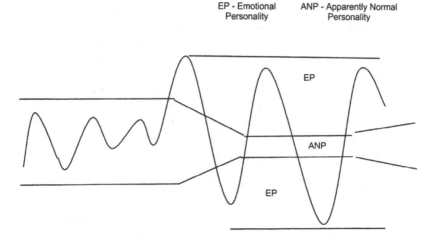

Figure 2.1 Window—after chronic trauma, with inability to recover between traumas
Note: Window of tolerance is smaller. Person reacts in keeping with unresolved trauma, hyperarousal reactivity, or hypoarousal response. In dissociative disorders, EPs and the ANP may be separated by amnesic barriers, or may interact, experiencing different parts of the self as "me" and "not me".
Source: Lynette Danylchuk, Ph.D.copyright, 2012.

system. Sometimes these strategies work fairly well to keep the person close to their window of tolerance. Sometimes they don't work at all and have the effect of exaggerating the swings between hyper and hypo-aroused states, chaos and rigidity, and the person's inner conflict becomes obvious. One of the reasons why dissociative clients may not be identified as often as they should be is that a dissociative system, when functioning well, is virtually invisible. It's so adaptive to the environment that others may not notice the shifts that happen internally to match the external demands on the person. That's why it may be helpful to think of Dissociative Identity Disorder as Dissociative Identity Adaptation, identifying the adaptive function of the dissociation.

People with dissociative issues other than DID may manifest their distress through shifts in consciousness or through somatic symptoms. Consciousness may be impacted by trance states, depersonalization, derealization, fugue states, and catatonia. Somatoform dissociation, as defined by Nijenhuis, "designates dissociative symptoms that phenomen-ologically involve the body. The adjective 'somatoform' indicates that the physical symptoms suggest, but cannot be explained by a medical condi-tion or by the direct effects of a substance" (Nijenhuis & van der Hart, 2011, p.12). Somatoform dissociation can manifest through analgesia, anesthesia, freezing, motor inhibitions, submission, and delayed pain (Nijenhuis & van der Hart, 2011, p.169).

Models of Complex Trauma and Dissociation

The Ego State Model

The Ego State Model was originally developed by John and Helen Watkins. They described it as follows.

> We define an ego state as an organized system of behavior and experience whose elements are bound together by some common principle but that is separated from other such states by boundaries that are more or less permeable. Such a definition includes both true cases of multiple personalities and those less rigidly separated personality segments that lie in the middle of the differentiation-dissociation continuum and that may be more "integrated" and hence more adaptive.
>
> (Kluft & Fine, 1993)

In this model, it is seen as normal for people to have ego states they are aware of and can access at will, such as shifting between relaxing with friends and performing at work. In this case, ego states are often role related, conscious, and appropriate. In traumatized people, ego states may need to be more defined and varied, according to the needs of the situation, and some of those ego states may need to be unaware of others, their roles or functions so incompatible that they cannot function in a single consciousness. Severely traumatized people may have many ego states that emerge to deal with good and bad events, work, school, family, etc., and they may have varying degrees of dissociation between those states.

In the picture below, the first circle represents ego states in a normal person. The boundaries between them are permeable, and the person experiences all ego states with the same consciousness, aware of shifts and able to shift on purpose if the need arises. In the second picture, there is an ego state that is separate from the rest of the person, walled off within. That could represent an experience that hasn't, or can't, become part of the whole person for some reason, a blocked memory from a single trauma, a set of memories from complex trauma, or a dissociated memory. The third picture shows how the separated ego state can feel removed from the rest of the self. A good example of the third picture would be Marilyn Van Derbur's split mentioned earlier between Day Child, present most of the time, winner of the Miss America beauty pageant, and Night Child, present in the incestuous relationship created by her father. (Van Derbur, 2003)

The fourth picture illustrates dissociation, many separate ego states, with rigid boundaries, and the possibility of operating independently of other ego states. Still, the person is still one person, and the ego states with their clear and solid separateness all reside in one body and brain. It's critical to remember this while interacting with people who have DID. All those separate parts are different experiences within the same person. Their sense of separateness is very real, but they are all part of one person. The next to last picture illustrates that reality.

Notice, also, that the first picture shows permeable internal boundaries with a circle that has a solid line separating it from the outside. That represents a person with an internal locus of control, which means that the person has a coherent sense of self from which he, she, or they can make decisions about likes and wants that are genuine, coming from within. In the last picture, the circle has solid lines dissecting it and a permeable line surrounding it. That reflects an external locus of control which means the person is organized to respond to what others want and need, and may not even be aware of their own desires and needs. An external locus of control often goes along with hypervigilance, the need to pay attention to the outside world and meet the needs of others in order to survive.

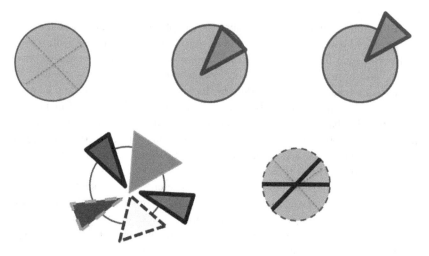

Figure 2.2 Ego State Model

The BASK Model

Another way to conceptualize complex trauma and dissociation is through a component model created by Bennett Braun who describes traumatic experience across four domains: Behavior, Affect, Sensation and Knowledge. When a person is traumatized, their memory can be retained in one or more of these domains, effectively fragmenting or blocking out part of or all of the experience from normal conscious integration.

Braun's model is a continuum.

> The continuum runs from full awareness—through suppression, which is a conscious putting-out-of-mind of something we don't want to think

about— through denial, which is a mechanism we use until we have the capacity to cope in other ways—through repression, which Freud identified as being due to pathological psychological conflict—to dissociation itself, which I believe includes repression, but unlike the classical definition of repression, has a major NPP (neuropsychophysiologic) component.
(Braun, 1988)

When people are traumatized, the experience can be so overwhelming that the brain cannot process all the information flooding the system. That information remains, but not integrated into a coherent narrative (see a discussion of the neurobiology of memory formation in Chapter 3). The trauma may show up in behaviors, affects, or physical sensations that don't match the current situation. Similarly, the person may experience thinking and feeling in ways that are inconsistent with their present surroundings and the current event.

A mild and common version of this dynamic is to feel like a child in trouble and called to the principal's office when receiving a summons to talk to one's boss. There's a feeling of emotional regression, often accompanied by anxiety and even shame, as if one had done something wrong, emotions from the past triggered in the present. Most adults can laugh at themselves and meet with the boss without difficulty. Some people can't do that unless they manage to push away the old feelings or have them blocked out of consciousness with dissociation. In more intense situations, behavior from the old trauma may leak out and sabotage the person, as when one trauma survivor was stopped for questioning by the police and started physically fighting with them, flashing back to a time when she was attacked and had to fight for her life. In each of these cases, a portion of the old trauma was felt in a current situation, impacting the person to varying degrees.

The disconnected elements of the traumatic experience, Behavior, Affect, Sensation, and Knowledge remain in the mind like pieces of a puzzle. In therapy, each piece is an important part of a larger "gestalt". At the beginning of the process, the individual pieces may not make sense, just as attacking the police made no sense at all in current life. Eventually, the pieces fit together well enough that a coherent narrative emerges. This process takes patience and acceptance of how the mind holds on to trauma. Once the pieces are put together, the reality of the trauma may be confronted.

A crucial consideration is whether or not the client has the skills and support to deal with the trauma, the conflicting feelings and cognitions, and the potentially overwhelming affects. If so, they can tolerate attending to the memory, grieving the experience, and exploring new ways of understanding the event. If not, the client may feel revictimized, unable to withstand the onslaught of intolerable thoughts, sensations, and feelings. In the latter case, they may need to re-dissociate the material using whatever means possible, such as self-injury, drugs, alcohol, and/or interpersonal crises in order to regain a sense of equilibrium. Often, new clients are caught up in a maelstrom of dissociated bits of the traumatic events breaking through to conscious awareness without the prerequisite support, skills, and understanding to manage the experience. Their use of these dissociation enhancing behaviors earns them the unwarranted title of "difficult".

The Sequential Model

The Sequential Model is a model of a dissociative process. It focuses on the process within the person, how dissociation, both DID and OSDD (Otherwise Specified Dissociative Disorder), works in the person's life. When the function is identified, it can be easier for the person to see how the dissociation has been helpful in responding to traumatic events, and that can lower shame and help the person learn to value all parts of the self.

The very simple illustration below shows how this model works. Annie is the child in an untraumatized state. In this state, she's fine. Then her father comes home, smelling of alcohol, and Annie shifts into Betty, a part of the self that tries to placate Dad. When Betty's strategy doesn't work, Chuck emerges, a part of the self that feels and acts like a boy. Chuck engages Dad like a son and pal, because if Dad gets into sports or other male bonding activities, things will be ok. However, Dad isn't interested in Chuck. Dad has a particular gleam in his eye, which is Dora's cue to come out. Dora has learned to flirt with Dad when he's in this state, which may keep him happy until he passes out. This time, though, Dad doesn't pass out and starts to sexually abuse Dora who instantly shifts into Baby Eek, a terrified pain-ridden little girl who collapses under the abuse. That triggers Florence to come forth with anger and strength allowing the body to survive, and pushing the most traumatized state out of consciousness. The Dad has now passed out. Time goes by and Annie "wakes up", with little or no memory of the abuse, and hopefully disconnected to the point of not feeling the pain in the body, so she can proceed with her day.

The Sequential Model shows how different Self States work together to get through traumatic events. Note that by keeping "Annie" unaware of the trauma, unaware of Dad's abusive behaviors, "Annie" is able to engage in regular life as much as possible. She can approach her father, seeking affection, approval, or simply basic means of support such as lunch money for school. The different parts of self maintain different levels of awareness of each other, the behavior of the father and the nature and extent of the abuse.

Without an integrated, comprehensive, and coherent narrative pieced together by the various parts of self relevant to the experience, clients are unable to make sense of their lives. Their worldview, their organizing strategies for relating to peers, their ideas for setting boundaries and expressing needs and wants are hopelessly skewed, distorted and deficient.

In healing environments, the different parts of self will usually have familiar sequences, and the person can begin to know how their system works.

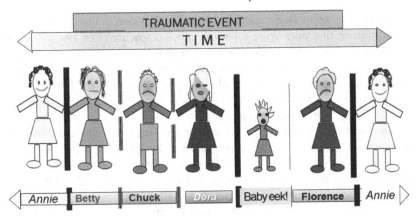

Figure 2.3 Sequential Model of Dissociation

Therapists and helping professionals can help the person soften the need for strong defenses and find other ways to manage powerful emotions by seeing how each part has been necessary and helpful in the past.

The Trauma Model

Colin Ross (2007), in his book *The Trauma Model*, noted that the major consumers of psychiatric treatment do not fit the gene-single disease model which is prominent in inpatient psychiatric treatment. They are repeatedly diagnosed with varying diagnoses, many of which seem, at the time, to be accurate. However, the diagnoses change, over and over. Why? What is usually missing in the treatment of those patients is the taking of a comprehensive trauma history. The gene model of psychopathology did not consider the impact of traumatic experiences on the individual. Ross' Trauma Model is built on a postulate of nature combined with nurture, recognizing the influence of both genes and behavior on a person's mental (and physical) health. This is the piece that he found missing in psychiatry, and he goes on to propose that chronic childhood trauma is to psychiatry what germs are to medicine (Ross, 2007, p.55).

One of the key points Ross makes in his writing is that there is a dose response to trauma; the higher the dose, the more impact on the person. This ties with the increase in awareness of cumulative trauma, of trauma including not only specific events, but also the context in which those events happen. Are there other stressors on the person? If so, how many and how strong are they? How might those "prime" the person for a higher reaction to any specific trauma? Combine this thought with the growing awareness of the impact of Adverse Childhood Experiences (ACE) scores on mental and physical health. The higher the ACE score, the more problems the person is likely to have, and the shorter that person's life may be.

Another key point Ross makes is that, "The Problem is not the Problem". The problems that may bring a person into therapy are often not the actual problems that need to be identified and healed. The presenting problem is usually a problem arising out of an attempt to manage something else. For example, he cites purging as a way of getting rid of bad feelings. It follows that in order to deal effectively with purging, there would need to be some better, healthier, way to manage "bad feelings".

It is not at all unusual for the presenting problem to become the sole focus of treatment, and that can often fail because that problem is not the actual problem that needs to be addressed. People working as family therapists are very familiar with this way of noticing behavior. In families, the children or teens may be the family's focus of attention, drawing everyone in with their acting out behavior. However, the children and teens may be acting out because they sense stress in their parents, and the insecurity of that is what is motivating their behavior. Unless, and until the issues creating the stress are recognized and addressed, the acting out behavior may shift, but will continue.

Ross also highlights the dilemma of the client's attachment to the perpetrator. When the perpetrator is also the child's care-giver, the child is put in an impossible situation. It is essential for the child to attach to the care-giver, and that makes it intolerable to hold on to the reality of the abuse by the perpetrator. To not know what is known becomes a survival strategy, and dissociation a survival mechanism.

Another survival strategy involves shifting the locus of control from the people outside, to the survivor. Children will take responsibility for trauma, even when it's obvious to all that the child had no power to either cause or stop the trauma. They do this for a reason. If, somehow, the trauma stems from something they've done, or not done, then they can strive to do better, and then maybe their parents will love them and not abuse them. They are not powerless. As they grow, learn, and heal, the reality of their actual powerlessness as children becomes clear, and the loss of any hope of love from their parents becomes the focus of therapy. They grieve, deeply.

There is another side of this locus of control problem, which we'll discuss more fully later. When children take the responsibility for the abuse, and make it their fault, they do two things—feel responsible when they're not, and, also, become highly attuned to the expectations and reactions of their parents or other authority figures. This high attunement to external cues helps them modify their behavior to please others and stay as attached as possible. It also interferes with their ability to listen to their own wants and needs. One of the main goals of therapy is to move from focusing on adapting to what others expect or need, an external locus of control, to being able to actualize the self, a true internal locus of control.

Ross' work focuses on integrating psychiatry and all that he's learned about trauma. The result is a model for treatment that incorporates the resources from both areas of knowledge and experience.

The Structural Model of Dissociation

In the Structural Dissociation model, the personality is divided between the ANP (Apparently Normal Personality) and EP (Emotional Personality), terms first used by C.S. Myers in 1940, writing about his observations of shell-shocked WW1 combat soldiers (Myers, 1940). This theory has been further developed by Van der Hart, Nijenhuis and Steele (2006). In this model, there are three levels of dissociation identified: primary dissociation with one ANP, and one EP, secondary dissociation with one ANP and several EPs, and the most complex, tertiary dissociation, with several ANPs and several EPs.

The ANPs may function fairly well. They appear normal. The EPs, however, are in various emotional states, which may, or may not, be helpful or appropriate. Usually, the parts of the self, ANPs and EPs, are activated by the emotional needs of the person, to protect the self and to stay connected to others. For example, if the person becomes angry, an angry part may surface to express that emotion. If the anger expressed drives the therapist or other important person away, an adorable child part may emerge, drawing the other back. That would be an obvious attempt to both express intense emotion and maintain connection in a relationship, but it is done in parts and may be jarring and confusing to the therapist or others. Switches between ANPs and EPs may be as obvious as that, or very subtle shifts that may not be perceived from the outside at all.

One of the difficulties experienced by dissociative people is that the ANP may be taught skills to be used to deal with life situations and emotions, but that information may not be available to the person when EPs are activated.

One of the challenges of working with dissociative people is to continue to see them as single people while simultaneously dealing with all the different aspects they present, many of which may present with different names, histories, and ways of perceiving themselves. All those varying aspects of self are still expressions of one person and his, her, or their life experience. The Structural Model of Dissociation helps people, both clinicians and clients, see the system as a whole person, with experiences of self that are within the Window of Tolerance, seen as "Apparently Normal", and those who carry the intense emotions and memories of abuse that are outside the person's Window of Tolerance, the "Emotional Personalities".

Summary

Each of these models—ego state, sequential, trauma model, and structural—have different ranges of applicability, and different strengths in explaining dissociative phenomena. These conceptual models can be combined to help understand our clients' experiences. For instance, ego states or alters can, and often do, appear in a sequential manner, with varying behaviors, affects, sensations, and knowledge. It may be helpful to think of trauma models like maps. Different maps serve different purposes, showing the topography, or the cities and streets, or where the nearest services can be found. Just as different maps can help to plan and to take a journey, all these trauma models are very useful for working with the many and varied challenges faced by people healing from severe trauma.

As helpful as these conceptual models are for thinking about and understanding the phenomenological experience of our clients, at the end of the day, they are merely conceptual models - constructs. An essential element to recall is the human being sitting across from us is one person struggling to cope with myriad overwhelming experiences, emotions, conflicts. Their ability to manage these extremes is weighed down under the variety and intensity of the memories and feelings.

Chefetz (2015) describes the sense of me and not-me as another way of looking at our client's struggle to cope with unresolvable conflict and unknowable feelings. The experience of overwhelm parallels what Bateson described as a double-bind, the need to respond to two mutually exclusive demands, neither of which can be ignored or avoided (Bateson et al., 1963). In a double-bind, the person cannot comment on, talk about, or acknowledge this inherent state of conflict. A dissociative response is an elegant solution, allowing the person to be me, not-me, and other-me simultaneously. To handle the multiple, conflicting demands of abusive and dysfunctional relationships, dissociative responses are the required, optimal, modus operandi.

The therapist needs to see the client as both existing within the context of the double-bind and as a person living in the world. There is value in appreciating and understanding the complex inner world of alter personalities/ego states and in seeing the client as a whole person struggling to manage what often feels unmanageable.

Etiology

Trauma is a common occurrence in life, and it has, by definition, an impact on a person. Sometimes, the person is able to recover from the trauma sufficiently to not have it impact his, her, or their overall mental and physical life for a prolonged period of time, over one month for PTSD. Delayed onset of PTSD shows up six months or more after the event. If the trauma is a single event, it is likely to be remembered well, although some peripheral details may not be accurate. (Chu, 2011; Terr, 1991). When traumatic events happen repeatedly, people don't remember as well. Children with complex trauma histories, what Terr would label Type II trauma, often forget, losing long periods of time, and showing massive denial and psychological numbing (Terr, 1991). Judith Herman describes the most exaggerated features of complex trauma as avoidance and restriction (Herman, 1997).

People who have experienced a single trauma tend to have a place to return to, an environment in which they can process what happened to them. The impact to them, to their brains, bodies, and relationships is identifiable and exists outside of their normal life. Having a normal life before and after the trauma helps the person to heal, and can help mediate the effects of the trauma over time.

People whose trauma continues have nowhere to go that will allow them enough time and support to recover. They may never have had a normal environment, and lack the resources that would have given them. The ongoing nature of the trauma also forces them to develop and maintain ways to survive, defenses against pain and betrayal. Their brains and bodies shift to accommodate to a hostile environment. Their path is much more difficult than that of the person with a single trauma. Traumatic stress symptoms stemming from this kind of continual trauma are increasingly viewed as "survival-based adaptations that draw on, and can greatly alter, the brain and body's self-regulation capacities" (Ford & Courtois, 2020, p. 35).

In the middle of these two categories is the person whose trauma caused massive changes in his or her life, like the death of a parent, an accident with disabling results, or other events that involve a permanent shift in how life can be lived. The people in this middle category may have had only one trauma, but their difficulties continue, much like those people with multiple traumas.

An environment that makes it intolerable to stay present can contribute to a person becoming dissociative. In many cases, it's physical and sexual abuse that push the person beyond their limit. In other cases, it's the absence of contact that becomes intolerable, being betrayed, neglected, or abandoned. For some, it's the chaos of caregivers that are in chaos themselves, through their own mental anguish, situations beyond their control, illness, death of someone close, or war. In those cases, a small child may end up with a disorganized attachment, a common prelude to dissociation. Still others learn to dissociate because of dysfunctional family dynamics, learning, for many reasons, to not think, feel, or talk.

In recent years, people have become more aware of socio-cultural trauma, the impact of race, religion, sex, gender roles, economic disparities, and other aspects of life that lead to micro and macro aggressions. The on-going and cumulative effects of these constant aggressions impacts individuals, families, communities, and whole countries. The added stress from these situations can be demoralizing, or catastrophic. Kimberlé Crenshaw defines this as "intersectionality". (Crenshaw, 2018).

Medical trauma can also contribute to dissociative difficulties. In this case, the interventions may have saved the person's life, but they were too painful and/or frightening for the person to tolerate, and dissociating became necessary. Not all the causes of dissociation are known, so it is important to keep assumptions out of the picture as much as possible.

3 Neurobiology and Research of Trauma and Dissociation

Trauma survivors often hear well-meaning friends say to "just put the past behind them". As one client said, "I tried to put it all behind me, but it kept following me home."

Trauma alters the way our brains operate. For one-time traumas, that alteration may be relatively small, not impacting the person beyond the immediate time to recover. With complex trauma, the ongoing nature of the trauma causes adaptations in the brain and body of the victim. The person needs to adapt in order to survive, and healing from this kind of long-term existence in a hostile environment requires sufficient time to create new neural pathways that will allow the person to have the option of experiencing and behaving differently.

Trauma results in hyper and hypo arousal, waves of emotions and reactions that are far beyond normal, and difficult to manage. Hyperactivation means too much is happening. Our brains shift out of a calm and rational state and fall back into more survival-oriented mechanisms. We react by going through several stages—freeze, run, fight, and collapse. These are all automatic, instinctual reactions to serious threats. The freeze response stills us, hopefully making us invisible to a predator. If we're seen, if there is an actual threat, we will run, if possible. If running isn't possible, or doesn't work, we will fight. If fighting isn't possible, or doesn't work, our bodies will go into a kind of collapse called tonic immobility. In that state, we are aware, but unable to move. Our bodies are filled with natural pain relievers, and we may appear dead to the predator/abuser. That's our body's last-ditch attempt to survive, and it often works.

Collapsing into tonic immobility is often the experience of people who have been assaulted and/or raped. They become immobile, unable to fight, not because they wouldn't want to, but because their wise minds have registered a threat that feels lethal and has accessed an ancient feigned death response over which the person, while aware, has no control. It would be helpful if those people, when asked, "Why didn't you fight?", could answer, "I went into tonic immobility, and I knew what was happening, but couldn't do anything to stop it. It was surreal and horrifying." Also, when people are traumatized repeatedly, their body/minds may learn to skip the middle steps of running

DOI: 10.4324/9781003217541-4

and fighting because those have proven to not work, and may actually have made things worse, so they go immediately into collapse/submission (and may dissociate) in order to survive and limit the harm as much as possible.

The following is a short and very rudimentary description of a few neurological systems and structures that operate interdependently within the human brain and how they react and respond when exposed to on-going abuse or neglect. Our discussion shall focus on the amygdala and the hippocampus, both within the limbic system, and the prefrontal cortex. We will also briefly take note of the hypothalamus, Broca's region, and the role of the corpus callosum.

In the middle of the brain is the limbic system, containing the amygdala, which is the focal point of our strong emotions such as pleasure, fear, and anger, and the hippocampus which is involved in the storage of memory. When confronted with a traumatic event, the amygdala is charged, and information sent to the hippocampus for memory storage overwhelms the hippocampus, resulting in traumatic memories failing to be stored in an integrated manner. The hippocampus simply can't work fast enough to take in all the parts of the memory and store it as a normal, coherent narrative. Consequently, some or many of the elements of the memory remain unconnected to others, like fear with no memory of what caused it, or a strong reaction to a smell without the knowledge of the cause of the reaction.

The amygdala is located deep within the center of the brain, in the temporal lobe. This is part of the limbic system that helps alert us to danger and to threat. LeDoux (1996) suggests that the amygdala is essential to understanding and experiencing fear. Studies have demonstrated that trauma survivors have increased blood flow to the amygdala in comparison with non-traumatized controls. The theoretical implication is, in part, that trauma survivors have adapted, become "hard wired", to be more on guard than the average person.

The hippocampus, situated right next to the amygdala, helps to integrate memory so that it can be consciously retrieved. When there is a decrease in the functioning of the hippocampus, memory can be affected to lesser or greater degrees. The importance of the hippocampus in memory retrieval was illustrated by the well-known and well-documented case of Henry Gustav Molaison, known to the world as 'Patient HM'.

"Patient HM" had his hippocampus removed in 1953, and was studied for over 50 years, until his death at age 82. Once his hippocampus was removed in an attempt to stop severe, unrelenting, epileptic seizures, he was left with implicit memory, but no explicit memory. During the 50 years he was studied, he never remembered the names of the people around him, or the experiments that were done on him. However, he did have some implicit memory, not conscious, but there. One experiment that was done with him was for a man to greet him, and shake his hand while wearing a ring with a pin that pricked HM's hand. This greeting was repeated daily, but on the fourth day, HM said he didn't want to shake hands, and didn't know why. His mind/

body evidently retained the memory of shaking hands leading to pain, and his body refused to shake hands.

Every time HM performed the task, to him, it felt like an entirely new experience. He had no memory of doing it before, but with practice he became proficient. Observing him, scientists saw that there were at least two systems in the brain for creating new memories. One, known as declarative memory, records names, faces and new experiences and stores them until they are consciously retrieved. This system depends on the function of medial temporal areas, particularly an organ called the hippocampus. The other system, commonly known as motor learning, is subconscious and depends on other brain systems.

> This explains why people can jump on a bike after years away from one and take the thing for a ride, or why they can pick up a guitar that they have not played in years and still remember how to strum it.
>
> (Carey, 2008)

Traumatized individuals have overstimulated and hypersensitive limbic systems that react to perceived threat very quickly and, unfortunately, with less discrimination than the average person. When the limbic system is over-activated there is a corresponding decrease in the functioning of the hippo-campus and the prefrontal cortex. When in a dangerous situation, fast reactions may make a significant difference in a person's ability to escape or otherwise decrease risk (LeDoux, 1996).

The prefrontal cortex, the front most region of the cerebral cortex, is involved in movement, decision-making, problem solving, and planning. There are three main divisions of the frontal lobes. They are the prefrontal cortex, the premotor area and the motor area. The prefrontal cortex is responsible for personality expression and the planning of complex cognitive behaviors. Broca's area is one of the main areas of the cerebral cortex responsible for producing language, located in the lower portion of the left frontal lobe. Hypoactivation of Broca's area results in an inability to find words, to speak. When a person becomes highly upset, speech fails. This can happen during traumatic events, and in therapy, when emotionally connecting with past events.

For example, a woman gets a call, telling her that her child has died. Suddenly, there is nothing but pain, the mind is blank, speech evaporates, and she starts to keen and wail. The emotions override everything, and she is unable to speak. Much later, speech returns, and the memory of that event is vivid with feeling but empty of language.

That was an example of a single trauma. Now, imagine the experience of people in war zones, where terror and losses like this one come one right after the other. There would be no time to settle, body and mind, no time to retrieve and use language to connect with self and others, and the impact would never have the time to soften. A state of constant hypervigilance becomes the norm, an adaptation necessary to survive.

Combining the endocrinological influences that keep the survivor in an aroused and alert state with the exacerbating influences from the amygdala and the limbic system, our clients are biologically disposed to exist in a state of hypervigilance. With the impact of trauma on the hippocampus and memory, people may not remember why they are on hyper alert so often, responding to cues that don't trigger explicit memory. While still in the threatening environment, this is helpful. Once out of that environment, however, the constant state of hypervigilance impacts social relationships and physical health.

In normal, healthy situations, painful experiences are acknowledged, the person is comforted and supported appropriately to heal. He, she, or they learn what needs to be learned to prevent or limit a repetition of the event if that is possible. In unhealthy situations, many or all of those factors may be absent, and the only strategy left for the person is to avoid similar situations or people, or if that's not possible, to create as much psychological distance as possible by becoming numb or dissociated. The brain adapts to make this possible, and will do that automatically if the opportunity to heal is not present.

The Neurobiology of Complex PTSD and Dissociation

The neurobiological substrates of complex trauma, chronic post-traumatic stress disorder, and dissociation are themselves as complex and complicated as humans can be. Our intent is not to provide a comprehensive discussion of the myriad details, structures and relative functions that comprise how the mind operates under trauma. Rather, we will discuss two important and central elements that drive complex post-traumatic stress disorder (c-PTSD) and dissociation: affect dysregulation and impaired memory formation. Within those areas, our purpose is to highlight how a person's responses to shock, abuse, and on-going trauma are neurobiological events and outside of direct conscious control. Accordingly, platitudes like "Put it behind you" or "Get over it" are meaningless, failing to address the neurophysiological underpinnings of the trauma response. In addition, informed therapists, understanding these mechanisms, can better assess the needs of their clients in formulating treatment plans and interventions.

Affect Dysregulation

At the risk of oversimplification, the neurobiological experience of emotions is a series of bottom up events while affect regulation is a top down process. When exposed to shock or trauma, the dorsal raphe nucleus (DRN) responds by releasing 5-HT to the dorsal periaqueductal gray (PAG) (Maier, & Seligman, 2016). The PAG is an important interface between the lower brain stem and the forebrain, coordinating reactions to stress, pain, and defensive behaviors, playing a significant role in how a person learns about fear responses to life threatening events (Kincheski et al., 2012). In turn, the PAG transmits the information to the amygdala and the ventromedial hypothalamus (Deng, Xiao & Wang, 2016).

The amygdala is central to detecting and responding to actual or potential threats as well as encoding implicit emotional memories. Teicher & Samson (2016) noted early childhood emotional or physical neglect tends to increase amygdala volume. Adults and adolescents with multiple forms of trauma may show significant reductions in amygdala volume; suggesting early exposure may sensitize the amygdala while subsequent exposure may result in reduced volume (Kuo, Kaloupek & Woodward, 2012; Whittle et al., 2013 as cited in Teicher & Samson, 2016).

For persons with c-PTSD, the amygdala, when exposed to stress or trauma, shows increased activity. However, unlike people who weren't traumatized, there isn't a subsequent reduction in amygdaloid activity associated with an increase in activity in the right anterior cingulate cortex (rACC) (Andrewes, & Jenkins, 2019). For the trauma survivor with complex PTSD, the amygdala hijacks the brain, leaving the person in a state of hyperarousal.

At the same time, the hypothalamic-pituitary glands adrenal (HPA) axis increases the production of adrenocortical hormones, notably cortisol, to facilitate the body's defensive responses. Trauma survivors live with increased levels of these hormones leading to cortisol toxicity, contributing to impaired cognitive functioning, problems with memory formation, diminished executive functioning, language difficulties, and neurotoxic stress on the hippocampus (Ounes & Popp, 2019). Limited studies (Edwards et al., 2014) have correlated elevated night-time cortisol levels with impaired learning and memory formation.

Diminished executive functioning and impaired cognitive processing is indicative of the difficulty c-PTSD survivors have in managing intense emotions. As noted previously, trauma survivors do not demonstrate the same level of activity in the rACC as non-traumatized persons.

Reinders and colleagues observed, "a significant negative correlation between neuroanatomical deficits and measures of dissociative symptom severity" (Reinders et al., 2018, p. 162). Reinders and colleagues found, "Women with DID show significant and extensive volumetric reductions of regional gray matter in the insula, the cingulate cortex, the dorsolateral, superior, medial, and orbitofrontal prefrontal cortex, and the superior and inferior temporal lobe" (Reinders et al., 2018, p. 165). Parietal and insular regions as well as limbic-prefrontal connections are thought to help modulate emotional regulation. All of this suggests that our clients, struggling with c-PTSD and dissociative disorders, are "hard wired" to have increased, intense emotional reactions due to having been traumatized. Further, in addition to environmental, developmental deficits in learning how to temper and reduce their affective reactivity, our clients' have neurological complications exacerbating this condition. It is important to note that this physiologically based complication is itself a product of the abuse they suffered and not an inherent defect. They were wounded. They are not disordered.

One theory regarding dissociative processes posits that affective hyper arousal is a defining element of c-PTSD. In turn, affective numbing or hypo arousal is indicative of dissociative processes. Daniels, Frewen, Theberge, and Lanius (2016) studied gray matter volume in patients with the dissociative subtype of PTSD; observing dissociative severity was positively correlated with gray matter volume in the right middle frontal gyrus, an area of the brain that helps with downregulation of emotional arousal. They suggest dissociative severity may be linked to excessive down regulation reactively triggered by excessive emotional arousal. Daniels and colleagues also found less gray matter volume in the right inferior temporal gyrus, a part of the brain involved with visual recognition of shapes, patterns, faces and objects. They suggest reduced gray matter volume in this region may be associated with symptoms of derealization.

If we view this within the context of Siegel's Window of Tolerance, we can see that healthy expression of emotion requires a dynamic balance between neurobiological networks that affect arousal and affective modulation. Weems and colleagues (2021) discuss a shift from modular conceptualizations of neuroanatomical functioning to a greater recognition of how different structures may serve as hubs for information transfers and processing within larger networks that manage more complex and nuanced behaviors. Two important networks are the salience network (SN) which help focus attention on external events of importance and is active in response to threat, pain, and uncertainty, and the executive control network (EN) which facilitates top down affective modulation and is engaged in tasks involving attention and working memory (Seeley et al., 2007; Seeley, 2019). PTSD responses may be due to excessive activity of the SN combined with diminished activity within the EN (Peters, Dunlop & Downar, 2016).

Impaired Memory Formation

The hippocampus is crucial in forming and retrieving long-term memory by integrating proprioceptive and external sensory information into spatial and temporal models of events. Teicher and Samson (2016) reported trauma tends to reduce hippocampal volume. They described studies showing affluence or poverty mitigated by supportive or hostile parenting impacted left hippocampal volume while right hippocampal volume was less impacted by affluence-poverty factors but remained impacted by parenting styles (Luby et al., 2013 as cited in Teicher & Samson, 2016).

Two cortisol receptors are prevalent throughout the brain: mineralocorticoid receptors (MR) and glucocorticoid receptors (GR). Both types are found in the hippocampus while only GRs are located in the prefrontal cortex. MRs are correlated with enhanced executive functioning, while GRs are associated with diminished cognitive performance. In the hippocampus, moderate levels of cortisol tend to affect the MRs enhancing memory formation. However, when cortisol floods the brain due to intense shock or abuse, or when a person lives with chronic cortisol toxicity due to a lifetime of trauma, the MRs in the hippocampus become saturated and the GRs are triggered, leading to progressively greater impairment of memory formation (Ounes & Popp, 2019). Further, higher amounts of cortisol are associated with diminished hippocampal volume. Conversely, elevated cortisol levels can lead to increased development of dendritic spines in the amygdala which may lead to hyper-sensitivity and increased reactivity of the amygdala (Edwards et al., 2014; Tatomir, Micu & Crivii, 2014). Because only GRs are located in the prefrontal cortex, increased cortisol levels may result in diminished declarative memory (Ounes & Popp, 2019).

Trauma also impairs cognitive functioning and declarative memory in other ways. Teicher & Samson noted parental verbal abuse decreases gray matter in the left auditory cortex and interferes with the left arcuate fasciculus linking Broca's and Wernicke's areas, resulting in language processing impairments (Tomoda et al., 2011 as cited in Teicher & Samson, 2016). Wernicke's area is associated with the ability to make sense of incoming verbal information, while Broca's area is linked to the ability to find language to express feelings, thoughts and experiences.

Another neurobiological element in the interplay between trauma, PTSD symptomology and dissociation centers, is on sleep disturbances—notably the disruption of REM sleep. Disturbed sleep, with interrupted REM sleep, has been suggested to be both a defining feature and a causal factor of PTSD. The HPA, via adrenocorticotropic hormones, initiates the release of both cortisol and norepinephrine which oppose REM sleep (Edwards et al., 2014). REM sleep is thought to be essential to learning, memory consolidation, and the reduction of the emotional charges associated with stressful events (Fink, 2020).

Pulling this together, we see that c-PTSD and dissociative disorders share a neurobiological basis where the salience network (SN) is overstimulated, while the executive control network (EN) is impaired. The result is both increased difficulties in modulating affective responses to past and current events as well as learning new means of coping with situational conflicts and relationships.

Learned Helplessness

Often our clients express a profound sense of shame that they did not, could not stop the abuse that was being perpetrated on them. Frequently, they confess to being unable to move, to push back, or even cry out as they are being assaulted. They may be told by the abuser that this inability means they actually wanted or enjoyed being hurt. Traditionally, therapists speak of learned helplessness as a response to being in an inescapable position. Clients learned that no action on their part was going to stop, or could stop, the attack. Still our clients cry, bemoaning they didn't try at all.

Soral, Kofta, and Bukowski (2021) posit loss of control results in learned helplessness. Their idea suggests that after repeated instances having no control, no ability to effect change, our clients have an impaired ability to detect or conceive methods of challenging or coping with abusive behaviors. From this grows a diminished sense of agency, diminished beliefs regarding their ability to influence events.

Maier and Seligman (2016) note a key element of learned helplessness is the subjective experience of perceiving one's self as helpless. Inescapability itself only produces a sense of temporary helplessness. The person's explanations as to the causes of their helplessness predicted the duration, course, and the extent of helplessness. Their review of neuroscientific studies on learned helplessness shows the dorsal raphe nucleus (DRN), under conditions of shock or trauma, releases 5-HT to the dorsal periaqueductal gray inhibiting fight/flight and to the amygdala potentiating fear/anxiety. If the person can perceive a possibility of control, if they have been taught how to create change, then, via their ventromedial prefrontal cortex and posterior dorsal medial striatum, they can inhibit DRN neuronal activation. Helplessness and freezing, fear and anxiety are the default responses to shock and trauma. Control, and the expectation of control, are learned responses based on experiencing the ability of creating change (Maier & Seligman, 2016).

Consider clients who have suffered chronic, complex relational trauma. They have been repeatedly placed in situations where they were physically unable to stop abuse. More so, they grew up in dysfunctional families where the parents or caretakers denied and discounted the existence of abuse, failed to take measures to help stop the abuse, and undermined or overwhelmed any emerging attempts by the child to stop the abuse or to assert autonomy.

The corollary between learned helplessness and an external locus of control is noted by several researchers (Burger, 1984). Restructuring the paradigm from "fight or flight" to a "fear, freeze, flight, fight, or collapse" response as both a neurobiological response and a pro-survival, behavioral response is an essential piece of psychoeducation to share with survivors of profound abuse and helps to reduce self-blame and shame. Further, we suggest a new "label" for the behavior/condition we're describing. Rather than "learned helplessness" might we think of this as "reinforced helplessness". Our clients were rarely taught how to stand up for themselves. They weren't shown that options and opportunities for control existed.

Consider the "Mother in the Mall" incident we referred to earlier. That mother offered her crying child a viable solution. More so, by asking which hand he wished to hold, she gave him a choice appropriate to his age and judgment. Through innumerable experiences like that, healthy parents teach their children that control/solutions exist and they can find and enact them. Those experiences are not only empowering, they build expectations of efficacy and hope. Contrast that with the experiences our clients relate wherein their efforts were quashed, denied, and discounted. Small wonder our clients come to us filled with shame. Small wonder they struggle with dysfunctional, chaos inducing attempts to resolve conflicts and moments of inchoate collapse.

Another Short Story

Little Laurie (age four) is watching Mommy cook in the kitchen. Mom tells her to not touch the stove as it is hot. Little Laurie keeps looking at the stove longingly; she saw the cookies go in there. When Mom isn't watching, Little Laurie touches the hot stove and, unfortunately, burns her finger. Good Mom to the rescue, treats the burn and calms our heroine. Little Laurie learns to avoid all big white boxes in the kitchen. She won't touch the refrigerator, the washer, or the dryer and certainly not the stove. Over time and with careful explanations from Mom, Little Laurie learns that the refrigerator, washer, and dryer are safe to touch. Later, she learns that even the stove is safe, when it's not turned on.

This example teaches the process of avoidance and discrimination. It also highlights the interplay between the interpersonal, relational aspects of the child/parent dyad and the internal, neurobiological mechanisms.

Imagine if Little Laurie had an abusive and non-nurturing parent. Having touched the hot stove and burned her finger, she would not have been comforted and taught, but could have been yelled at and hit. She would end up with more physical pain and additional emotional pain. In addition, her curiosity would suffer from the punishment. Also, she might not learn when and why the different big white boxes were safe to touch, which ones were safe to touch, and when certain ones should be avoided.

When there is no known safe person or place, the need to constantly be on guard is heightened and highlighted. Constant fear impacts the ability to learn new cognitive, emotional, and relational information. It stifles the child's curiosity and openness to explore. The child's mental and emotional focus is on protection and damage control, not learning new and exciting things. Fear of being hurt or shamed inhibits the child, and the child stops trying to learn. (Nathanson, 1992)

In relationships, the child needs to learn to distinguish the safe relationship from the dangerous one. When abuse comes from many different quarters in the household, when no one remains a safe and secure caretaker, then how does that happen? The child can't rely on any relationship to be safe, so they will assume all relationships are dangerous, and it will take a long time to realize that some can actually be safe.

In studying children, Martin Teicher identified how the effects of childhood trauma can be seen in brain scans. He looked at the brain scans of children of different ages who had been physically, sexually, or emotionally abused and noted how different kinds of abuse damaged the brain in different ways. Teicher found that the impact of abuse was both inward and outward. Inward, the child was more prone to depression, anxiety, suicidal ideation and PTSD. Outward effects were aggression, impulsiveness, delinquency, addiction, and hyperactivity. There are both sensitive and critical periods in a child's development when abuse can have a more serious effect. The sensitive period results in a maximum effect, and the critical period marks an essential effect

(Hubel and Wiesel, 1970). The hippocampus was particularly sensitive to abuse reported to occur at 3–5 and 11–13 years of age. In contrast, the rostral body of the corpus callosum was affected by abuse reported to have occurred at ages 9–10, and the prefrontal cortex by abuse at ages 14–16 (Teicher, 2008). For instance, if a child is abused at age four, hippocampal volume is reduced by 13.2%, and is associated with DID, PTSD, Borderline Personality, and depression in adulthood.

The corpus callosum, affected by abuse most significantly at ages nine to ten, is the structure in the brain that connects left and right hemispheres, allowing people to integrate rational and emotional aspects of experience. It is significantly affected by early neglect, (as well as by physical and sexual abuse). With insufficient integration between the two hemispheres, it is easy to see why people who have a smaller corpus callosum may have problems with impulsivity. Stress may cause the right hemisphere to dominate, diminishing the person's ability to use rational thought to mediate their behavior.

The prefrontal cortex exerts inhibitory effects, limits the response to stress and exerts inhibitory feedback control on the HPA (Hypothalamus, Anterior Pituitary, & Adrenal Cortex). The prefrontal cortex, which myelinates primarily between adolescence and the 20s, is impacted by stress most from the ages of 14 to16, producing precocious maturation but stunted final capacity (Teicher, 2003). So, the neurological attempt to inhibit stress responses starts early from necessity, but because of the push, never reaches its normal capacity.

In researching the impact of stress and abuse on the developing brain, Teicher is hypothesizing that "early stress signals the nascent brain to develop along an alternative pathway adapting itself to survive and reproduce in a malevolent stress-filled world" (Teicher, 2003, p. 34).

Ulrich Lanius describes the effect of trauma on the brain as there being two actions going on at the same time, the sympathetic nervous system (hyperarousal) dominates, with simultaneous parasympathetic (hypo-arousal) activation. He says, "At some point, if the stressor is ongoing or too great, parasympathetic tone becomes dominant and the organism moves into a passive defensive response." The person's cortical functioning shuts down, and "the brain moves from smooth state changing to switching abruptly between defensive responses without attendant mindful awareness" (Lanius, 2015). In other words, the brain is both activated to confront the danger while shutting down on non-essential functions and filling the body with pain-reducing chemicals. If the trauma goes on too long, the mind and body shut down the activated processes (sympathetic system), leaving only the parasympathetic system which helps to minimize blood loss and pain, and slow everything down to facilitate healing. In doing so, consciousness is also affected, and the result is somewhat like being mildly anesthetized, lowered pain levels, and lowered consciousness. This is a survival mechanism, a product of evolution. It is not under conscious control.

Switching abruptly between defensive states, over time, can result in the development of substrates within the brain, different patterns of behaviors and cognitions that are regularly accessed for particular situations. Like Marilyn Van Derbur's "Night Child", these substrates emerge as ways to deal with repeated traumas, containing survival strategies that have proven to be helpful in these situations. The more challenging situations the person needs to survive, the more substrates their brains will develop. These are altered ways of being, created to allow the person to survive and live as best as possible in extremely difficult situations.

When a trauma passes, the body and mind seek a return to normal. When there is on-going trauma, the body shifts into a constant defensive state, and that becomes the new "normal". Basically, the brain and body adapt to a dangerous environment. When learning about all the effects of trauma on the brain, consider the people who have been repeatedly traumatized throughout their childhoods. For those people, the adaptations they've needed to make in order to survive involve all of those areas of the brain, and all of those automatic instinctual responses. They are prepared to survive as best possible in a hostile world, but they are not adapted to peace, and that makes it difficult for them to live in and enjoy the safety they have found. In therapy, our clients need to work on becoming conscious of their cognitive and physical states and responses, and through learning and practice, reset their brains to adapt to a safe environment. The neuroplasticity of the brain allows it to adapt, so new adaptations are possible. This process does take time, however, and is not something that happens in a few therapy sessions. It also requires that the environment actually be safe enough for the brain to allow for adaptation out of hypervigilance or dissociative processes.

4 Diagnosis and Research

Diagnosis: How Do We Find Out If Someone Is Dealing With Complex Trauma Or Dissociation?

The symptoms of trauma are becoming increasingly well-known and integrated into more clinical diagnoses. In the DSM-5, PTSD has four symptom clusters instead of three: intrusive symptoms, avoidance symptoms, negative alteration in mood and cognitions, and arousal and reactivity symptoms. The new changes include a clinical subtype "with dissociative symptoms". The dissociative subtype is applicable to individuals who meet the criteria for PTSD and experience additional depersonalization and derealization symptoms.

Supporting this revision was research that suggested a dissociative subtype of PTSD, identified by the experiences of depersonalization or derealization. Causes of these symptoms are from experiences of abuse, torture, or war that put a person in a position of no escape. The lack of any external escape possibility results in internal forms of escape, altering consciousness to manage to not be fully present in intolerable situations. These may include feeling the world to be unreal (derealization), not feeling like a real person (depersonalization), or experiences of leaving the body and viewing the experience from an "out of body" position (Lanius et al., 2012).

The DSM-5 also included a revised section on dissociative disorders, eliminating the need for evidence of alters taking executive control over the person and substituting, "marked discontinuity in sense of self and sense of agency, accompanied by related alterations in affect, behavior, consciousness, memory, perception, cognition, and/or sensory-motor functioning. These signs and symptoms may be observed by others or reported by the individual" (American Psychiatric Association, 2022, p. 331). The DSM-5 also included that, in some cultures, the experience may be described as possession. In the DSM-IV, the diagnosis included having parts of the system take executive control, with amnesia. Those criteria forced many people into the DDNOS category, with the result that there were more diagnoses of DDNOS than of DID, the opposite arrangement from other diagnoses. The NOS (Not Otherwise Specified) in the DSM-IV, and the OSDD (Otherwise Specified

DOI: 10.4324/9781003217541-5

Dissociative Disorder) in the DSM 5 were meant to designate those people who did not fit well in the major categories listed. In the other diagnostic categories, the "Otherwise Specified" groups was always smaller than the diagnostic groups in that category, and changing the criteria for DID and OSDD was meant to include more people in a regular diagnosis, fewer in the unspecified category, and an awareness of the cultural interpretation of some of these experiences.

Prevalence: How Common Is Complex Trauma, and How Prevalent Are Dissociative Disorders?

It is not uncommon to hear clinicians report that they do not treat clients with complex trauma or dissociative disorders. Believing their practices are limited to people with family conflicts, substance abuse issues, or eating disorders, they may acknowledge that there is likely some trauma in some of the clients' histories. However, the nature of the trauma, the extent of the traumatic injuries, and the pervasiveness of any dissociative defenses goes unrecognized and, therefore, untreated.

The contribution of trauma to many current personal and relational issues is just beginning to be recognized. One of the largest investigations ever conducted to assess associations between childhood maltreatment and later-life health and well-being is the Adverse Childhood Experience study (ACE). This study started as a collaboration between the Centers for Disease Control and Prevention and Kaiser Permanente's Health Appraisal Clinic in San Diego. The initial phase of the ACE Study was conducted at Kaiser Permanente from 1995 to 1997. More than 17,000 participants completed a standardized physical examination, and their physical health continues to be monitored.

The results of the first ACE study showed two thirds of the 17,000 people had an ACE score of at least one and 87% of those had more than one. That reveals a large number of people dealing with multiple traumas.

> The ACE Study findings suggest that certain experiences are major risk factors for the leading causes of illness and death as well as poor quality of life in the United States. It is critical to understand how some of the worst health and social problems in our nation can arise as a consequence of adverse childhood experiences. Realizing these connections is likely to improve efforts towards prevention and recovery.
>
> (Center for Disease Control and Prevention, 2014)

The ACE Study reports the following results of research done on the impact of high ACE scores on psychological and behavior problems. In one long-term study, as many as 80 percent of young adults who had been abused met the diagnostic criteria for at least one psychiatric disorder at age 21. These young adults exhibited many problems, including depression, anxiety, eating disorders, and suicide attempts (Silverman, Reinherz, & Giaconia, 1996).

In addition to physical and developmental problems, the stress of chronic abuse may result in anxiety and may make victims more vulnerable to problems such as post-traumatic stress disorder, conduct disorder, and learning, attention, and memory difficulties (Dallam, 2001; Perry, 2001).

Children who experience maltreatment are at increased risk for smoking, alcoholism, and drug abuse as adults, as well as engaging in high-risk sexual behaviors (Felitti et al., 1998; Runyan et al., 2009). Those with a history of child abuse and neglect are 1.5 times more likely to use illicit drugs, especially marijuana, in middle adulthood (Widom, Marmorstein, & White, 2006).

Taking this information into account, it's clear that clinicians dealing with family conflicts, substance abuse, and eating disorders are most likely also dealing with the impact of trauma, and the ways in which the victims are attempting to deal with intolerable affect. The waves of hyper and hypo arousal, intrusive and blocked memories and emotions, and dissociative defenses may all be present in these people, and being able to identify those dynamics and help the people learn to deal with them effectively can make the therapy far more effective while also reducing the shame often felt in being out of control.

People with substance use disorders often have a history of multiple psychological traumas and suffer from PTSD and complex PTSD.

> Among adult addiction treatment outpatients with self-reported trauma histories, 50% had PTSD alone, 41% had comorbid PTSD and complex PTSD, and 4% had complex PTSD alone. Compared to PTSD alone, comorbid PTSD/complex PTSD was associated with a history of childhood sexual trauma, sexual retraumatization in adulthood, and more severe PTSD and depression symptoms. Patients with alcohol-related SUDs were at increased risk for PTSD, while those with cocaine or opiate SUDs had a reduced risk of comorbid PTSD/complex PTSD. Complex PTSD may warrant clinical and research evaluation, particularly for patients with histories of childhood sexual trauma and retraumatization.
>
> (Ford & Smith, 2008)

Within the substance abuse community, two other studies have suggested one-fourth to nearly one half of the sample population endorses a significant number of items on the DES. Benishek and Wichowski (2003) administered the DES to 51 people with a history of substance abuse. They found 25% scored 15 or higher. In a study from Turkey, Karaday, Sar, Tamar-Gurol, et al. (2005) with a sample population of 104 found 4 % scored higher than 30 on the DES.

Gielen and colleagues (2012) found patients with substance use disorder (SUD) are more than five times as likely to have PTSD than patients without SUD. Further, patients with both SUD and PTSD were more likely to have depression or other axis I disorders. Similarly, Najt and colleagues (2011) found patients with PTSD experienced more problematic substance abuse issues and more frequent comorbid diagnoses of mood or anxiety disorders and suggest that PTSD is a clinical indicator for SUD. Giordano et al. (2016), in a study across three outpatient treatment centers noted that 85.45% of women and 84.62% of men experienced at least one traumatic event, with women experiencing an average of 3.15 traumatic events and men experiencing 2.89 such events. While the definition of trauma included criminal events, general disasters, as well as unwanted physical or sexual encounters, women were more likely to report traumatic experiences linked to forced intercourse or sexual assault while men more often experience witnessing serious interpersonal violence. Notably, approximately 80% of those reporting at least one traumatic event did not have a diagnosis of PTSD.

Among clients diagnosed with eating disorders there are similar figures. Beato, Cano, and Belmonte with a sample population of 118 reported 30.5% scored higher than 25 using the DES.

Vanderlinden, Van der Hart, and Varga employing the DIS-Q on a sample population of 98 eating disordered clients found 12% met the criteria for pathological dissociative experiences. While Dale and colleagues, also using the DIS -Q, noted 22% of their eating disorder patients (N=106) had severe dissociative symptoms.

Tagay et al. (2014) found that 23.1% of patients with anorexia nervosa and 25.5% of bulimia nervosa patients met the criteria for PSTD. Brewerton (2019) notes the prevalence of lifetime traumatic events among clients with eating disorders including anorexia nervosa, bulimia nervosa, and binge eating disorder is significantly higher than people without eating disorders. Further, that interpersonal trauma was the most common form of traumatic experience endorsed. Gomez and colleagues (2021) found that sexual trauma is an independent predictor of disordered eating and suggest clinicians working with eating disordered clients and clients with food insecurity issues be screened for trauma histories. Nilsson and colleagues (2020) found people with eating disorders endorse both psychoform and somatoform dissociation. They noted that the subjective sense of severity regarding disordered eating behaviors is significantly correlated to the degree of dissociative symptomatology.

Among clients reporting histories of intimate partner violence (IPV), Connors and colleagues (2008) in a multi-center study reported that 31.6 % of the victims of IPV scored 20 or higher on the DES. Utilizing the DES-Taxon

Table 4.1 Prevalence of Dissociation among Patients with Substance Abuse

Authors	Population	N	Tests	Results
Benishek & Wichowski	Substance Abusers	51	DES	25 % > 15
Tamar-Gurol, Sar, Karadag, Evren & Karagoz	Substance Abusers	104	DES, DDIS & SCID-D	46% > 30

Table 4.2 Prevalence of Dissociation among Patients with Eating Disorders

Authors	Population Studied	N	Tests	Results
Beato, Cano, & Belmonte	Eating Disorders	118	DES, Rosenberg Self-esteem Scale, Body Shape Questionnaire, Eating Attitudes Test-40	30.5 % > 25
Dalle Grave, Tosico, Bartocci	Eating Disorders	106	DIS-Q	22.6% had severe dissociative symptoms,
Vanderlinden, Van der Hart, Varga	Eating Disorders	98	DIS-Q	12% pathological dissociative experiences

protocol developed by Waller et al, they found 18.9% endorsed a pathological level of dissociative symptomatology.

Mantakos (2008) in attempting to develop the Dissociative Partners Violence Scale (DPVS) sought to establish a correlation between the DPVS and pathological dissociation. She found a significant correlation between 9 of the items on the DPVS and the DES-Taxon.

Kulkarni and colleagues (2012) studied male veterans entering a PTSD clinic. They noted that anger and dissociation predicted avoidance/numbing and total PTSD symptom severity. Further, they observed that dissociation alone predicted intrusive and hyperarousal symptoms and that 21.5% of their sample were above the clinical cut for dissociation among PTSD samples.

A review of published literature of various patient populations suggests that dissociative experiences are not uncommon across a wide number of diagnostic groups. "Several epidemiological studies over the past 15 years have shown that dissociative disorders may have been previously underdiagnosed and that with proper screening and diagnostic instrumentation, a much higher prevalence is encountered" (Foote et al., 2006).

In clinical studies done in North America, Turkey, and Europe, including populations in inpatient psychiatric units, adolescent inpatient units, and in

Table 4.3 Prevalence of Dissociation among Patients reporting Intimate Partner Violence

Authors	Population	N	Tests	Results
Connors, Kemper, Hamel & Ensign	Intimate Partner Violence – Victims	95	DES, CTS, CAT Trauma History	31.6 % > 20 18.9% > Taxon Score of .55

programs treating eating disorders, substance abuse, and obsessive-compulsive disorders, between 1% and 5% of the patients met the diagnostic criteria for DID that was set in DSM-IV-R (International Society for the Study of Trauma and Dissociation. 2011).

Intimate partner violence (IPV) impacts staggering numbers of people every year. PTSD is a common response to IPV. One study found over 60% of IPV victims having a diagnosis of PTSD (Gold, 1999 as cited in Lilly & Graham-Bermann, 2010). Further, the greater the degree of violence within the relationship, the larger the increase in PTSD symptomology (Lilly & Graham-Bermann, 2010). Coker and her team (2005) found among 5,654 IPV survivors they surveyed, 24% of the women and 20% of the men had moderate to severe PTSD.

A history of childhood abuse or interpersonal violence in adulthood is a risk factor for other forms of abuse as an adult, notably IPV. It is suggested that emotional numbing, associated with PTSD hypo-arousal, impairs the victim's capacity for detecting or responding to abuses associated with revictimization (Iverson et al., 2011). Perez and colleagues (2012) note PTSD symptomology interferes with the IPV victims' ability to make use of resources (emergency housing, legal aid, job training, etc.) and to interact with social service agencies. Iverson et al. (2013) found that dissociation, in addition to PTSD symptoms of hyperarousal and negative coping strategies, was predictive of revictimization. Dissociation may be a coping mechanism, helping IPV victims avoid loss of attachment with their perpetrator (Zerubavel et al., 2018). Dissociation is also thought to play a role in IPV perpetration where offenders are emotionally disconnected from their behaviors and from the impact of their abuse on their victims (Webermann, Brand & Chasson, 2014).

This very brief review of the literature is not meant to be exhaustive. Rather, the point is to draw awareness to the likelihood and prevalence of dissociative disorders across a broad spectrum of patient populations.

Screening and Diagnostic Tests for PTSD

The purpose of this short section is to overview some screening and assessment tools. For best results, seek training, consultation, or supervision in order to learn how best to use these tests.

The ACE (Adverse Childhood Experiences) study has been mentioned previously. It is well known, free, and easy to administer as a screening tool. Available in many languages, it can be a useful tool to open up a dialogue about the nature of a person's history and how that could be affecting their current behavior (CDC, 2014).

The Symptom Checklist, SCL-90-R (Derogatis & Savitz, 1999) is a 90-item self-report symptom inventory, evolved from the Hopkins Symptom Checklist (Derogatis et al., 1974). The SCL-90-R and BSI, with their matching clinical rating scales, form a set of brief test instruments for the assessment of psychological symptoms and psychological distress. "Sensitivity to pharmacologic, psychotherapeutic, and other treatment interventions, as well as to clinically meaningful variations in psychopathology and psychological distress levels, provides endorsement for these test instruments as effective for both psychiatric screening functions and clinical outcomes measurement." These test instruments are available in over two dozen languages, and have been utilized worldwide (Derogatis, & Unger, 2010).

The Los Angeles Symptom Checklist (LASC) is a 43-item self-report measure of PTSD and associated features. The LASC asks about the presence of problems in the past month, and does not identify any specific trauma. "The 17 DSM-IV symptoms of PTSD are embedded among other items that assess more general psychological distress. Items are rated on a 5-point scale ranging from 0 ('no problem') to 4 ('extreme problem')" (King et al., 1995).

The PTSD Checklist (PCL-5) was created by the staff at the Veteran Administration's National Center for PTSD. It is a 20-item self-report measure that assesses the 20 DSM-5 symptoms of PTSD. The PCL-5 can be used to monitor symptom changes during and after treatment, screen people for PTSD, and make provisional PTSD diagnoses (Weathers et al., 2013).

Dissociation Research

One characteristic of dissociative phenomena is how frequently it is misdiagnosed or not accounted for at all. Many people in the mental health profession do not know what dissociation looks like or how to assess for it. There's been too little training available. The result of that lack of training is that people with dissociative issues are seldom seen accurately, which results in treatments that are inadequate or fail completely.

From the moment of seeking treatment for symptoms to the time of an accurate diagnosis of DID, individuals receive an average of four prior other diagnoses, inadequate pharmacological treatment, have several hospital admissions and consequently spend many years in mental health services. (Reinders & Veltman, 2021). According to Madden, (2004), dissociative people spend on average, 3.6 to 6.8 years in the mental health care system with 3.2 wrong diagnoses.

One of the factors contributing to the long delay in diagnosis, and the high rate of misdiagnoses is that there is little taught in graduate schools about trauma & dissociation.

"Most mental health clinicians receive little systematic training in assessing or treating trauma in their professional training programs. This situation has created a widespread and unfortunate disparity between clinical need and availability of suitably trained providers" (Henning, Brand, & Courtois, 2021).

In addition to the relative absence in training to identify and treat dissociative issues, many people come into the mental health care system with high comorbidity with other mental health issues. With these people, it is often very difficult even for well-trained clinicians to sort out the various difficulties the person is experiencing. It's common for people who dissociate to be seen as Schizophrenia, Bipolar, Paranoid, Depressed, and/or Borderline. Often, they carry several of these diagnoses. Comorbidity is one of the main themes addressed in Colin Ross' *The Trauma Model: A Solution to the Problem of Comorbidity in Psychiatry*. "If the trauma dose is set high enough, virtually everyone will develop serious psychiatric comorbidity" (Ross, 2007, p. 67).

Differentiating DID from Fantasy

One of the misconceptions that has impacted the diagnosis and treatment of dissociative disorders is the idea that dissociation is fantasy gone awry. The trauma model (Dalenberg et al., 2012) views DID as a severe trauma-related disorder, often with comorbid PTSD (Putnam et al., 1986), related to early childhood trauma, disorganized attachment, chronic neglect, and abuse. In contrast, the fantasy model sees dissociation and DID as the interaction of high suggestibility and fantasy proneness combined with enactment, sleep disturbances, suggestive psychotherapy and/or sociocultural influences.

In a study designed to test these conflicting views, Vissia et al. (2016) concluded that

> Patients with diagnosed genuine dissociative identity disorder (DID) were not more fantasy prone or suggestible and did not generate more false memories compared to the other groups. Furthermore, a continuum of trauma related symptom severity was found across the groups. This continuum supports the hypothesis that there is an association between the severity, intensity, as well as the age at onset of traumatization, and the severity of trauma-related psychopathology. Evidence consistently supports the Trauma Model of DID and challenges the core hypothesis of the Fantasy Model.
>
> (Vissia et al., 2016, p. 4)

Dissociation is not the same as fantasy, and not the same as other diagnosis that people often receive in those "average of four prior other diagnoses, inadequate pharmacological treatment, ... several hospital admissions and consequently ... many years in mental health services" (Reinders, 2021).

The Structured Clinical Interview for DSM-IV Dissociative Disorders (SCID-D) and revised version (SCID-D-R) provide diagnoses of Dissociative Disorders and differentiate them from non-dissociative disorders as well as factitious and simulated dissociative presentations.

> The SCID-D interviews show good validity identifying and differentiating those with DDs as compared to those without DDs. The SCID-D interviews are valid instruments for diagnosing and differentiating DD from other psychiatric disorders and feigned presentations of DD.
>
> (Mychailyszyn, et al., 2021)

The SCID-5 is organized into diagnostic modules, assessing mood disorders, including;

psychotic disorders, substance use disorders, anxiety disorders, obsessive-compulsive and related disorders, eating disorders, somatic symptom disorders, some sleep disorders (i.e., insomnia and hypersomnolence disorders), "externalizing disorders" (i.e., intermittent explosive disorder, gambling disorder, and adult attention deficit hyperactivity disorder), and trauma- and stressor-related disorders.

(First et al., 2015)

The research behind the assessment tools available for dissociative disorders supports their validity and usefulness in being able to correctly identify the issues being brought into therapy. Use of these assessment tools, from the original screening tools to the more sophisticated structured interviews has the potential to save clients and therapists years of inadequate or misapplied treatments.

Treatment Guidelines

The American Psychological Association (APA), and The International Society for the Study of Trauma and Dissociation (ISSTD) are working together to produce guidelines for the treatment of complex post-traumatic stress, CPTSD. These organizations are in the final stages of review for their "Professional Practice Guidelines for the Treatment of Complex Posttraumatic Stress Disorders in Adults". When complete, the Guidelines should be available through either organization.

ISSTD has created guidelines for the treatment of dissociative disorders. The third edition of those guidelines, published in 2011, are currently available online. A fourth edition of the guidelines is currently in process and are due to be published in 2023 (ISSTD, 2011).

Treatment Studies

The field of diagnosis and treatment of dissociative disorders is relatively new. In order to identify effective treatment approaches and processes, a group of researchers and clinicians created a survey of expert therapists skilled in working with dissociative clients. The survey questioned the experts on their recommended treatment interventions for DID and DDNOS.

The results of that survey were that experts recommended a carefully staged three phase approach, emphasizing skill-building and maintenance of safety, impulse control, interpersonal effectiveness, grounding, and containment of intrusive material. Cognitive distortions were treated with cognitive therapy. While some abreactive work was done by these experts, it was modified and catered to the individual (Brand, et al., 2012).

Training programs for therapists working with clients who experience PTSD or dissociative difficulties are proliferating. There are courses, webinars, and conferences given by ISSTD, ISTSS, APA, and many other professional organizations. There are, however, few programs specifically designed for joint use by clinicians and clients. One of these is an online educational program put together by a team of researchers and clinicians. A study of that program showed significant improvement in all patient groups tested, with greater and faster improvement in individuals with higher levels of dissociation (Brand, et al., 2019).

The Randomized Controlled Trial (RCT) is the gold standard for research. The Treatment of Patients with Dissociative Disorders (TOP DD) group is starting an RCT to study the effectiveness of only treatment for PTSD and dissociative disorders in early 2022. It will be the first RCT of individual therapy for DID patients. The study will recruit therapists and patients from around the world who are willing to be randomly assigned to a 6-month wait list or to the group that gets immediate access to the online educational program. The study will include DID, OSDD, complex PTSD, and PTSD with the dissociative subtype patients.

Screening Tools for Dissociation:

The Dissociative Experiences Scale (DES), was developed by Carlson & Putnam in 1986. A 28 item self-report measure assessing the frequency with which an individual experiences different manifestations of dissociative behaviors. The DES is scored by tallying all answers, and dividing by 28. A result of 30 reveals dissociative issues. A score of 45 suggests Dissociative Identity Disorder (DID). Dr. Putnam also designed the Child Dissociative Checklist (Putnam, 1988). Also in 1990, Judith Armstrong, Ph.D., Drs. Carlson and Putnam developed the A-DES (Adolescent-DES).

The DES Taxon consists of eight items of the DES. These questions are used to evaluate the presence of a dissociative disorder, and correlates roughly to Marlene Steinberg's 5 factors of the SCID-D, as stated below: depersonalization, derealization, amnesia, identity confusion, and identity alteration. (Steinberg, 1993).

The Somatoform Dissociation Questionnaire 5 (SDQ 5) and Somatoform Dissociation Questionnaire 20 (SDQ 20) both look at somatoform disorders and their relation to dissociation. The SDQ 5 is a screening tool for identifying dissociative disorders, and the SDQ 20 evaluates the severity of somatoform dissociation. (The SDQ 5 items are included in the SDQ 20.) As one of the authors, Ellert Nijenhuis, notes, the SDQ is more sensitive than the DES in picking up dissociative symptoms in the group of persons with somatoform disorders (Nijenhuis et al., 1997).

It is important to note that the above measures are screening tools rather than diagnostic tests. Accordingly, they suggest the presence of dissociative phenomena, but do not offer a diagnosis. Should there be positive indications of dissociative symptoms or processes, use of more definitive diagnostic tests is recommended.

Diagnostic Tools and Structural Interviews

Multidimensional Inventory of Dissociation (MID 6.0) is a diagnostic inventory developed by Dr. Paul F. Dell in 2006. It is a self-administered pen-and-paper assessment with 28 items, taking about 30–50 minutes to complete, designed for research and to assess clients who present with a mixture of posttraumatic, dissociative, and borderline symptoms. It has discriminated between different diagnostic groups in the United States, Israel, and German. It comprehensively assesses the phenomenological domain of pathological dissociation and diagnoses dissociative disorders (Dell, 2006).

Structured clinical interviews represent the highest standard for diagnosing dissociative disorders. These clinical interviews should only be given by a trained, licensed professional, ideally one with a consultant or supervisor who are available if needed to help monitor the process and evaluate the results.

The Dissociative Disorders Interview Schedule (DDIS) was developed by Colin Ross is a highly structured interview which makes DSM-5 diagnoses of somatization disorder, borderline personality disorder and major depressive disorder, as well as all the dissociative disorders. It asks about positive symptoms of schizophrenia, secondary features of DID, extrasensory experiences, substance abuse and other items relevant to the dissociative disorders. The DDIS can usually be administered in 30–45 minutes (Ross, 1996–2007).

One of the challenges faced in diagnosing people who are dissociative is to find and use diagnostic tools that have the capacity to identify dissociative disorders and differentiate them from other potential mental diagnoses. Many people have several diagnoses before being properly diagnosed with a dissociative disorder. Years spent with a mistaken diagnosis are years without proper treatment, and, often, treatment that adds to the person's experience of not being seen.

The Structured Clinical Interview for DSM-5 (SCID-D) is considered one of the most psychometrically sound approaches for diagnosing dissociative disorders. In a meta-analysis, Mychailyszyn and colleagues concluded that, "the SCID-D interviews are valid instruments for diagnosing and differentiating DD from other psychiatric disorders and feigned presentations of DD" (Mychailyszyn et al., 2020).

The SCID-D is a semi-structured interview that includes five subscales: amnesia, depersonalization, derealization, identity confusion, and identity alteration. The SCID-D is very helpful in distinguishing dissociative disorders from other psychiatric diagnoses and feigned presentations. It can be used to assess dissociative symptoms in people with a variety of psychiatric illnesses, independently, or as part of an assessment battery. The SCID-D includes an "Interviewer's Guide to the SCID-D" outlining the procedures to be used in the interview (Steinberg, 1993).

A word of caution—not all mental and behavioral symptoms are caused by emotional problems. Some emotional problems are caused by physical disorders. Before assuming everything is psychological, make sure that the client has a thorough physical check-up, and that their physician is aware of any emotional difficulties the person may be having. Some of those may be symptoms of conditions or diseases that the physician can treat, such as feeling depressed being part of a hypothyroid condition. If there is any sense of the person having a somatization disorder, the need for serious medical evaluation becomes even more critical. Traumatized people may have both somatic issues stemming from their trauma and physical issues that may or may not be associated with their psychological traumas. Clients have at times felt that their reporting of physical issues was not being taken seriously because of their diagnosis of PTSD or DID. Some of those physical issues turned out to be life-threatening, and the delay in treatment made things more challenging for everyone.

In addition to the possibility of medical conditions complicating the picture, there are also cultural influences that need to be included in the evaluation of the person. Some cultures acknowledge and include possession in their religious practices and beliefs, and some have ways to provide for altered states of experience as part of their spiritual or cultural experience. For example, peyote is used in Native rituals. "Speaking in tongues" is an accepted ecstatic experience in some Christian churches. There are many examples of this kind of expansion of consciousness woven into cultural and spiritual traditions. This makes diagnosis more challenging, and highlights the need to get to know the client within the context of their culture and traditions.

Suggestions

Add to your assessment package:

- An open, and on-going, discussion of clients' experiences—what does it mean to them?
- What associations may they have to anything in their current life or culture?
- How do they feel about their own experiences? Which ones may be concerning or troubling to them, and why, and which one may be meaningful, and why?

History—Case Formulation or Who is the client?

Before being able to treat a client, the therapist needs to know who the client is, and that includes obtaining a comprehensive history. That history needs to include developmental stages, family, culture, traumatic events, medical issues, past treatment, and current presenting problems. As Tracy Eells states, "A formulation is more than a summary of history and presenting problems. It explains *why* the individual has problems" (Eells, 2015). In the midst of gaining that information, the therapist also needs to begin to build a therapeutic relationship and alliance with the client. It is this relationship, focused on developing trust, that enables the client to share at a deeper level, and helps both therapist and client identify issues and goals in therapy. The information gained in beginning dialogues with the client will also help the therapist discern which screening tools and diagnostic tests may be helpful to this individual client.

As cultures evolve, people find new ways to experience and express themselves. Those new experiences may confuse and complicate diagnosis. In addition to all the elements that contribute to the awareness of the diversity within cultures and individuals, roles, genders, races, beliefs, etc. There is also the emergence of new ways of interacting with others through electronics and imagination. Communities form online, and people begin to identify with others, creating group identities that are new, outside old categories. This raises more challenges for diagnosing a person's distress. It makes it very important for the clinician to ask what the client means by their description of themselves. For example, people may come into therapy with the belief that they have PTSD or are dissociative based on what they've read or heard about those conditions. Maybe they are, and maybe they're not. Clinicians need to take the time to know what that person means when they say they've got PTSD or DID, or any other diagnosis. Complicating factors may arise from the client being on the autistic spectrum, or from spending a great deal of time interacting with others through fantasy. In addition, some people get "lost" in maladaptive daydreaming which can be dissociative, or an indication of dissociative tendencies.

There are very helpful screening and diagnostic tools and protocols for interviewing new clients, but there frequently is also pressure on clinicians to make quick diagnoses and virtually instant treatment plans. That often results in the clinician not using screening tools or any kind of formal assessment. In addition, one of the most critical parts of the initial interview with a person is the development of a relational connection between therapist and client, the beginning of a good therapeutic alliance. With the increase in demands that the therapy move quickly and be done expediently, therapists may find themselves missing or giving very little attention to aspects of the client's life beyond the person's presenting problem. That's unfortunate, because the presenting problem may be the tip of the iceberg in terms of what is fueling the client's problematic behavior and distress. Also, when the therapist isn't able to take a thorough history, and build an alliance with the client, the outcome of the therapy can suffer. If the client is dealing with complex trauma or dissociative issues, launching into therapy too quickly can result in the person being overwhelmed and decompensating.

In *The Psychiatric Interview*, Daniel Carlat describes the four tasks of the initial interview as building a therapeutic alliance, obtaining a psychiatric database, diagnostic interviewing, and negotiating a treatment plan with the patient (Carlat, 2012). He talks about getting through these four tasks in the first hour together. The assumption may be that this process would continue, but it is not stated explicitly in this text. In an older book of a similar theme, *The Handbook of Psychiatry* (Guze, Richeimer & Siegel,1990), the initial psychiatric assessment was far more extensive, consisting of the subjective information related by the patient, and the objective information obtained by observing the patient. Taking the psychiatric history, the psychiatrist was advised to cover the patient's presenting problem, previous psychiatric difficulties, family psychiatric problems, medical history of both patient and patient's family, history of any drug or alcohol abuse, occupational history, and social and developmental history. This assessment would take as long as necessary, not limited to one session.

These two texts appear to have the same goals in mind, and the shift between these two handbooks may only be a reflection of the authors and their intended audiences. However, it also could be seen as illustrative of the overall shift in care available to patients over the last several decades. For complex trauma and dissociative clients, the need for speed in diagnosis and treatment is detrimental to their healing process—there is too much to cover in a short amount of time, and failing to understand the complexity of the person's difficulties impacts the effectiveness of the therapy.

It takes quite a bit of additional time to get to know the whole picture of what the traumatized client brings to therapy. At the beginning of therapy, many people will share only a little, and when asked about their history, may give only partial responses. That makes sense. There's a limited amount of time, and the client doesn't have a relationship with the therapist, so some information may feel too sensitive to share. History taking continues throughout therapy, with the groundwork set at the beginning, and more being added over time as the person remembers, and/or feels safe enough to share.

The need for a thorough history cannot be overstated. Taking the time to get to know the person sitting across from you, and using that as a means to assess their interactions and their style of relating provides a rich and complex view into their world. As with so many other elements of therapy with trauma survivors, proceed slowly and revisit this process as the opportunities arise.

Ask about the person's history, from the context of the family in which they was born, the birth, early years, adolescence, and up to present age. Take note of missing pieces, they may fill in naturally later, or be indicative of a period of time that is blocked from memory for some reason.

Given that trauma survivors often have gaps in their memory, a complete history is usually unobtainable at the onset. These memory gaps themselves are an interesting part of the discovery process. A gentle curiosity, supplemented by a supportive and non-shaming stance, allows for the therapist and client to join together in a collaborative inquiry as to why there would be such a gap, what purpose having a gap might fulfill, and whether or not there are similar gaps in present day memory.

Careful attention should be paid to the way the family functions and the roles that different family members played. Examining the relational status the client has with each family member currently and how they came to this place is important. What rules, spoken and unspoken, governed behavior within the family? Do these roles and relational styles correspond to other interpersonal relationships the client experiences in the present? Further, do these roles and relational patterns carry over into the therapeutic relationship, or past therapeutic relationships?

Within the family of origin, how was anger expressed and managed? Who, if any, was allowed to get angry and how did the rest of the family respond to that person's anger? Was the client able to express anger then? Are they able to do so now, and if so, how do they manage to do so?

How were other emotions expressed or rejected in the family? Was one person's emotional state more important than the others? Did the family and/or the client need to placate a certain family member? Were children allowed to be angry, sad, afraid or were they told that they needed to keep quiet and stop crying?

In a similar vein, how was power held and manifested in the family of origin? Did the parents collaboratively share power? Did they struggle, fight, and undermine each other? Did they encourage the child to develop a voice or did they stifle any attempt of the child to assert his, her, or their own needs? How did family members negotiate their needs and wants? Were the children given age appropriate chores and choices? What were they held responsible for?

Ask what forms of discipline were used. What could this person expect if they did something the family considered wrong, breaking family rules about behavior, emotions, sexuality, and responsibility? All of these conditioned responses will show up in therapy to some extent. For instance, if the family never discussed sexuality, and reacted with shame to any reference to sex, then the client may bring that hesitancy and proneness to shame into the therapy. Or, in reaction to the family stance, the client may take a rebellious approach and make talking about sexuality a priority in therapy.

Knowing family rules and the consequences to the child if those rules were broken helps both therapist and client anticipate potential reactions to breaking any dysfunctional rules that need to be broken in order to free the client. That allows for preparation for anticipated backlashes, and gives the client the knowledge needed to withstand the backlash until it diminishes and ceases to have control over the client.

When asking about the personal history, pay attention when people respond with:

"I don't remember",
"I don't remember anything before the age of...",
Very vague responses,
Overly idealized responses,
Complete avoidance whether articulated or acted out,
History of abandonment, neglect, physical, sexual, or emotional abuse,
Highly unstable early life (death of someone close, war, hospitalizations, etc.),
Medical trauma, especially in early years.

When someone says "I don't remember", check to see what the person means by that statement. In some cases, the person hasn't stopped to think about their past, so it doesn't feel immediately accessible. In these cases, asking about externals, things like where they lived, the town or city, in an apartment or house, with an intact family or some other combination of people, with siblings or without, home-schooled or attending a private or public school. Normally, people can access that information, and when they do, other memories from their past become more available. They discover they actually do remember quite a bit. In contrast, other people who say they don't remember may be able to know some externals in their lives, but the associations that would normally help them remember more don't seem to exist, or emerge in a nonlinear fashion, bits and pieces that lack a sense of coherence. In the beginning of therapy, this is something to notice, a piece of an unknown puzzle. Along with what is said in answer to this question, notice the person's body language, and the resonating emotions within you. All of that is information that helps a picture of the person begin to emerge.

If the client says, "I don't remember anything before the age of …", then a fairly obvious question would be, "What happened at that age?" There may be a decisive event of some kind that marks the boundary between knowing and not knowing. It may be a move, a death, a trauma to self or others, or it may be a point at which the person lost hope, or began to hope for something better. It could also be a time when the person made a personal decision of some kind, making a change within the self. In dissociative people, it may be the time of the emergence of the alter who is now in your office talking to you, that part of the person not having executive control before that time.

Vague responses may be given for many reasons, from disinterest to hostile withholding of information, from an inability to remember to fear of sharing too much that is remembered, from lack of trust in the therapist or therapy to fear of the strength of attachment already felt for the therapist, or from innumerable other reasons. Take note of what information is shared, and what areas remain relatively blank. Explore the experience of not knowing. How does it feel for the client to not have access to that part of their history? What does it mean to the client to have a gap in their memories?

At times, a client may report an idealized childhood. Human relationships, especially parenting is fraught with missteps and disappointments as well as successes and celebrations. Healthy relationships include acceptance of the other's foibles and an appreciation of their human-ness. There may be many reasons for idealizing one's own family, such as loyalty, an inability to perceive the family as good or healthy if issues are recognized, or lack of ability to articulate issues that may be present. People can have very good families and still need to deal with issues from childhood. There are also cases where the child did not suffer direct trauma but was born to parents whose lives were extremely difficult, like the survivors of the Holocaust. In these cases, the child can be impacted by the parents' history, either through epigenetics or by the changes in the parents' behavior caused by their trauma.

If a client completely avoids talking about the past, either by saying he or she won't talk about it, or distracting whenever the subject arises, it is safe to assume there's a reason why the subject is off-limits. However, it's not safe to assume to know what that reason may be. Staying with ambiguity, with not-knowing, can be very difficult, but far better than making up a story about things unsaid by the client.

The rule is, if you don't know something about the person, you don't know and have to hold that space open until the client fills it in. Living with ambiguity is a skill, and the therapist models that skill by allowing the unknown to remain unknown, by not rushing to fill the spaces but standing in them with the client.

While a history of abandonment, physical, sexual, or emotional abuse is very challenging to face, one of the most difficult experiences to work through is neglect. The pain caused by the absence of interpersonal connection is profound, and pain from something missing is more difficult to define than pain from something done to the person. Neglect in infants triggers failure to thrive, a life threatening condition. In older children, lack of adequate attention may stunt growth, physically and emotionally. Human beings were meant to be in relationships with other human beings. We are communal creatures, and when left completely on our own, we do not do well at all.

A highly unstable early life, whether that's due to the death of someone close, war, hospitalizations, or other circumstances beyond a person's control can result in problems for infants and young children. The death of someone close can impact a woman who is pregnant and, therefore, impact her infant's experience. That is no one's fault, an example of how life events can hurt without any intention of harm. People caught up in wars are also affected, often tragically.

Medical trauma, especially in early years, can have lasting emotional impact. The procedures used may be both necessary and painful. Sometimes parents are involved in helping with those procedures, which puts the child in the position of needing to be comforted by the person who has to care for the child in a way that causes pain. That is an awful experience for both people, but the adult has the knowledge and awareness of the need for the procedure, and the child may be too young for any knowledge to be helpful. For those children, coping with the pain and need for the closeness of the parent may evoke a dissociative process in an attempt to keep the two separate.

In order to grow in an optimal way, infants and young children need to feel that someone is always there to see them and care for them. The seeing and caring doesn't need to be perfect, but does need to be appropriate, genuine, consistent, and warm. Whatever disrupts that caring connection has an impact on the child, and the more severe the disruptions, the greater the impact.

Informal Assessment for Dissociation

Formal assessment tools are extremely valuable in helping to diagnose clients with complex PTSD and/or dissociative disorders. Often, however, the therapist will not routinely screen for these conditions until they have some obvious and outstanding rationale for doing so. In the earlier stages of treatment, attending to the process between client and clinician, and making a genuine connection with the person creates an environment in which the person can become known to him or herself and the therapist. Within the safety of a healthy and attuned therapeutic relationship the client can become willing and able to share what was previously unsafe to share. Only then can the roadblocks to progress be identified and addressed.

While clients are exquisitely and minutely scanning the therapeutic relationship, they are more highly attuned to what can go wrong rather than what can go right. The therapist has to gently and skillfully observe the difference between the therapeutic relationship and all previous relationships. The very act of talking about how you talk together is empowering and liberating.

There are several experiences that are common to therapists when working with dissociative clients. These experiences tend to be a reflection of the client's experience, picked up from being in the presence of the client, a subtle transfer of the client's state onto the therapist. Sometimes this comes across as a somatic transference, and sometimes it's an experience of re-enactment emerging in the midst of the therapeutic relationship. If the therapist has not already done a complete assessment, noticing any of these experiences would indicate that an assessment for dissociative issues would be helpful. The following descriptions offer a sense of what the therapist may find, especially in early stages of work with traumatized clients.

Confusion

Dissociation disrupts linear thinking, and/or emotional congruity. The client may shift from one subject to another, or from one emotional state to another, with no apparent reason. The therapist may not be able to follow what's happening with the client. Also, the client may not respond in anticipated ways, leaving the therapist confused about what's going on with the client, or what the diagnosis may be. When the therapist thinks, "I have no idea what's going on," or, "Who is this person?", it may be time for a formal assessment for dissociation.

Sleepiness In Session

Sometimes therapists do get sleepy in sessions, but they're usually aware of the reasons—not enough sleep, too heavy a meal for lunch, or the effects of stress or medication. There are times, however, when therapists feel very sleepy only with certain clients, and they cannot figure out any reason for that sleepiness within themselves. That's when they need to consider that the client may be dissociating, only partially present in the room, and partially absent. The feeling of struggling to stay awake may reflect the client's struggle to stay conscious in the way he/she/they want or need to be. Sometimes the client is both actively engaging with the therapist while also blocking intense feelings about things not said. If therapists senses that things are being withheld and that may be what is causing the feeling of sleepiness, they can ask the client, "What are we not talking about?" While that's a useful intervention for a lot of situations, in this case, it can open the door to look at the unspoken material that is in the room, exerting a powerful effect. If the client can share what's being withheld, no one feels sleepy any more.

Therapist Going Into a Trance State

Sitting with someone who is dissociating may cause therapists to begin to feel as if they were in an altered state, as if they were inside a dream. Notice any feeling of floating away, or trancelike sensations. That may indicate that the client is spacing out or leaving reality in some way.

Client Emotionally Fragmented

The sense that the client's personal "point of view" is shifting throughout the session. The client may move from a guarded description of events to a more emotionally complete description, from a blunted report to an angry or tearful recounting and then back. When asked to comment on their personal sense of the interchange, how they process the conversation, the client may report that they feel "all over the map" or that they are saying things without knowing what they about to say next, that the event feels out of their immediate control, as if they were a bystander to their own involvement. Gentle, continued exploration by the clinician may reveal that this is not uncommon for the client and they may report experiences of derealization or depersonalization.

Client Relating In Different Personality Styles

Similarly, the client may have a shifting style of relating to the therapist. Like the fluctuation between hyper and hypo arousal noted in PTSD, the client may shift between an engaged partner in the therapeutic process, to an irritable and guarded antagonist, then onto someone struggling to stay awake and involved. Shifting patterns of behavior, such as vulnerability followed by distance, or attack followed by appeasement, may be the person's only way to share vulnerable information and also protect the self, by doing one and then the other alternately. These variations in phenomenological presentation of the client, while creating degrees of distress within the therapeutic relationship, also serve as markers suggesting a more thorough examination for the presence of complex trauma and dissociative disorders.

Clients with dissociative issues may evoke conflicting emotions, perceptions, reactions in the therapist, reflecting alternate perceptions and experiences within the client. They may appear young and vulnerable, or hostile, or remote in ways that are subtle or alarmingly blatant. Therapists may have difficulty tracking the shifts and feel ungrounded in the therapy, not sure what's going on, how to track the client, and how to develop a treatment plan that will match the needs of the client. The needs keep changing.

Within the therapeutic relationship, the therapist may feel pulled to rescue the client, feel rescued by the client, or be perceived as being abusive to the client. These are all re-enactments of Karpman's Triangle. With clients who have dissociative disorders, the different roles in Karpman's triangle may come out in different aspects of the person. (We will further discuss aspects of Karpman's Triangle and other forms of role-driven behavior and relating in Chapter 6.)

Clients with complex trauma or dissociative issues may have obvious problems with emotional dysregulation and may be more easily dysregulated then most clients. Often their experience of emotional lability may vary to a greater degree. An example of this is a client who appeared very constrained, with limited emotional connection, who when gently asked about her twitching foot, went into a full flashback, ending up on the floor curled in a fetal position.

The client may have an inability to track from session to session and little sense of the on-going process in therapy. This is an experience that can sometimes be described as feeling like a new person comes to session each time. When asked, the client may not remember the previous session at all, or only small parts of it. The client may also miss parts of the current session, stopping in confusion unable to regain their train of thought, or appear to wake up in the midst of the session or at the end, unaware of the conversation up to that point.

Notice that while the client may not remember parts of sessions, or whole sessions, they still arrive at their appointment. In fact, while consciousness may not be linear, but very sporadic or coming from different places inside the person's psyche, there may also be ways in which the client is functioning in what appears to be a normal, consistent manner. For instance, the client may have gone to work and did all that was required, with little or no conscious memory. There is, however, procedural memory that is functioning in a reliable manner. Even people who are unable to work often have procedural memory that is working—to get up in time, get dressed, have a meal, travel to the office or get online, etc. It can be helpful to notice how much the person is doing that is working well enough. If the person is diagnosed with dissociative issues, this awareness of how they are managing well enough in some or many areas of their life can help soften the impact of hearing the diagnosis.

Therapy with clients who are dissociative often swings and fluctuates between seemingly contradictory extremes. The clinician may feel boredom, overwhelm, or both. The client may alternate between crises and shutdown. Both may feel that nothing is happening in therapy, or far too much. The client frequently has trouble maintaining an even presentation of material or affect, opening up too much and then shutting down involuntarily.

Memory and denial often play tag. "I made it all up. I'm a liar" is followed by flashbacks and then denial is a repetitive pattern. For some clients, these shifts are the only way they know to take a break from facing the reality of their lives. They use the same strategy that was used on them, a denial of their abuse. For those clients, learning to say, "I need a break" and taking one, decreases the frequency of this kind of dance between having a memory and denying it.

When the therapist observes such radically opposed shifts in attention, presentation, and/or language, it becomes vital to inquire about these phenomena with an authentic, non-judgmental curiosity. The focus is on better understanding and appreciating the client's experience. rather than shaming them for "not doing it right". Trauma survivors, having lived with shame and blame will be quick to assume shame and failure. Gentle curiosity must then be tempered with an acceptance of the client's limits and willingness to move forward.

When any of these situations arise in therapy, it may help to do a formal assessment of the client. The assessment can enhance the therapeutic process, giving the client the opportunity to share his or her internal reality in an open and accepting environment.

When Something Else May Be Part of the Picture

Sometimes people present with behaviors, thought processes, or experiences that feel "different", but don't quite fit within the categories of traumatic stress or dissociation. Sometimes, even when the person has some clear indicators of dissociation, it doesn't seem to be experienced as disruptive, or doesn't meet the criteria for PTSD or dissociative disorders. The confusion may come from the person being on the autism spectrum, or the person may be engaged in maladaptive daydreaming. Those are only two possibilities. Others include medical reasons, medication effects, or cultural influences. In these cases, it may take additional assessments to gain enough clarity to create a treatment plan that will fit for this person.

"Helpful, Hurtful, Missing"

While taking a history, it can be helpful to notice what the person learned that has value, what was harmful, and what was missed. Think of this as a three-column list, "Helpful, Hurtful, Missing" that can be added to throughout the therapy as the person learns what happened, how they developed skills that are still helpful, what kinds of harm they suffered (physical, sexual, emotional, spiritual, relational), and what they missed (secure attachments, opportunities to develop skills and talents, and the possibility of healthy relationships). For example, many clients learned to be responsible far beyond what would be role or age-appropriate, like being the family cook at age six, then were punished for not doing well enough. So, they learned how to take responsibility, and that is a common characteristic of people who manage to leave abusive situations, so, in one way it helped. They were also hurt in that situation, emotionally and/or physically abused, and that was harmful. And in the last column, they missed being able to move through normal developmental stages outlined by Erickson: building trust, autonomy, initiative, industry, identity, intimacy, generativity, and wisdom (Orenstein et al., 2021).

When people are able to see their experiences in this way, they become aware of how what they learned that was helpful, combined with learning what they missed, helps in dealing with what harmed them. For example, knowing how to be responsible, combined with authentic support from therapists and others, works together to heal the pain, shame, and neglect that came from the abuse.

Suggestions

Add to your assessment toolkit:

- Assessment of autism, or referrals for that assessment
- Assessment for Maladaptive Daydreaming, available online: https://da ydreamresearch.wixsite.com/md-research/measures
- Create an on-going list of "Helpful, Harmful, and Missing", adding to each and noticing how the "Helpful" combined with filling in the "Missing" contributes to helping heal the "Harmful".

5 Overview of the Three Stage Phasic Model of Treatment and Tasks of Each Stage

Working with complex trauma and dissociative clients is analogous to an old vaudeville style of performance—plate spinning. The performer would have a row of thin vertical wooden dowels, each approximately five feet tall. The performer would place a dinner plate on the first dowel and start spinning the plate. When the spinning of the plate achieved a fast enough pace, the plate would remain balanced on the pole and the performer would start the next plate spinning on the next pole. After getting two or three plates rotating rapidly on their respective poles, the performer would return to the first pole and gently shake it in a circular manner to keep the plate spinning at the proper speed. From there the performer might add another plate or two to the growing row of pre-cariously spinning platters. Then the performer would quickly dash up and down the line to shake a few sticks less a plate should slow below the critical speed to maintain its balance. Alternating between launching new plates and maintaining the currently spinning ones, the performer would attend to the row of whirling china until every dowel was topped.

Similarly, while we talk of treatment being a three stage phasic process, the client never stops working on the tasks of Stage One even as they move onto addressing the tasks of Stage Two. When the client has progressed to meeting Stage Three goals, they will often find that they are moving back down the line to address Stage One or Stage Two tasks. Describing trauma treatment as a non-linear process does not do justice to the intricate dance of responding to the complexities of the needs and emerging issues of trauma clients.

Trauma treatment is thought to be best done in stages, starting with safety and stability, moving through remembrance and mourning, and ending with the integration of the trauma and a realization of the authentic self in the world (Herman, 1997). In reality, those "stages" are more like aspects of the process that may need to be dealt with at any time during treatment. As much as possible, it's best to focus on stability at the beginning, to help the client calm down and create as firm a foundation as possible from which to do the deeper work of intentionally facing the trauma. Also, in working with safety and stabilization, the client learns skills that help with the processing of the traumatic material, making that aspect of therapy move more quickly and effectively. The maxim that "the slower you go, the faster you get there"

DOI: 10.4324/9781003217541-6

(Kluft, 1993) is based on the experience that the skills learned in what is traditionally thought of as the first stage of therapy enable the client to move through the second stage much more easily, with less disruption in all areas of life, and a greater sense of mastery while moving through the effects of the trauma. Without the safety and stabilization skills, therapy can be destabilizing and potentially re-traumatizing. The third aspect of therapy, integration of the trauma and authentic expression of self, emerges to some extent periodically throughout therapy as people work through issues and take growth steps forward, and becomes the natural focus towards the end of therapy.

It is not uncommon for people to come in for help when they are in a crisis. It is often imperative that the therapist deal with that crisis immediately. When that's the situation, the skills and knowledge normally taught in the first stage of therapy need to be taught simultaneously, while dealing with the crisis. Simple grounding tools, some cognitive-behavior skills, psycho-education, and pacing can all be done in the midst of working through a crisis. It's preferable to have these skills prior to dealing with overwhelming emotions and a disrupted life, but it's still essential and very helpful to learn the skills as part of bringing down the overwhelm, and the more those skills are taught, the more empowered the person will be to continue in his or her process.

There is a sense of these aspects of therapy being interwoven. The stability provides the space and ability to face the trauma, and facing the trauma allows for it to become part of a coherent narrative, and, appropriately, in the past. Having worked through a trauma, the person is often open to acknowledging and facing whatever other traumas may have occurred in their life. Thus, people who have complex traumas may find themselves automatically wanting or needing to heal other traumas once they've felt the relief of healing and integrating one.

In dissociative systems, a trauma processed by one part of the person will need to be acknowledged and integrated into the whole system. Sometimes that happens easily, with different parts of the person witnessing the work and following the process with some co-consciousness. In those cases, dissociated parts may actually support or assist in working things through. In more severely split systems, there may be amnesia or an emotional barrier between the part in therapy and the rest of the system, resulting in a more prolonged therapy as the parts become known, and the person is guided through the therapy necessary for a dissociative system to become co-conscious, cooperative, and eventually as integrated as possible.

With dissociative clients, the aspects of therapy are often all happening simultaneously. Even then, however, it's helpful to emphasize stability first, and the other aspects of therapy afterwards. There may be times when parts of a system emerge in a flashback, or come forth believing that the only way to do trauma work is to recreate the feeling of the original ordeal. When these things happen, another part of the person may step in to put on the emotional brakes. Stopping the process can happen by stating the need to slow down directly, or indirectly, by coming too late to an appointment, or skipping sessions. It can also happen with protective alters coming out in session and telling the therapist to stop, sometimes rationally, and sometimes with panic or anger. In other people, a self-helper part or function may step in and let the therapist know it's important to stop. There are many ways for the person to self-regulate when the therapy is going too fast or too intensely. It's helpful in those times to thank the part of the person who slowed or stopped the therapy, and come up with a signal for that part to indicate to the therapist whenever things are not ok inside. This builds a collaborative feeling and helps keep the therapy within the client's overall window of tolerance.

While trauma treatment is described as a three stage model, this presents a false sense of it being a linear process. Trauma treatment is non-linear. Each stage builds upon the previous ones. Return to the image of trauma therapy being like a performer spinning plates on sticks. In order to keep all the plates from crashing, he'll need to give each a push in turn according to the needs of the moment to keep it all going.

Stage One: Safety and Stabilization: Finding a Place to Stand—Setting Up the Context of Therapy, Boundaries, Expectations, Contracts

"The value of a treatment method is inextricably bound to the relational context in which it is applied" (Norcross, 2011).

Other than the client's personal resources and honest and authentic motivation to change, the most significant factor predicting growth and healing is the strength and quality of the therapeutic relationship. This therapeutic alliance is created through a consistent practice of key principles. Foremost is the therapist having excellent interpersonal skills and engaging the client in a welcoming fashion. To be met with empathically attuned, non-judgmental, open curiosity is to create a profound sense of acceptance. When clients feel that the therapist genuinely cares and wants to work with them, they are more open to engaging and feeling empowered to engage.

To create the therapeutic alliance is to create an attachment, a dyadic bond. In this case, the attachment evolves out of a process of reciprocal engaging behaviors between therapist and client, where each recognizes, elicits, and responds to the other in a mutually attuned, ongoing process. The therapist does this to the best of his, her, or their ability, modeling it while also teaching the client about healthy attachment and how this is fundamental to healthy relationships.

The initial task in creating the safety and stability to support the work of trauma recovery is to define the therapeutic relationship as a safe environment in which to meet and to explore problematic feelings, memories, and relationships. Defining the relationship as "safe" is only the first step in a process that will, hopefully, provide sufficient experiences of safety for the client to begin to actually know that the relationship is safe. Survivors are often very familiar with people being warm and kind at the beginning of a relationship, and then using the closeness that develops to harm the client. This is a way in which people are "groomed" to be abused, and therapists need to know that experience is behind a lot of survivors' hesitancy in trusting people who call themselves "safe". Many therapists who work with severely traumatized people have learned to not use the word "safe" without checking to see what that means to the client. Often, the therapist and client choose other words to describe the experience of not being in imminent danger.

The creation of a safe place (or *"danger-free zone"*) starts at the first moment of contact and is a collaborative process with the client engaged as a partner in defining the goals of treatment and understanding and setting the guidelines for engagement. The therapist works with the client to specify what healthy therapeutic boundaries will be and how to talk about any difficulties that may emerge for either the therapist or the client during therapy. Carol Mayhew (Connors & Mayhew, 2006) described the purpose of boundaries as creating a "negotiation space" in which it was safe to talk. She noted that good boundaries are consistent and predictable; neither too rigid nor too fluid. As in all human relationships, empathetic flexibility in response to shifting needs and situations needs to be balanced with a desire for stability and certainty. From the beginning, clients should be empowered to express their expectations and needs. Together, therapist and client define and refine the boundaries and expectations as the therapeutic process continues.

People who are coming to heal complex trauma or dissociative issues frequently have great difficulty stating what they need in a way that works. In traumatic situations, their needs didn't matter, and they had no voice in what was happening. In therapy, both of those things are addressed immediately at the onset of the therapeutic process. The client and therapist collaborate as much as possible. The rules they both need to be aware of and adhere to are spelled out clearly. Most therapists include those in their original therapy contract, including rules about confidentiality and the laws that dictate when the therapist must share information about the client. Also included in most therapy contracts is information about the availability of the therapist, payment policies, office or agency policies, HIPAA compliance forms, and, hopefully, information about the therapist's professional will, a document that lets the client know what will happen to the therapy and the client's records if the therapist becomes disabled or dies (Frankel, 2015).

What also should be conveyed at the beginning of therapy is that issues between the therapist and client need to be addressed in the therapy as soon as possible from the time they become known by either person. This places the relationship between therapist and client on the table as something to be discussed whenever necessary and gives the therapist the opportunity to share the importance of this with the client. Unresolved issues can derail the therapy, while issues identified and worked through can add immeasurably to the success of the therapy.

The more severe the abuse, the more the client's boundaries are impacted, and the more often boundaries will need to be discussed, and sometimes slightly altered. In most cases, the boundaries may need to be stretched to accommodate the level of distress and need in the client. In some cases, however, a therapist may make the boundaries more rigid, in an attempt to contain the desperation and need of the client. A survey done by Adah Sachs (2013) compared the boundaries that practitioners kept with clients who suffered Dissociative Disorders (DD) to their boundary practice with all of their other clients. Boundaries were deemed modified when professionals treated their dissociative clients differently than their other clients. The results showed a marked tendency for the modification of professional boundaries when treating people with DDs (Sachs, 2013, p.159). These results appeared to be independent of country or profession but were more pronounced among the more experienced professionals.

For instance, weekly sessions may periodically become bi-weekly sessions, or even daily sessions to work through acute crises and prevent the need for hospitalization. After the crisis has passed, however, the frequency of sessions would diminish, moving back to the norm for that person and therapist. Personal and agency policies may dictate what level of care is possible, and the limitations of the provider need to be clearly stated at the beginning of therapy.

Creating Safety

Safety in sessions includes both emotional and physical safety for both client and therapist. "Do no harm" is a rule everyone needs to follow to the best of his or her ability. With some clients, that may be very difficult. Self-harm and other unhealthy or dangerous behaviors may be the only way the client knows how to handle certain problems, and it may take a while to learn skills that eliminate the hurtful behavior. It takes time to extricate oneself from addictions, and to learn to deal with emotions in non-reactive ways. The therapy will need to involve both harm-reduction strategies and limits for the kinds of behavior that would sabotage treatment.

While most therapists clearly state that it is not acceptable to harm anyone in session, they also normally state that the client may not destroy the office property. Ironically, some clients will intentionally break something in the office in order to be sent away, having no other means of letting the therapist know that they cannot stay in therapy any longer. It is helpful to let the client know that when therapy becomes too difficult, it's acceptable, and a good idea, to tell the therapist. The pace of the work can be slowed down or the direction of the work can be changed to help the client continue with a process that feels productive and not overwhelming.

An important aspect of establishing safety within the therapeutic relationship involves stressing a sense of "I–Thou" mutuality, a deep respect for one another. Too often expectations are simply handed down for how the client is to behave in therapy, and what he or she can, and cannot do. This can be perceived as another set of rules to follow (and challenge) as passed down by yet another authority figure. A more collaborative approach is to have expectations emerge out of a respectful conversation, apply to both client and therapist, and become a behavioral contract between the two people, setting things up to go as well as both people can imagine. As the therapy progresses, expectations may change, and both people can initiate conversations about the need for change and how they can manage that in a mutually satisfying manner.

Clarifying these expectations becomes an embodiment of two people respecting each other, respecting the valuable work they are doing together, and ultimately respecting themselves.

In order to work on difficult material there needs to be an atmosphere of profound respect and safety between therapist and client. This is embodied in the following expectations:

The client will not break any of the therapist's property.
The client will not break the therapist's furniture or otherwise mess up the therapist's office.
The client will not hurt other people.
Clients will not hurt themselves.
And Safety Rule Number One, the Client will not hurt <Insert name of therapist here>.

The therapist goes on to say that this set of expectations is a mutual process and that:

The therapist will not break any of the client's property.
The therapist will not hurt other people.
The therapist will not hurt their own self.
And Safety Rule Number One, the therapist will not hurt <Insert name of client here>.

Creating Stability: Collaboration, Communication, Comforting, and Containment

Creating a context of safety and stability involves creating collaboration, communication, comfort, and containment. These are vital in setting up an environment in which complex trauma clients can heal, and the need for these things is even more pronounced for the dissociative client. Each one of these begins with the first contact between therapist and client, with the therapist continually modeling collaborative communication which is both comforting and containing. Mary Jo Barrett from the Center for Contextual Change describes therapy as "a collaborative process at the very onset and throughout". That therapist and client work together to establish goals, framework and a collaborative relationship (Barrett & Fish, 2014).

Collaboration and Communication

With dissociative clients, that first contact may be repeated with different parts of the person, greeting and connecting with each part genuinely and with respect, no matter what their initial presentation. For the therapist, to continue to keep the whole person in mind is critical. Whether the person is dealing with a single trauma with a sense of self as "before and after", or a lifetime of trauma resulting in no consistent sense of self, the client is still one person, and the therapist needs to keep that reality in mind.

Within the client, the challenge is to come together, retrieving or creating a unified sense of self. Doing that requires learning how to communicate and collaborate within the self. In order to do that, the person needs to be in an environment that allows the client to relax defenses enough to work on difficult material. The presence of the therapist witnessing the client's journey is also essential. Trauma often feels extremely lonely and isolating, so to have a person who sees, hears, understands, and cares, makes a big difference in the client's experience of healing.

The genuine connection with a safe and caring person provides the context in which healing can happen. According to Porges' Polyvagal Theory, sociality is the core process underlying mental and physical health (Porges, 2021). The creation of a safe relationship allows the client's automatic defense mechanisms to relax over time.

In the early part of therapy, there needs to be an openness to allow the client to express the disconnect within, and their genuine reactions to that. Being able to discuss the client's experience from within that framework and to acknowledge and validate their experience without judging or requiring them to accept or acknowledge other parts is an initial step in creating a safe means of communicating in general.

It's common for people to want to distance themselves from their trauma, wishing it could just go away. They may do that through denial, or self-loathing. Some people attempt to rid themselves from their pasts with drugs or alcohol, self-harm, and any other way they can find that might work to relieve their agony and despair. They often hate and fear their vulnerability. In the beginning, it is more helpful to listen to how the person feels and try to understand why he, she, or they would feel like that than to begin to try to change that feeling. Hearing the motivation behind the avoidance helps put both therapist and client in a position to learn how best to build a bridge between internal splits.

To create collaboration within any divided system requires communication between the splits, whether it's a split between traumatic experience and consciousness, or splits within the self. In the case of a complex PTSD client with limited dissociative defenses, this might be creating a sense of awareness between the person's conscious desire to heal and the blocks inside that make that healing difficult. For example, the most difficult part of the trauma may have been the feeling of powerlessness. If that can be named, and that feeling is then validated; it becomes easier to address. No one likes feeling powerless.

Noticing patterns of avoidance or distraction is helpful when done with compassion. Many survivors automatically feel exposed and shamed when their defenses become conscious, as if they were flaws instead of protections. There's also the potential for shame when the traumatic material begins to surface. Accordingly, comforting and containment skills need to be modeled and taught all through the process of healing.

Splits in consciousness protect the person from flooding with intolerable affect and knowledge. They also help keep irreconcilable experiences separate. They protect the person from the annihilation of being betrayed and alone in the face of the abuse. It is common to hear the survivor of abuse describe shock when the abuse begins, the desperate feeling that carries the message and experience of, "this can't be happening, this can't be happening to me, this is not happening to me, I'm not here, I'm up on the ceiling (out the window, etc.), and it's happening to him/her/them down there". When the abuse is followed by denial, with family or others acting as if it didn't happen, the split becomes more profound. The person may have a surreal feeling, losing the sense of confidence in their own reality, increasing the sense of disconnect inside and out.

Having grown up in dysfunctional households, coping with multiple conflicting demands of disorganized caregivers, or reeling from several tours of duty in war zones, the complex PTSD client is ill equipped to manage the challenge of holding two or more conflicting feelings at the same time. They tend to have a narrow Window of Tolerance, and need to learn how to deal with their intense emotions one step at a time. Having someone present and witnessing the person helps to ground the person in the reality of what they had to endure.

Validating the client's feelings and subjective sense of the experience is not the same as validating or confirming the client's history. The therapist is seldom in a position to do that, and that is not the point of listening and witnessing. The point is to hear the person's experience, what impact it had, and then work together to heal from that impact. This is a slow and gentle process of moving from respecting the splits of consciousness that were necessary to survive to supporting the survivor's ability to tolerate and explore a widening circle of conflicting yet related thoughts, feelings, and perceptions.

For the client with more elaborate dissociative parts, this initially appears as a form of "shuttle diplomacy" where the therapist speaks with different self-states, listening to each one as they emerge. At the opportune moment, the therapist begins to help the client become aware of and share alternate points of view held by different aspects of the self and gently assesses the client's (and the separate self-states') readiness to explore and acknowledge those varying ideas and feelings. Gradually, the need for separateness softens. It is no longer necessary to not know what is known, and the person learns to hold conflicting feelings, such as both loving and hating their abuser.

Involving the different aspects of self in discussion takes a great deal of sensitivity and tact. The complex PTSD client may be more comfortable talking about their rage than the terror or shame that was part of the trauma. In dissociative systems, DID or OSDD, some of the aspects of self are often kept "out of the loop" to prevent them from being overwhelmed by the traumatic material or intensity of the conflict. Often those are the aspects of the self that are the ANP or the "host". Carefully engaging that part of self in the process is essential, so the therapist needs to be mindful of situations where one or more parts of the self may affect the pace of therapy in a way that could be harmful to the whole person. Engaging those self-states in a discussion, those who may want to push the pace of the therapy, or those who may block it by "holding the secrets", allows more of the person to be included in the discussion of the purpose and process of the therapy. The conversations with the therapist provide a model and a valuable experience in creating positive communication patterns within a dissociative system which help to build a collaborative internal community.

Bearing in mind that the self-states are dissociated parts of a whole, moving from externalized, concrete means of communication to internalized states of knowing one's self is another important goal. Mid-steps along the way include shifting from externalized communication through the therapist or through tangible means such as written expression to internal forms of communication, such as internal cell phones or imagery of meeting spaces and group discussions. Later in the process the therapist can ask the client to "ask inside" or to "listen intuitively", or move to a place where the ANP can imagine what the EP might be feeling. For the client without such a delineated dissociative system, one might ask if the client can name the feelings that are most difficult to face, and explore why they are so difficult.

Double Binds

One of the common difficulties for traumatized people to face is having been put in a double bind. A double bind exists when two options are offered and neither one is acceptable. People remain stuck in double-binds because to accept one side is to lose the reality of the other, and yet both exist. For example, children may need to lose themselves to remain attached to an abusing parent. If they step back in order to preserve themselves, they are abandoned by their parent. It's a lose-lose situation. Each side of the conflict is held separate and in a state of tension with respect to the other sides of the conflict. To acknowledge both sides is to risk being overwhelmed and to feel "crazy".

Gregory Bateson (Bateson et al. 1956) described this as the classic "Double-Bind Theory". Acknowledging one side apparently requires denying the other.

Yet neither can be denied and neither can be wholly accepted. To complete the trap, the client cannot leave (escape) the conflict; nor can the client talk about or observe the conflict as a whole.

The double bind may also be presented as the illusion of choice. In this situation, the person is told he or she can choose between two or more options. However, all options are horrible, and there is no option to say "no". This is another form of a no-win situation. To be forced to make what appears to be a choice but isn't, results in the client taking on a responsibility for something they have no authority or responsibility for. The abuser who says or implies that the victim, "made him do it" puts the victim in this no-win situation. To acknowledge one's own personal power would be to agree that the abuser was powerless to resist, and to acknowledge that it was the abuser who really had the power is to confront the feeling of powerlessness. Often victims take on the pseudo-responsibility rather than be left with the reality of their own powerlessness to stop the abuse.

For the DID client, each side of the conflict is manifested as a separate self-state, such as a part who loves the abuser, and another part who hates the abuser. The different self-states can neither acknowledge one another nor cooperate without risking the overwhelm of the whole internal community. In highly conflicted "systems", the self-states seem at war with each other and threaten the community or other self-states should they acknowledge an opposing view. There may be alters who feel attached to the parent, and other alters who have disengaged from the parent to preserve the self. The two alters (or sets of alters) typically stay very distant to each other and may even "hate" each other—which helps to keep them apart so they can continue to manage an untenable situation.

Collaboration among the different and divergent parts of self is critical to moving forward. When the person is in a state of internal conflict, the experience is like a civil war. Lincoln's quote about "a house divided cannot stand" rings true here.

Gaining awareness of and sufficient access to these self-states or differing aspects of the client allows the therapist to begin to work through the careful process of educating and normalizing the richness of human experience and emotional responses. Children growing up in "good enough" households learn that they can hold these different feelings; that they can be mad at Mom for setting a limit while still loving and being loved by Mom. They learn that they can like their best friend Tommy while being hurt that Tommy outscored them playing pinball.

Learning to respect the different self-states and their contradictory roles is another aspect of building a sense of collaboration. People learn to respect the need to have another part of self (or self-state) hold some of the crushing load. Analogies that seem useful include references to team sports where each player has a specific job to do. Similarly, describing orchestras or choral groups where each musician plays or sings a different part to create a total experience more beautiful than any individual element.

Comforting

There is tremendous loss and pain in facing the horrors of abuse, the devastating sense of betrayal or abandonment. People need respite, shelter from the storm, in order to be able to recover enough to be able to face what happened to them. Sadly, for many people, there was little comfort to be found in their early lives, little chance to have experienced being cared for by another. When abused, they often had no one to turn to for help, having to carry the trauma alone. In a dysfunctional family, children may be abused by the parent they would normally go to for help. That parent may be alternately abusive and nurturing. Unable to predict which presentation of the parent will greet them at the door, a caring mom or an abusive mother, a molesting dad or a playful father, or any number of paradoxical presentations, the child may feel that it is not safe to seek help from others, and will learn other ways to try to comfort the self. Rocking, head-banging, regression, trancing out, or dissociative shifts to alternative ways of being are some of the ways people try to comfort themselves when comfort from others is not available.

As these children grow, they lack experiences of healthy ways to soothe or nurture themselves. Worse, they may not even be able to identify soothing activities. In addition, the perception of soothing activities they do have has been influenced and informed by the behavior of the dysfunctional family. As a result, they may have learned to use harmful means to try to calm themselves, like alcohol, drugs, risky or painful sex.

Being traumatized increases the need for comfort by others and the ability to actively soothe the self. As both of those sources of help are compromised or absent for some people who have been chronically traumatized, the needs of the traumatized person frequently exceed the resources available, both internally and externally. When that happens, caring friends may become frustrated and burned out, leaving our clients dropping into despair.

To further complicate matters, for clients with Dissociative Identity Disorder and/or strong internal conflicts, there may be multiple conflicting ways that they identify as nurturance; some which may be helpful, and some that are not. Compulsive activities, self-harm, avoidance, and dissociation are some of the ways people attempt to self soothe. In people with DID, some parts of the self may be capable of healthy self-soothing, or asking for comfort from others. Other parts of the self may block or react destructively against the vulnerability inherent in asking for help and support. Others may engage in a myriad of self-harming behaviors as a means to turn emotional or relational pain into physical pain or trigger an endorphin enhanced dissociative episode. (Other reasons and uses of self-harm behaviors will be discussed in Chapter 9.) All of these options may be cycling through simultaneously.

Every person and every dissociative internal structure is different, so care must be given to not make assumptions. The careful therapist needs to check in and ask about the person's self-soothing behaviors.

Comforting (and containment) work best when the dissociative person has developed internal collaboration. For people with complex PTSD, a different kind of collaboration needs to develop, involving a willingness to deal with the trauma and sufficient skills to tolerate the intense experience of working things through.

Without internal methods of communication and a respectful, collaborative approach, the client will remain locked in an intrapsychic civil war. For the complex PTSD client without the pronounced dissociative defenses, this manifests as being frozen between two mutually exclusive ways of being, shut down to the trauma or overwhelmed by it.

Containment

Dissociation at any level, from depersonalization, derealization, dissociative trance states, or dissociative amnesia to polyfragmented Dissociative Identity Disorder can be seen as a means to keep the client from becoming over-powered by the effects of the abuse. As with other intrapsychic defenses, these methods are limited in effectiveness, and ultimately fail to prevent the person from escaping the torment of their internal war.

The "Good News" is that dissociation works and the survivor need not fully feel the abuse or know the trauma. The "Bad News" is that dissociation works and the survivor cannot learn, grow, or develop a sense of self.

Developing skills to contain the intensity of the emotional storm and cog-nitive maelstrom is essential to facilitate the process of keeping our clients in the here and now and able to develop critical coping skills and insights into their behaviors, reactions and recovery.

Specific containment strategies will be discussed in a later chapter. The key point here is the need for our clients to address this crucial task as an integral part of the healing process. Furthermore, these skills are interconnected and interdependent. Without a sense of collaboration, the disparate self-states will not communicate nor engage in proactive self-soothing behaviors. Without developing containment skills and adaptive comforting strategies, the client needs to rely on on-going forms of divisive defenses.

Suggestions

Have clients make a list of self-soothing behaviors, things they can do when alone. Add to the list as new things are discovered.

Have clients make a list of how they can be comforted by others. Include the names and contact information for those people who have demonstrated that they can help the client calm down, feel safe, and regain equilibrium.

Have clients get different magazines or pictures from the internet and make a collage of comforting objects and activities.

To work with resistance to self-soothing or being comforted by others, it can be helpful to have the person write, draw, or simply share the possible negative consequences of self-soothing behavior. Actually being kind to one-self, or accepting kindness from another can be painful. People connect with the pain of the absence of that kindness in their personal history. Grief and upset may emerge when true comfort is given and received. The realization that the abuse was as bad as it was, and the lack of concern and care by others can be very difficult to face.

One process that can help discover and potentially widen the client's range of acceptable experience, is to engage in internal dialogues. Similar to the famous empty chair technique of Fritz Perls (Perls, Hefferline, & Goodman, 1951), having the client manifest the different sides of the dialogue (or multi-logue as the case may be) allows for the therapist and client to follow and process the discussion together. The empty chair technique involves imagining another person, or a part of the self, on an empty chair, and having an imaginary dialogue with that person or part. Talking and listening to another part of the self externalizes an internal dynamic and helps the person learn more about what's going on inside.

A useful intervention for clients who are unable to identify positive nurturing behaviors, is to create a collage of what they perceive as positive images. The instruction is to find a variety of different magazines covering a variety of interests. Without judging or evaluating, select and clip out any image that gives the client a warm (perhaps wistful) feeling, or ones that the client wishes to experience. The client is encouraged to assemble these apparently random pictures on one or more sheets of paper (perhaps a different sheet of paper for different parts of the self-system) and bring them into session for discussion.

In the follow-up therapy session, client and clinician explore what themes might emerge, why certain items seem as possible or desirable nurturing experiences, and how they could be experienced. Internal conflicts are examined and potential compromise solutions are offered for consideration.

Other strategies include a letter writing campaign or a form of serial journaling. Make a list (sometimes with the assistance of the therapist and/or friends) of things that are normally perceived as healthy ways to self-soothe or be comforted by others. Then choose one each day (or at whatever interval sounds possible) and practice doing that one thing.

Stage 2: Remembrance and Mourning: Facing What Happened

The traditional second stage of therapy is focused on addressing the trauma, and the impact of the trauma on all aspects of the client's life. The skills learned in the first stage of therapy come into play in this stage—the ability to be consciously connected to knowing and feeling what has happened in a way that allows the trauma to be acknowledged, tolerated, and disempowered. Intense emotions surface, and the person has the ability to work through them for the amount of time that is tolerable. The window of tolerance has grown large enough to incorporate the person's experience, and the work of facing the trauma, grieving the losses, acknowledging parts of self that were unavailable or inaccessible, and finding a way to create some meaning out of the tragedy make up the work of this stage.

Remembering and mourning any trauma is difficult. For single traumas, there is a "before" and "after", marking whatever changes within the person and how the person relates to the world. Trauma shatters a person's worldview, and that can be a shift in how the world is experienced, or a devastating rupture leaving the person struggling to find a completely new way of being in order to survive.

When there have been multiple traumas, the second stage of therapy is more complicated. Trauma needs to be faced and dealt with, but with multiple traumas, the person needs most to deal with the common themes of the traumas, such as powerlessness and shame. For some people whose lives have been defined by on-going trauma, it's not possible, or advisable, to try to deal with each traumatic event. Some specific trauma memories may serve as representative of many others; containing behavior and effects common to a lot of the traumatic events in the person's life. Those traumas, when dealt with effectively, carry over into the others, spreading the healing through to those traumas that were similar.

Trauma clients do not need to recall and process every bad thing that ever happened to them. To attempt that would overwhelm both client and therapist. The key is to address pivotal points that speak for many parts, reflecting the core themes of the abuse. The goal is closer to consciousness raising, achieving a "critical mass" that in turn triggers a paradigm shift in the client's understanding of him, her, or themself. The need to address every traumatic incident is based on a fear of not doing therapy "right", of avoiding a mistake and then being punished.

Knowing the history of the person is critical to planning the second stage of therapy. Too often, therapy begins with an insufficient knowledge of the client, and working on the known traumas may activate those that were not identified and overwhelm the person. When that happens, the therapy needs to shift back to emphasizing stability and safety, giving the person time to become calm enough to feel more in charge of the process and less at the mercy of it. The emergence of old coping mechanisms may indicate that therapy is moving too fast for the person, and newly acquired skills are not strong enough to handle the emotional impact of the work. Slowing down is often a good idea. It allows both client and therapist to take stock, revisit the treatment plan, and make any revisions that both feels would be helpful.

Work in Stage Two can be very intense. Trauma treatment triggers trauma (Connors & Mayhew, 2006). This is a challenge for both the client and the therapist. Not many therapists have been trained to deal with intense emotions, like shame, rage, grief, and terror. In Stage Two of the therapy, those are the emotions that emerge when the trauma is faced directly. In dealing with such powerful emotions, it becomes important for the therapist to understand an inverse relationship; with increased affective arousal comes decreased cognitive functioning. Additionally, as dissociative defenses are dropped, there is often an increase in PTSD symptomatology. Failure to titrate these effects frequently undermines therapeutic success.

The therapist must resist the tendency to turn therapy into an ordeal. Trauma is subjectively experienced as if there is no beginning, middle, or end. There is only the never-ending now of terror and pain. Learning to pace oneself is part of healing from the effects of trauma.

Traumatized people have suffered great losses, of many kinds. Some of the impact of trauma can be restored, such as healthy self-esteem. Other things are gone forever, such as the assumption that all people can be trusted. When the trauma comes with betrayal, relationships may be permanently damaged or lost.

A fundamental reality to trauma treatment is that we are not changing history. Therapy cannot undo what has been done. The goal is integration of disowned and dissociated aspects of self and one's experience. Therapy is not exorcism. Rather we are helping our clients deal with what was and grieving what was not.

In processing memories, a growing awareness of what feels bad and scary is necessary and ultimately helpful. Connecting with the past yields vital information about what was learned and what was missing. Clients will then have the opportunity to choose whether or not to hold onto the lessons of the past and what they need to learn (healthy attachment, relationship skills, self-care, etc.) in order to move forward.

The trauma itself may be extremely difficult to share, and to hear. Both the client and the therapist may want to save the other from the devastating reality of what happened. Some clients have felt that telling their truth would contaminate whoever listened. Because so many people may have recoiled and left when the client tried to share previously, there will need to be reassurances given that are followed up with the behavior of listening, staying present and continuing to see the client with respect and compassion. Some therapists may have difficulty hearing their clients' traumatic memories, wanting to save the client from the intensity of what already happened. Even if that is not stated, the client will pick it up and have more difficulty sharing.

A core theme throughout this discussion of trauma treatment is the importance of the authenticity of the therapist and the strength of the therapeutic alliance. As the client is recounting their experiences, in the depth of the pain and torment, the therapist cannot remain the neutral blank screen. Silence is the hallmark of the uncaring other, the enabling parent. An attuned therapist needs to demonstrate and express appropriate levels of compassion and a sense of moral outrage regarding the abuse.

Memories are best dealt with in small amounts. Attempting to process an entire traumatic event at once can easily push people past their ability to assimilate what happened and the impact it left. Taking the time to step into the memory and back out, with resources available to handle each section of the trauma, allows people to move through it step by step; seeing, feeling, understanding, and moving past each section.

There are many techniques that can help in this process. Dr. Kluft writes about his fragmented abreaction technique, using hypnosis to help the client tap into memories and come back out successfully (Kluft, 2013). Catherine Fine and Amy Berkowitz (2001) developed a very effective Wreathing Protocol, using hypnosis and EMDR. Anabel Gonzalez,Dolores Mosquera and Miriam Morrison (2012) have also studied complex trauma and dissociative difficulties and found ways to use EMDR effectively, advising therapists to start with the least upsetting event rather than most upsetting when the client has a long history of abuse and has dissociative issues. Pat Ogden, Kekuni Minton, and Clare Pain (2006) have worked to help people process traumatic memories using somatic techniques. Rich Chefetz (2015), and Elizabeth Howell (2011), work successfully using psychoanalysis. There are many ways to help clients through this stage. The more ways the therapist learns, the better able they will be to match the technique to the client. All of the people just mentioned have a great amount of experience and training, and are able to use many different techniques. Each one will automatically use the approach that will best meet the needs of the client. That is the hallmark of a master clinician.

An important caveat: specialized techniques, specific schools of thought or treatment methodologies are tools, not panaceas. They must all be used with wisdom and caution reflecting the therapist's best clinical judgment based on the unique and individualized needs of the person sitting before them. Many specialized techniques can work well with severely traumatized people, but they must be used with the awareness and cooperation of the client's internal "community". Severely traumatized people are avoiding their pain for good reasons. The desire to be "fixed" quickly and without pain or discomfort can cause therapists and clients to use a technique too often or too soon with tragic results.

As Phil Kinsler has stated, "Any intervention can be harmful if you don't know your client" (Kinsler, 2018). This is particularly important for therapists working with people who are dissociative. People with Dissociative Identity Disorder have adapted to living in situations where they need to not know their own experiences. Those experiences are too traumatic and they lack the safety and supportive relationships that could help them heal. They don't fully know themselves, and, therefore, the therapist can't fully know them, either. The focus of therapy is to help clients get to know themselves safely, in the context of a healthy, supportive relationship. The therapeutic relationship is known to be the most significant factor in healing (Norcross & Lambert, 2014). Trauma that happens within a relationship, from people within a family or close to the person in some way, has a more severe impact, adding betrayal and damage to significant relationships to whatever trauma has occurred. In these cases, which includes many of the people with dissociative disorders, the importance of a solid therapeutic relationship becomes crucial. The traumatized person needs to both deal with the trauma and have the experience of a genuine, healthy, supportive relationship. This is not, and can't be, a "quick fix", and it's not uncommon for premature use of techniques to plunge people into their trauma beyond their capacity to cope. Therapy needs to stay in step with the person's ability to manage the facts and the affect around what happened to them. Every therapy needs to be personalized, designed to work with the whole individual, including any and all self-states known and potentially not yet known.

Most clients have their own way of doing the work of Stage Two. The therapist's job is to make sure the process is fundamentally healthy and allow for individual differences in how it's done. This continues to be a collaborative process, with client and therapist working together to create the best healing path for this particular person. Some things for the therapist to notice is whether clients tend to stand too far back from emotions and experiences or tend to jump in over their head and feel that the process won't work without a crisis. The former is on the avoidant end of the scale, and the latter is on the ordeal end. Somewhere in the middle is the balance point, where the trauma is addressed at a manageable level, within the client's Window of Tolerance.

If there's a difference between the client's ability to tolerate affect and the therapist's ability, that will need to be addressed. The therapist can explore with clients what they can tolerate. The therapist may need to seek supervision or consultation to deal with their personal discomfort with the client's way of working. There are a few ways this can turn out. In some cases, the client may be a bit too avoidant, or trying too hard. In other cases, the client's process may trigger the therapist in ways that make it hard for him or her to remain in a therapeutic position with the client. In the former, the therapist can focus on helping the client find ways to face what happened and move through it successfully. In the latter, the therapist will need to do whatever is necessary to take care of personal issues so they do not impede the client's progress.

One of the advantages for the therapist of working with trauma survivors is that they are continually pushed to deal with their own issues in order to be available to their clients. In doing their own work, therapists also gain insight into how it feels to work on internal issues, and they tend to improve as therapists.

When intense traumatic events are confronted, people may react with the emotion that was not accessible during the event, or they may react with the realization of the effect of the trauma on their lives. They may sob, rage, or shake while speaking. In some cases, the reality of their loss may result in keening, a delayed response to their loss. The therapist needs to be able to gauge whether the client is staying with the window of tolerance or not. In stage two, the client may be able to express this level of intensity and remain in their window of tolerance. They are using the skills learned in stage one. If the client is going over the line, outside their window of tolerance, the therapist will need to gently interrupt the process and help the client calm down enough to continue. Affect tolerance, pacing, self-soothing skills, and the ability to be comforted by others are extremely important during this stage of therapy.

Unbridled expression of emotion without attached context and meaning is unhealthy and retraumatizing. Recounting an experience without the attendant affect remains disconnected and dissociated. An essential element of Stage Two work is to assemble all the dissociated parts of traumatic memories into a coherent and understandable narrative that can be integrated into the client's personal history and on-going sense of self.

Also, during this stage, the client is confronted with the imperfections of memory. It's very difficult to know some of what happened and not all of it. The therapist needs to help the client let the unknown be unknown until it becomes clear from within. In most cases, enough of the memory comes back to be able to make sense of the client's symptoms. However, it's not necessary for the memory to be complete for the person to heal. It's not the details of the memory that are important, it's the effect of whatever happened on the person. So, whether the memory can become clear or not, the client can still heal. Even without details, the impact of the trauma remains, and that's the focus of the therapy.

What does it mean to process a memory? As mentioned above; one essential element of memory work is to assemble all the dissociated parts of traumatic memories into a coherent and understandable narrative. Integrating this more complete understanding of the traumatic event into the client's personal history and on-going sense of self is a second and equally essential aspect of processing the trauma.

There are several steps in the process. In the beginning, the memory may emerge in many ways, as images, sensations, feelings, or knowledge. These fragments may have been part of the person's life for a long time, or may be relatively new. There is usually something familiar about what comes up, and it's helpful to notice that. Sometimes, what was originally breaking through in flashbacks in the first stage of therapy now comes out in more accessible form.

Thinking back to the models of dissociation and how traumatized people block or avoid awareness of different elements of the trauma experience, the need to assemble the previously dissociated components of the event becomes clear. In exploring the event, there are a few guidelines to facilitate a careful unfolding of the dissociated material.

Let the client choose which events to focus on. Use the present to tap into the past. Be attuned to recurrent themes that confound the client's life in the present. Explore the historical aspects of on-going relational conflicts by asking if specific behavioral patterns seem familiar and when or how they were treated in a similar fashion. All of these opportunities provide a doorway into the client's trauma history.

Asking non-leading questions is essential to helping the narrative unfold. Experienced clinicians will have a sense of what might have happened based on their experience and understanding of how trauma impacts people. However, they weren't there and it is the task of the client to piece their history together. An important skill for therapists to model at this juncture is the ability to tolerate ambiguity and uncertainty.

As the client recounts their story, there is often a profound need for them to be believed. The elegant and careful dance of the therapist is to acknowledge the client is reporting their history as they believe it to be at this point in time without validating what the therapist has no means of authenticating. It is important not to get caught up in the details and lose sight of the experience of loss, abandonment, and betrayal.

Often the initial experience of trauma is a repetitive loop of a portion of the event. The goal is to develop a coherent narrative, identifying a context and a frame of reference for making sense of disparate images, feelings, and sensations. Allow for non-linear processing by asking, "What happened before that?" as well as "What happened next?" Ask if other parts of self can contribute to filling in gaps. Move forward and backwards to complete the beginning, middle, and end.

If the client is not at risk of decompensating, it is helpful to have him, her, or them explore whatever has surfaced, paying neutral attention to it, noticing it, jotting it down or sharing it. Let the client talk about it. As the person talks about the piece of memory, monitor their emotional state. Notice the things that seem to be easy to relate, and those that are difficult. Also, notice if there are gaps in the memory, parts that seem to be completely missing, like the awareness of entering a room, and then leaving it feeling devastated, but no memory of what may have happened in the room. Start with what is known and let the person reflect on it. Having distance from the event, and a lot more emotional skills, telling the narrative may be a completely new experience, with insights coming out spontaneously.

In exploring the recalled event, the purpose is to empower the person to examine the beliefs that arose from this and similar experiences. What did this teach them (or more accurately, what did this teach the child that underwent the trauma) about themselves, others, and the world? To facilitate pacing, periodically step out of the recalling to identify and acknowledge dysfunctional and manipulative tactics of the perpetrators, missed opportunities, and distorted beliefs that were either imposed by the abusers or developed by the child as a magical means to try to avoid further abuse. This is a key opportunity to develop the client's ability to question and view experiences from alternative perspectives.

Another way to deal with complex traumatic experiences is to take one feeling common to most and deal with that. For instance, a person may talk about the experiences of being tricked, or betrayed, noticing how that felt and how it impacted their ability to trust others. Or, they may look at the fear they carry, all the reasons for it, and begin to be compassionate to themselves rather than put themselves down for not being brave enough.

When the memory is extremely horrific, leave the worst parts for last. The person will need to confront the trauma, know it, feel it, be able to talk about it in an integrated manner, and then be able to leave the office fully capable of getting home safely. That means that the trauma will take many sessions of work, keeping the amount of emotional material limited at each session.

It is helpful to prepare for what may be an intense session. Without preparation, the most intense parts of the work may come too close to the end of therapy, leaving the person at a vulnerable place when it's time to go. If the session is planned, the client and therapist can move into the work early in the session and allow sufficient time to come back to the present in a grounded way before leaving. It can also be helpful to have a support person available to help the client before and after therapy. This could be the client's friend, roommate, spouse, etc., anyone available who is stable and cares.

Sometimes, Stage Two includes sessions with a little or a lot of abreaction. An abreaction is an outpouring of emotion, the expression of intense feelings that were not able to be expressed at the time of the trauma. For example, a woman who saw her father killed in a car accident froze at that time, and years later, in telling the story of that event, began to wail with grief. She was strong enough for that to happen, so the therapist supported her, and the client was finally able to grieve the loss of her father.

Abreactions can be very helpful, as long as they can be in line with the person's healing. When they are, they come out as a natural part of the process. In the example above, the woman was talking about her father, and herself at the time of the accident. She had a coherent memory, just a lack of emotion, and that felt odd to her since the time of her father's death. This was a single, devastating trauma. Her life changed from that point on. Still, she had spent most of her childhood with two parents who loved her and took good care of her. When she began to keen and wail, the therapist was not concerned about her being unable to return to a stable place. The release of emotion felt "right", as if the missing piece had been found.

It's more challenging with people whose trauma has been on-going. Allowing those people to freely release intense emotions may not be a good idea. Each of their traumas may contain emotions that pop up in other traumas, creating a connection through the similarity of extreme emotional states. To drop into one of those emotional states may take the person on a wild ride through many memories of trauma and become too much to take in and work with successfully. In those cases, the portion of the memory needs to be limited to the amount of energy and time the person and the therapist have to address the emotions that emerge. Techniques such as hypnosis, EMDR, TIR, and others, can help the therapist focus the client on small enough portions of the trauma to ensure success in moving through and coming to a better place. That place is known by the feeling of being present and relatively calm while also being aware of the trauma and the impact of it on the person's life.

As mentioned previously, developing a coherent narrative is important. Understanding how those events impacted the person's life is equally important. As client's come to recognize the depth and extent of what has happened to them, they begin to truly count the cost. With that comes intense grief and a host of existential questions.

The intensity of the grief cannot be adequately expressed in words. The therapist's ability to sit with and bear witness to the client's pain will be tested.

Clients are highly attuned to the therapist's reactions and responses and will stop themselves rather than push the therapist too far.

We help our clients move forward by acknowledging their pain and helping them see that the grief, as all powerful emotions, comes in waves. We remind them to look for relief between the waves, reassuring them that the pain will not go on forever. It is important to help our clients to learn to accept support and to care for themselves. Appropriate self-soothing skills developed in stage one work will be called upon. Comforting that should have occurred when they were younger can happen now.

Frequently, clients ask to understand why this happened to them. Why were they targeted for the abuse? What is inherently so wrong, so bad, about them that people would treat them in such horrific ways? Understanding the dynamics of abusers can shed some light onto this difficult area.

Recognizing that perpetrators are often narcissistic and unable to truly care for or about another person is an important realization. Seeing that a narcissistic abuser does not hold anyone as an equal or a peer deserving of respect; that other people are reduced to the status of an audience or a prop may be helpful.

Another avenue to understanding why abuse can happen over and over from multiple perpetrators is to see the client, their family of origin, and many of the others they interacted with as members of a highly specific and exclusive subculture. Within that subculture people were assigned very defined and limiting roles. It may prove useful to examine the roles of other family members within that same subculture. Of specific interest to dissociative clients is to examine if their internal "system" reflects these same roles.

It is important that the therapist both normalize the early childhood reactions and learned behaviors while encouraging change. Examine how the initial set of responses made sense in the "war zone" that was their childhood home life. Validate the intent and attempt to seek safety and develop some degree of mastery and control in an otherwise unmanageable and unpredictable environment.

While acknowledging how the trauma and abuse impaired developmental growth as a child, stress the need for change as an adult. Key questions focus on the emerging authentic self. As the client can see the attempts to manipulate and limit their expression of self, so can the client let go of false "selves" maintained to appease the abusers. This stage is ripe with opportunities to find unique strengths buried among the ruins. What did the client foster to better survive—keen observational skills, adaptability, compassion?

With dissociative people and others who have long lasting abuse, it may be helpful to take one section of those traumas and work with that, such as the moment of realization that it's going to happen again, or the feeling of relief or abandonment when left alone at the end. Some people may choose to start with noticing how they managed to survive, by leaving their body, shutting down in some way, or, with dissociative people, switching into another part of the self. Noticing the patterns that contributed to survival can help the person appreciate their spontaneous survival mechanisms and notice inner strengths that kept them alive.

Stage 3: Integration and Reconnection

The third stage of therapy involves the integration of the trauma, with the growing sense of being able to be present and authentic, in touch with what happened, but no longer controlled by it. As one person said, "I am no longer my past". People often experience a burst of post-traumatic growth, finding meaning in their suffering that allows them to move forward, frequently involving ways to transform their trauma by helping others or by finding themselves at a new level of compassion and maturity.

Stage Three is often given too little notice in the literature of working with trauma survivors. This is unfortunate because it is the stage in which the trauma is integrated in such a way that the survivor knows and feels it to be past and is focused on living his, her, or their present and future life without the trauma being a necessary focal point requiring time and energy and influencing identity. Learning to live consciously in the world beyond the trauma challenges the person to evolve, in consciousness, relationships, and meaning. With the trauma having left center stage, all aspects of life shift, and the person now has the ability to have some conscious effect on how those shifts happen.

When a person has had many traumatic experiences, healing has probably taken a long time, and the last stage of therapy becomes a marker for a life transition. They take what they have learned about themselves and the world and put their energy into living in the present and being able to envision a future.

The identity of the person changes. For people with complex trauma and PTSD, they move out from under those labels. Their experiences have impacted them, but they have moved through the experiences enough to have them become part of their past and not something controlling their present lives. Generally speaking, their need to protect themselves, the constant vigilance associated with unresolved trauma, softens and they become more comfortable being closer to other people, more vulnerable. Intimate relationships gain in importance and begin to grow. Old relationships built on the connection through trauma tend to fade unless the other person has also grown.

For people who have integrated from being dissociative, there's an entirely new experience of being a whole self. Those people speak of the need to adjust to the quiet inside, the absence of internal companions. They may feel unusually lonely and realize how much they need to develop relationships with others outside of themselves. Without internal companions, the person may feel very vulnerable in the world, and it takes time to adjust to that new reality. Dissociative defenses are gone, and the person is steadily confronted with being present and dealing with others outside the self. Internally, normal emotional conflicts are all in one place, not divided into separate parts of the self, so the person can feel positive and negative emotions at the same time and needs to learn how to work with that kind of ambiguity. As a result, the manner in which the person makes decisions changes. They tend to move away from either/or responses and be able to consider the mix of variables that normally appear in significant decisions.

The person's relationships change. Some relationships may change for the better, becoming richer, and more intimate. Other relationships may fall by the wayside, with the gulf between people widening to the point of no longer being able to sustain a connection. Survivors often find each other and cling to each other, having no one else who can see them and comprehend their pain. When one person has grown and is no longer trapped in pain or fear, the connection dissipates.

In the third stage of therapy, people grapple with how to deal with the relationships that have been changed in the process of their healing; which ones will continue, and which ones show no hope of becoming healthy. The relationships that are lost need to be grieved. The ones that continue may need to be nurtured to become what they are possible of becoming. Old relational patterns emerge and new ones are practiced. Roles are examined, and consciously evaluated.

In dealing with abuse, relationships of all kinds are impacted. For example, it's not unusual for people dealing with incestuous abuse to be targeted by the family when they first speak up. Families often flee from the truth, blaming the victim and even defending the perpetrator. When survivors continue to hold onto the truth and heal, they may become the turning point for their entire family. Some family members may ostracize them, but others may see the truth that is finally being told and move towards the survivor. In telling the truth, the survivor is actually behaving as a very loyal family member, speaking a truth the family needs to hear in order to heal. They are seldom recognized in that manner, however, and are frequently labeled "disloyal", the opposite of what they actually are. In the third stage of therapy, the person may need to grieve the loss of the fantasized family, and consider what kinds of relationships might be possible with different family members. The third stage also includes forgiveness (forgiveness "in" —see Chapter 10), and the realization of what would be necessary for any kind of reconciliation in the future.

Often people experience post traumatic growth in meaning and spirituality. Post traumatic growth includes moving beyond the trauma in a way that uses the experience to deepen one's understanding of life, and that often includes an enriched spirituality. People glean meaning out of the trauma, learning to notice and appreciate life, love, kindness, and connection—all the things that were threatened or destroyed in the trauma. They are also often stronger for having survived and confronted their abuse.

For people who have complex trauma and dissociative issues, therapy may have been a part of their lives for years. The third stage of therapy includes ending therapy, something some people may have never thought would happen. Coming to the end of her process, one client and her therapist went over all the goals she had for therapy, those she came in with and those she added as she got into her process. Jointly, she and her therapist checked off all the goals. They had covered them all, and the person was doing well in her life. When it became evident to both that the therapy was done, the client said, "You mean I don't have to be in therapy forever?" The therapist assured her that she didn't, that she had done what she came to do. She could return at any time if she needed to, but she was able to deal with her life on her own now. The client had learned skills that allowed her to address her issues on her own. She had the internal resources she had discovered and learned in therapy, and those were serving her well. Face alight with joy, the client left the office for the last time.

Not all therapy ends that well. Sometimes, for many reasons, people never get to the third stage, or never get to complete it. People move, lose their insurance, become ill or in other ways unable to continue. Therapists also move, retire, become ill or disabled and may not be available to the client for the last stage of therapy.

When the client leaves, if there is time it's helpful to summarize the therapy as much as possible. That includes the reason the person came in, what was covered in therapy, and what still needs to be addressed. The client may need to return to his or her source of insurance to find another therapist, or the therapist may need to give the person referrals. Either way, letting the client know how to proceed to get back into therapy if he or she chooses to do so is an important part of the process of ending.

Some clients leave not out of external necessity but for other reasons, such as fear of facing the enormity of their own trauma, or fear of becoming attached to the therapist. Some may leave in order to maintain a feeling of control, a flight into health, or the need to take a break. Not everyone leaves for the same reason, and it is helpful if the client is able to share the reason with the therapist. That may not be possible, either because the departure is too swift, or because the client may not know why he or she is leaving or may not want to share that information with the therapist.

When the therapist needs to leave, it's helpful to let the client know as soon as possible. Moving, or retiring usually allows plenty of time to gather what is needed together to end as well as possible. Sometimes, however, the therapist leaves because of sudden illness, disability, or death. In these cases, having a professional will can make all the difference for the client and his or her ability to deal with the loss of the therapist and connect with a new therapist. A professional will includes a designated professional to call the clients, notify them of the loss of their therapist, and give them the referral that the therapist had written down for them. Records are then transferred to the new therapist. (Frankel, 2015)

Complicating Factors: Heads up—The Person You Will Be Treating Comes With More Than You Know

Dr. Rick Kluft:

> Good and knowledgeable clinicians are driven by the need to address what is there. Mediocre clinicians are driven by the need to find their models and theories confirmed in what they observe and do. Thereby

they sacrifice reality testing for statistical significance. They get reliability and lose ecological validity.

(Kluft, personal communication, 2015)

When working with complex trauma and dissociative issues, the three stages of therapy are more intense and complicated. Simple models and single theories seldom fit. The more the therapist can learn about trauma and dissociation, and the individual person coming for help, the more likely the therapy will succeed. Every trauma is different, and every person is different, so formulaic approaches rarely work. The most influential part of the therapy will be the relationship between the therapist and the client. It is within the relationship that the therapist gets to know the client at a level deep enough to determine which therapeutic tools may be helpful. It is also the presence and reality of the relationship that gives the client an experience of being seen and attuned to that facilitates healing beyond techniques and tools. A conscious therapeutic relationship is intensely respectful, continually bringing a sense of dignity into the process.

The necessity is to have a different relational experience from which to learn a different perception, one that is healthier, based on safety and trust. A lot of therapy tends to be top down—attempting to shift a person's way of perceiving and believing, without necessarily exploring the client's experience. With trauma survivors, a typical top-down approach is to ask them to have a thought or belief that would be healthier than the one they currently hold. However, since there is no experience to support that thought or belief, it has no foundation inside and will not stand up to real situations or emotions. A bottom up approach uses the new experiences in a healthy therapeutic relationship to allow the person to have a new experience. For example - asking a person to imagine a safe place inside when there has never been a safe place in his or her life is a top-down approach that often fails with survivors of severe trauma. For them, there's no reference point for what "safe" feels like. So, the therapist needs to work from the bottom up, providing a safe enough relationship from which the client can learn the feeling of safety. Milton Erickson described therapeutic interventions that allowed the client to imagine the therapist's voice going with them into emotionally charged situations (Rosen, 1982). The therapist's voice would connect with a new feeling, one of safety, that the client could then incorporate and practice.

The stages of therapy may not be clearly defined and in perfect sequence, but the relationship can remain consistent throughout the process. The therapist moves in concert with the client to create safety, process trauma, integrate and understand the past and be open to the future, moving back and forth through these tasks to help the client continue to move forward at an optimal pace. It's never a completely smooth process, with misattuned moments, ruptures, and repairs being both challenging and offering some of the greatest opportunities for growth. Working together with a competent and compassionate professional can make healing from complex trauma and dissociative issues happen at a deep level, giving the person experiences of a genuinely caring relationship that he or she may never have known to be possible.

Complex Trauma Disorder is a cluster of different and divergent symptoms and defenses that are manifested in ways that exacerbate and aggravate each other. This is one reason why the stages of therapy need to cycle back and forth so often. On-going trauma causes systemic breakdowns and distortions across multiple developmental dimensions. Key lessons and critical tasks are not taught or worse, deliberately filled with misinformation or patterns that work against the person. While therapy is progressing, time is taken to learn lessons and tasks missed while focusing on survival. Working in relational skills, boundary setting, self-care, autonomy, affective regulation and expression may reveal the distortions learned in dysfunctional settings. Emotional needs may be expressed through a variety of direct and indirect means, some appropriate, and some not. All of this comes out in therapy, and the damage that has been done becomes evident over time in many areas. Knowing the areas impacted by trauma helps the therapist set up the context for therapy and create treatment plans that can address these developmental issues. While there may be common patterns and issues, each client is unique. The more therapists learn about the client in front of them, the better they will be able to create therapeutic experiences.

In clients who have dissociative issues, there may be many different levels of development that manifest during the therapy. Childlike states may emerge in session along with very sophisticated adult states, demonstrating the absence and presence of developmental steps in an unintegrated manner. Knowing that there's an internal variation in the person's ability to respond means that the therapist cannot assume mental or emotional consistency and will need to learn to work with the person knowing that interventions may be "heard" by any or all aspects of the person. The technique of "talking through" (Caul, 1978) is based on the awareness that the person may have few or many aspects of the self that are attending to what is being said so the message needs to be given in a way that is appropriate for the whole system. The language may vary between talking to the part of the person currently presenting and the whole person, parts known and unknown. The intention is to consistently use inclusive and integrative language to invite the whole person into therapy. It is very similar to working with a family in therapy—whatever is said to one person, is heard by all. When this inclusive communication is not done well, the result may be more entrenched internal divisions. One of the worst things a therapist can do is label parts of the person as good parts or bad parts, and attempt to rid the person of the bad parts of self. All the parts of the person belong, although some behaviors may be harmful and those behaviors do need to be addressed in whatever state they emerge. As fragmented as clients may be, they are still one embodied person and need to know and include and integrate as many aspects of self as possible to become whole.

6 Foundational Issues: What They Bring

Attachment; Rupture and Repair; Boundary issues; Dependency vs Support; Karpman's Triangle; Role driven relationships; Stockholm Syndrome

Attachment

In normal development, a secure attachment creates an emotional foundation for the child. The mother or other regular caregiver is there consistently enough to feel reliable, to give the child the sense of safety and warmth that allows the child to move freely in the world, stepping away and coming back as necessary, never abandoned or lost. Life becomes more manageable with a secure attachment. When difficult things happen, someone is there to help. The child's energy can be focused on internal development and an exploration of the world. That child is free.

It's only been fairly recently that people have made the connection between a person's attachment style and their behavior in adulthood, and in therapy. John Bowlby and Mary Ainsworth studied the nature of the relationship between mother and child, creating theories and studies seeking to understand the impact of the attunement or misattunement of the mother to the child on the child's emotional development. Ainsworth's "Strange Situation" (Ainsworth et al., 1978), was a classic experiment into how babies respond when presented with different scenarios—mother present and playing with them; stranger in the room with both mother and baby; mother leaving baby with stranger; mother leaving baby alone; and baby in room with only stranger. In each situation, the mother returned and attempted to comfort the baby. Babies responded differently to these situations. They varied in their distress when their mother left, in their amount of interaction with the stranger, and in how they reacted to being reunited with their mother. Out of this research, the babies' reactions were categorized into secure, ambivalent, and avoidant responses. The secure group expressed distress at mother's leaving, were friendly with the stranger when mother was still present, but avoidant of the stranger when left alone with her, and were happy when mother returned. The ambivalent babies were intensely distressed when the mother left, fearfully avoided the stranger, and approached the mother when she returned,

DOI: 10.4324/9781003217541-7

only to push her away again. The babies labeled "avoidant" were not distressed when the mother left, were fine playing with the stranger, and were not particularly interested in the mother when she returned.

There is another style of attachment beyond these three. Disorganized attachment is characterized by a confused response to the mother, running towards her, then away, as if not able to decide whether she's safe or not. One of the causes of disorganized attachment is child abuse, where the child is abused by the mother in some way, and, therefore, needs to be comforted by the mother. The mother being the abuser, however, leaves the child in an impossible situation—the need to be comforted by the person who was abusive. This is also true in relation to the father, or any other close person in the child's life with whom the child needs to stay attached but is also afraid of that person. Disorganized attachment may lead to a dissociative disorder, with dissociation providing amnesiac walls between awareness of the parent or other significant person as abuser and alternately as comforter (Liotti, 1992).

A secure attachment is one of the fundamental hallmarks of health. With a secure attachment, people are able to connect with each other, and maintain that connection when apart, providing them with an ongoing sense of connection and community. They feel like they belong, and that frees them to move about in the world, exploring within themselves, making contact and developing relationships with others. When the early childhood attachment process is disrupted, the impact may be felt for years, or an entire lifetime. An insecure attachment results from the primary care-given being unavailable enough to cause the child significant stress. The child becomes clingy, unable to venture far from the caregiver, insecure in the belief that the caregiver will be there when needed. An avoidant attachment results from caregivers being unresponsive or unattuned to the child, and the child becomes anxious and avoidant of relationships, not trusting that he/she/they will be seen and responded to adequately. Disorganized attachment comes from the caregiver being inconsistent, alternately warm and cold, nurturing and abusive or absent. People with disorganized attachment may go on to develop a dissociative disorder, which enables them to have different parts of them available to respond to different presentations in the caregiver, maximizing their opportunities to be both attached and protected.

The impact of abuse on attachment and relationships shows up in many ways. For some people, whose abuse has been part of their lives since early childhood, their attachment to others will be compromised with insecure, avoidant, or disorganized attachment behavior. They may become avoidant of others, or enmeshed, either way unable to stand apart and relate emotionally on an equal basis. Sometimes there's a split seen in the manner of relating and the experience of others—they are either good or bad, and sometimes they are seen as moving from one extreme to the other, their behavior seldom seen as complex or multifaceted. This may be a direct manifestation of having a parent or parents model that kind of behavior. For example, in situations where there's substance abuse or domestic violence, people may behave very badly, and then feel terrible about their behavior and become especially good to try to make up for being bad. The child in this situation sees the two ways to be, good or bad, and nothing in between, so that is what is learned.

Normal relationships include ambiguity and the ability to tolerate and deal with a range of emotions, including ways to deal with upset and anger that result in moving through issues and returning to a calm, connected, stable place. Traumatized people are often not able to do this emotional work well. They may accommodate others, or distance themselves in one way or another because the emotions are too difficult to feel, or they may simply lack the vocabulary to express themselves in those situations because they never had the opportunity to learn it.

What does this mean in therapy? It means that clients will use the ways to attach to the therapist that have worked for them in the past. They may attempt to become overly connected to the therapist, or avoid any kind of authentic emotional connection. Or, they may shift between attachment styles, being vulnerable and close, and then disappearing for a while. These shifts may happen over months, days, or, sometimes, within the same session.

Securely attached people form trusting relationships with their therapists, and can be supported, taught, and encouraged to explore new knowledge. Ambivalently attached people resist the help they seek, keeping the therapist engaged at a safe distance. People with an avoidant attachment don't seem to care whether the therapist is there or not, and can take assistance from whomever is available. However, their connection to people seems guarded, with an absence of deep interactions.

John Bowlby, one of the pioneers of attachment theory, once said, "…the therapist's role is analogous to that of a mother who provides her child with a secure base from which to explore the world" (Bowlby, 1988). The role of mother, or caregiver, is similar, but the client is not an infant with no previous experience, who can absorb and learn with fresh eyes and an open heart. The client has lived through that impressionable period of time having a very different experience, one in which the caregiver was not safe, available and attuned, so the therapist's job is far more complex and challenging than that of the new mother. It is very important that the therapist be reliable and consistent, attuned to the client, able to teach, guide, and console the client. It is also important that the therapist recognize attachment attempts that will not lead to health and work with the client to confront those old attachment attempts with kindness and gentle wisdom.

Attachment styles show up in the client's boundaries, how close or distant they hold themselves, and what they expect from the therapist. Some survivors seem to have no boundaries, or boundaries that are porous and easily collapsed (insecure attachment). Others have developed walls instead of boundaries, keeping others at a distance, unable to connect (avoidant attachment). In people with dissociative issues, there may be many boundaries expressed, with different aspects of the person relating with different boundaries (disorganized attachment). The goal in all of these is to both connect and be safe.

Since the person did not grow up in an environment that allowed that goal to be met, he, she, or they are still seeking connection while needing to protect themselves. The result can sometimes be experienced by the therapist as "come here and never leave" (insecure attachment), "stay away from me" (avoidant), or "come here, go away" (disorganized), as the client seeks to find a way to both engage and be defended at the same time. Noticing the boundary styles and being curious about why they needed to develop in that manner can help the client notice the behavior, connect with the purpose behind the behavior, and slowly learn more adaptive ways to relate in the present moment.

The other layer of the boundary problems may be an underlying desire to repair the damage done in childhood by using the therapist as a substitute parent. In a way, the therapist can help with that dynamic, by being aware of it, sharing with the client the normal longing underneath the behavior, acknowledging that the needs from the past will never be fully met, and helping the client grieve that loss. In doing so, ironically, the therapist is giving something to the client that is similar to what a good parent would have given - presence, compassion, understanding, and support to face difficult realities. In some cases, it can help to make this more overt by saying something like, "If your parents had been healthy enough to do this, they would have said to you...", with the therapist then modeling several things that could have been said to the client that would have been helpful, with appropriate affect and tone of voice. Since therapists are often seen through the lens of a parental transference, this is a way to work with that transference while being clear that the therapist is not the client's parent. It's also a way for the client to hear what a helpful response would have sounded like, and get a sense of how it would feel to have been treated that way. That good-parent modeling can help clients learn to treat themselves with greater kindness when distressed. Asking the client how they can share a similar message with themselves may facilitate the internalization of a positive parent model.

Rupture and Repair

There are times when mistakes help move therapy forward. Usually, that's when the mistake is the result of a misattunement or human error. Those are two of the kinds of situations that are common to all people. When people have a sufficient amount of emotional health and a secure attachment, they can tolerate these mistakes. They have the skills to work them through, let them pass, or learn something of value from them. People who have come from a lifetime of trauma, however, without a secure attachment, may experience these ruptures in the relationship as catastrophic, evidence of abandonment or betrayal. Therapists may have difficulty reconciling the difference between the event and the reaction to it. It can feel like the client expects the therapist to be perfect, unable to accept common errors of understanding or behavior.

Put in the context of the client's life, this reaction can make sense. For example, if in the client's past, a minor misattunement signaled a shift from safe to unsafe, the prelude to genuine abandonment or abuse, then the therapist's error may trigger the fear and/or rage from those experiences with the abuser.

Ruptures elicit attachment issues, and when the therapist and client can repair the rupture, the effect of that can be far beyond the scope of the actual event. To be able to repair a rupture may be a completely new experience for the client, another skill never learned before and critical to staying in long-term healthy relationships.

Any misattunement can be experienced as a rupture. Noticing the 'miss' and exploring it with the client makes both the therapist and client more aware of each other, more sensitive to each other's cues, and better able to address relational issues in the therapy. A rupture may be a missed cue, a misunderstanding, a change from what was expected and what happened, or an event that disrupts the therapy. The client's needs to be seen and heard, and to have the presence of the therapist be consistent and reliable are not met, and the client will react in some way. Some clients shut down, and some may even leave therapy. Other clients become upset, hurt, or angry. Their reactions may make no sense to the therapist, and that can trigger the therapist to become defensive. Ruptures are sensitive events in the therapy. Handled well, the crisis passes, the client becomes stronger, and the relationship between therapist and client becomes healthier.

The first step in repairing the rupture is to recognize there is one. Checking in with the client when a rupture has happened or may have happened opens the door to talk about it, but some clients may not be willing or able to admit a rupture has happened. For the therapist, the signal may come from the sense that things are "off" between the therapist and client. The communication may not feel as natural, and there may be a sense of strain in the relationship. Sometimes, the rupture produces an obvious result, a withdrawal or confrontation with the therapist. When confused or confronted, the therapist needs to slow down and explore what has happened. That can be difficult when therapists find themselves perceived in an inaccurate, negative way. Acknowledging the difficulty may give the therapist a chance to regroup and respond, rather than react out of defensiveness. Saying something that reflects the reality of the therapist's reaction without blame or shame might sound like, "I'm shocked, really surprised, and I'm not sure what's going on. Let me catch my breath. I want to know what your experience has been, what has upset you so much. I truly did not mean to upset you, but, obviously, I have. Tell me about it." Clients may or may not be able to share their feelings in a way that's not blaming or shaming, so the therapist may need to sort through what's being said, picking up on the feelings and dynamics and noticing how the client expresses their upset. When therapists are able to do that, they learn what has impacted the client, and may learn some of why the client would be upset by what happened. By noticing how they feel in response to the client's upset, the therapist may also learn how the client was treated if they upset parents or original caregivers. Clients are likely to express upset to others in the ways it was expressed to them.

Ruptures and repairs take place throughout therapy and provide some of the richest learning experiences. They are challenging, for both therapist and client, and it takes courage and patience to work them through. When ruptures are repaired, however, they contribute to the development of "earned attachment", the experience of a secure attachment that is created in adulthood.

Boundary Issues

In the extreme, boundary issues can be very disruptive to therapy. The client who begs to be adopted may not be able to tolerate staying in a relationship where appropriate boundaries exist. Or, the therapist may not be able to sit with that client's pain and continue to hold the boundaries, resulting in boundary crossings or violations. When the boundaries are too rigid, essential work may not progress, genuine connection may not occur, and either or both therapist and client may feel stuck, ineffective, and frustrated. Therapists who feel unable to deal effectively with the client's overwhelming pain and incessant demands may flee the sense of failure and inadequacy resulting in a premature termination of the therapeutic process. This leads to the client's increased sense of shame and self-blame.

Conceptualizing boundaries as the means to create a safe environment, offers a working guideline to allow people to meet and address complex issues. Boundaries need to be flexible enough to respond to the needs of the therapeutic task at hand while consistent enough to offer stability and predictability. To achieve this, both therapist and client need to be aware of and open to talking about the issues involved, the longing and needs unmet, the wishes unfulfilled, and the ways and means for addressing them. Clarifying roles and responsibilities of each party in the interactions as they play out is essential to the on-going process.

Initially, the client may be unaware of what needs are being expressed and how the demands and pleas for special treatment are self-limiting and trauma perpetuating. The ability of the therapist to provide a consistent presence, to engage the client in identifying and understanding the dynamics at play in the therapeutic moment, and to ultimately educate and inform the client as to how to meet and express those needs appropriately within the context of differing relationships is at the heart of setting boundaries and creating safety and stability for the client. This process requires the willingness and courage of both therapist and client to be vulnerable to spending time in a space that is real, open, and amenable to change.

Boundary issues frequently come up with requests for more contact, more sessions, requests for hugs, presents, non-payment of bills, and inappropriate emotional or sexual advances. More contact may mean ways to connect between sessions, through email, texts, phone calls, etc. Sometimes clients push for more sessions, not because they're in acute crisis when additional sessions may be more beneficial than hospitalization, but because they may be looking to therapy to fill the need in their lives for more safe human contact. While this is understandable, it may actually backfire, relieving the need to move into the world and establish friendships and intimate relationships outside of therapy.

Requests for physical touch, holding hands, asking for hugs, requesting to be held are common, and the dynamics behind the request need to be identified before deciding how to respond to the request. Touch is truly a touchy subject in the therapeutic field. Professionals tend to divide themselves between those who are open to therapeutic touch and those who have decided never to touch their clients. In between these two extremes is a missing dialogue between therapist and client. Dalenberg has framed it as a result of therapists not being trained to talk things through with the client (Dalenberg, 2013). Rather than talking, they tend to state their position, and the client has to adjust to that, or leave. Again, the vital message is the on-going need for therapist and client to talk about all aspects, great and small, of the therapeutic process.

In talking about touch, the therapist and client would need to look at what kind of touch, under what circumstances, for how long, and for what reason. For example, one client asked to be able to reach out and hold the therapist's hand if she was feeling like she was going into a flashback. The therapist's hand was grounding, and even if it didn't stop the flashback, the physical connection kept the person in the room as much as possible and made it easier to ride out the flashback and return to the present. Other people might be further triggered by touch at that point, so it is better to ask and talk it through then make assumptions that may cause more distress.

In a dissociative system, talking about the meaning of the touch needs to include the whole person, and not just the part that is presenting at the moment. If that doesn't happen, the benign touch meant to be stabilizing or reassuring may be experienced by a part of the person in a completely different way, and the person may shift inside in response to the touch. An adult aspect of the person may shift into a child part, or a part that was conditioned to respond to touch sexually. If that happens, the therapist will need to work with that part immediately, listening to the client's reactions and letting the person know what the hug meant and didn't mean.

Suggestions

Pay attention to the feeling of emotional closeness or distance in the relationship with the client. Notice how you feel—whether you lean forward or back, drawn in towards the person, or seek distance. When the relationship seems to move back and forth, track the shifts or patterns of connection and disconnection. Involve the client in figuring out the amount of closeness that feels "right", and notice when he/she/they need to move closer or further away. If the client is dissociative, sometimes there's a part or parts of the client that track these things and will be able to inform the therapist about how this aspect of the relationship is managed by the client. It is a case of self-management, attempting to have a connection that is good enough, not too threatening. Once a pattern is identified, the client may begin to anticipate the need for a shift of some kind. At that point, the client and therapist can talk about ways to manage the attachment consciously, with either one noticing a pattern and stopping to have a chance to talk about it and choose whether to continue with the topic or not.

Talk openly about boundaries and how they help keep the therapy safe for both therapist and client. In most cases, it's easy to understand why the client may be pushing the boundaries in some way, and if that's so, it can be helpful to share that with the client. "It makes so much sense to me that you feel the need to have this be different than it is. That need is serious and deserves our attention. However, if we just go with it, without looking at what we're doing and why, we may make things a lot harder for you in the long run. So, let's talk about this and look for the best way for you to be able to heal." This gives both the client and the therapist a chance to explore what's going on and find ways to work with it that are respectful of both people and have the greatest chance for success. In a lot of cases, what is possible will not fully meet the person's needs. Those needs may have been unmet for the person's entire life, and healing will mean having some of those needs met realistically and appropriately, and being able to identify and mourn the losses in the person's life.

Notice the excessive demands or lack of normal demands at the beginning of therapy. The client who immediately wants unlimited access to the therapist needs to know that's not possible, and the client will need to have other resources. The therapist can help the client learn what resources may be helpful, but clients will need to take responsibility to do as much of that work as they can. When clients cannot function with the limitations of outpatient therapy, they need help in finding other resources, if those are available. If other resources are not available, then both therapist and client will need to make the best of what they can do together, acknowledging that it is less than the client needs. It can be very difficult for both people to be in this situation, so they will need to be able to talk about the challenge of their situation openly. When therapists try to do more than they normally do, there is a risk of burnout for the therapist, or dependency for the client, or an ever-increasing sense of not being able to do enough that leaves people feeling depleted and hopeless, a feeling that may have been too familiar to the client in the past. It's better to know and stay within workable limits and be honest about what can and can't be done than to create a pattern of trying to over-stretch to make things better.

Secure attachment comes from the caregiver being reliable and consistent. Therapists can do that, and their conscientious attempts to do that will help the client move towards an earned attachment, the experience of having a secure attachment that is created in adulthood. The way to do this is fairly simple—say what you do, do what you say, be respectful of the client at all times, and when you make a mistake, say so and apologize. The concept is not hard to understand, but may require a great deal of courage to actualize in a relationship.

Dependency vs Support

Trauma survivors grow up with developmental deficits and distortions arising from the dysfunctional dynamics of their family of origin, and often lack a secure attachment figure with whom to bond. Frequently the empathically attuned therapist is the first solid secure attachment figure in their lives.

Similarly they have deficits in coping skills and life management skills. The issues of shame and autonomy (discussed in Chapter 10) are muddled and confusing. The conflicts of only knowing how to relate through control, by trying to control others while not knowing how to control themselves, creates distraught and distressing relationships characterized by repeated victimization. The tendency to engage in role driven behaviors and relationships stymies the development of mastery and self.

Another complicating factor is the tendency for some trauma clients to be avoidant or to withdraw from social interaction. Their social circle shrinks. They lack an adequate support network. Many of the people whom they have relied upon have left. The friends report feeling used up and drained. Our clients once again feel abandoned and shame filled. Hungry for connection yet fearful of rejection and criticism, trauma clients may cautiously seek increased time and interaction with the therapist.

Within the three stage phase oriented treatment model, creating safety and stability is Job One. Clients have numerous means and behaviors to create chaos and confusion. Bessel van der Kolk (Van der Kolk & Greenburg, 1987) suggests that creating chaos is a means of avoiding the overwhelming emotions associated with the trauma. Into this maelstrom enters the intrepid therapist seeking to help the client find safety, stability, and security.

A common dynamic that arises is the attempt by the client to look to the therapist to be the idealized parent, the "Rescuer" who can set all things right. The trap is many layered and multifaceted. The therapist is trying to help the person, and that person may only think of help as rescue, not knowing the difference between being rescued and being helped to become empowered to help oneself. Failure to provide sufficient information, education, making the steps too big results in repeated failures.

Sometimes, an underlying expectation of the client may be that all the effort on the part of the therapist to teach the client how to manage life is a big trick designed to trip them up and show them to be a failure yet again. For clients who have been continually set up to fail in childhood, hoping to succeed feels foolish. The risks of trying cannot be overstated. The client may experience an internal civil war, wishing to trust and try these new strategies, distrusting and doubting the commitment of the therapist, and longing to be comforted and cared for in an infantilized way while terror-stricken at that thought.

With dissociative clients, this civil war challenges the therapist to not take "sides" but help the alters talk to each other and decide how to deal with needs to be close and needs to be distant.

The therapist walks a tightrope. Providing sufficient information, direction, and emotional availability to help the client succeed and master the task at hand, while maintaining sufficient distance and separation to empower the client to grow internal resources.

The stance of the therapist is often analogous to the relationship between coach or director and athletes or actors in sporting events and theater. World class athletes have coaches who spend hours helping them analyze the game, the strategies and tactics that might be applied in a given situation. However, on "Game Day", the athlete takes the field and makes the play. Coaches pace the sidelines, occasionally calling in suggestions. Famous actors have directors and acting coaches who rehearse lines, focus on specific gestures, and analyze subtle shifts in emphasis from word to word, from one syllable to another. On opening night, the actor takes the stage, while the director waits in the wings.

No athlete wins every game. No actor delivers award winning readings every night. Together, coaches and directors review the players' performance. Both mistakes and victories are dissected and explored, all with an eye to improving the next performance, all within a context of on-going support and encouragement.

The challenge of the trauma therapist is knowing how to stand behind and support clients as they try out new coping skills and strategies, giving enough encouragement and education to facilitate success.

Many clients have no experience of a relationship that gives this kind of support. The area between enmeshment and abandonment is unknown and they will assume one or the other for quite a while as they experience something new in the middle. In this process, therapists attend to their own internal sense of involvement, balancing it with listening to the client's needs for engagement within an open discussion by both parties. Evaluating and re-evaluating roles and responsibilities is critical to navigating this dynamic successfully.

Once again, we must recognize that the core of the therapeutic process lies in the relationship between client and therapist. To facilitate a client's growth requires the therapist to find an authentic way of walking with the client through many different minefields. Together, client and therapist must define how they can engage in a "good enough" and "empathically attuned" manner.

Observing the process can transform the interaction and teach a new way of being. Saying things like, "Looks like we have very limited choices here. Just like in your family, we get to choose between victim, abuser, or rescuer. That's sad, because none of those roles allows you to fully be you or free. Right now, we're just talking with each other, and that's another way of being that you weren't able to experience at home. When we talk like this, both of us are looking at how to be connected in a way that feels ok to both of us, no harm to either, free to express ourselves, and mutually respectful. How does this feel to you?"

The therapist reflecting back to the client the experience of being drawn into a reenactment can also be powerful. The therapist describes the experience they are having with the idea that the person has communicated through behavior the feelings that were never spoken. For instance, after a very frustrating and unproductive exchange, the therapist may connect with their own internal process and recognize what may be the underlying message the client is trying to express, and say, "I'm wondering if this is familiar to you. Feeling frustrated, angry, trying everything you know and having nothing work out, then feeling powerless and hopeless that anything you do will make a difference, and wanting to give up—do you know those feelings?" In that situation, the therapist, caught in a re-enactment gives a voice to the experience of the person, sees and genuinely knows a bit of what that person felt in the original traumatic situation. Being seen, having those feelings named and validated often stops the re-enactment, or at least makes it conscious for a moment, a building block for change. From that point onward, the experience is something that can be addressed and talked about in a healing manner.

Being curious about re-enactments can also lower the shame people feel about their out of control behavior. Over the years, it has not been uncommon to hear people describe needing to be physically restrained, and then, when looking at that pattern, discovering that the experience of being restrained mimicked the original abuse, the person was caught, physically overpowered, and rendered helpless. In several of these cases, the trauma had never been shared verbally and behaving in a way that ended in being restrained by others was seen as both an unconscious attempt to show what happened, and to master it, hoping for a different outcome.

If there's a pattern to the re-enactments, notice that, and wonder about when the pattern began, what might have prompted it, and what did it accomplish. Sometimes the only way people can get attention and care is through acting out behavior. They may have blocked out the trauma and be disconnected from their own experience. They may not know how to ask for what they need, or they've been taught that asking will result in not getting what was needed but something else entirely, like shame, neglect, or abuse.

Karpman's Triangle

Karpman's Triangle identifies set roles in relationships, and is also known as the Drama Triangle because of the action inherent in its dynamic (Karpman, 1968). Since that time, it has become a very popular and useful representation of a common dynamic in dysfunctional families and systems. Karpman describes a subculture of roles that bind a person into behaviors that ultimately don't work to provide personal growth and empowerment.

The survivor usually presents with these roles active in their psyche and life. In therapy, the process of becoming self-witnessing and conscious creates another perspective, which may be called a spiritual perspective, consciousness, an

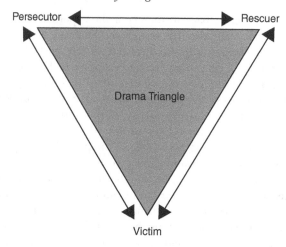

Figure 6.1 Karpman's Triangle

observing ego, a mindful state, internal self-helper, or some other version of something beyond this triangle. Whatever the person calls that state, it is very helpful to see the power and wisdom that state provides for healing—it allows the person a way to step out of the triangle and initiate new behavior, consciously and purposefully.

As long as the survivor only has the three possible roles, he or she is trapped in re-enactments. The only way to stop the re-enactments is to step out of the triangle, to see it as the limited, miserable container that it is. There is no freedom in the triangle. Like the proverbial Bermuda Triangle, people get lost. They can disappear forever, their true self/spirit circling the roles that don't provide any way out.

When the survivor does step out of the triangle, able to separate self from roles both in terms of identifying with them and behaving within their constraints, they will be able to say:

> I have been traumatized—I am not my trauma. I have been victimized—
> I am not a Victim. I have hurt others, intentionally or not—I am not an
> Abuser. I have helped others—I am not a Rescuer. I am a human being,
> a unique person, separate from and connected to all around me. I am not
> in control, but I do have personal power. I do not know everything, but I
> do have wisdom. I have within me the capability to love and be loved. I
> can continue to grow and learn for my entire life, and that will enrich me
> and the people around me.

People who have lived in dysfunctional families, and learned one of three fairly rigid roles, abuser, victim, or rescuer, will bring those roles into therapy.

Helping professionals are often looked to for rescue. When that doesn't happen, they may be seen as powerless, like victims, or powerful and deliberately not helpful, like abusers. While this is often very frustrating for the therapist, it is not intentional, it's the only way the person knows how to relate. For the therapist, it can be frustrating to see the client move from role to role, and put the therapist in one of those same three roles over and over, the only roles known to the client. The therapist is often the target of the client's anger or desire to be rescued, and through this, is given a sense of what it felt like for the client to be trapped in those roles, being hurt, or trying to help self or others. The result of all of this is to feel overwhelmed with pain and despair, just like the client.

To take on one of these three roles is the only way these clients have learned to manage their relationships—to just be present is not part of their experience, and is too frightening. In an abusive situation, to be authentic is scary— "if I'm seen, then I can be hurt". The more honest information that is given, the more can be used against the person. Pulling back and learning to relate only through roles is adaptive and gives the person some sense of being able to anticipate what is likely to happen. If the person were to become fully present and authentic, they would be living in the moment, not controlling what is happening, but actively interacting with it. These are skills learned in the context of safety and trust, skills which involve being vulnerable. There needs to be enough safety and trust to allow for the person to be vulnerable. Without that, being vulnerable can feel masochistic.

One client used to open her Christmas presents on Christmas morning, sort, and stow them, putting the ones she really liked back under the tree as if she weren't interested. The so-so ones she would play with a little. The ones she didn't like, she'd play with a lot. That afternoon, dad would get drunk, throw things around, and eventually grab something of hers, whatever she was playing with, and break it. He was then in the role of abuser, and she (through her toys) was the victim. She knew the pattern, so she rescued her toys. She made sure he broke something she didn't like. Then she'd get ordered to her room, where she'd put her best toys in the toy chest and the not so great stuff on top, continuing to try to protect the things she liked the most. In the middle of the night, however, her child alters would get up and play with the good toys, causing her to be anxious, afraid she'd lose the good toys. So, to be real and honest, would lead to loss. To play a role was safer, much safer. It prescribed her behavior, and others', too, and made things predictable. Roles limit and describe what can and can't go on.

Escaping the Triangle allows for growth and freedom, and involves the ability to reflect on current processes. Mindfulness, curiosity, and the ability to observe self and others are very helpful in slowing and eventually stopping old, dysfunctional patterns.

Suggestions

Drama triangle exercise: draw and explain the triangle, then show how that template is the lens with which the person experiences self, others, and the world.

Have clients identify roles in their family, and how they may have shifted between family members. Then, have the clients look at their own internal system to see how it had to adapt to those roles, and which roles were taken most often. For dissociative clients, have them explore how their internal system reflects those roles from their original family.

Have the person go over each of the four roles: abuser, victim, rescuer, and observer. The observer is not in the triangle, but is able to see each role and the dynamics in the triangle. The role of observer in this exercise helps people experience a sense of self-witnessing, noticing what's going on in interpersonal dynamics. If possible, have the person designate one chair for each role. Begin with whatever role the person chooses first. Have the person sit in that space and connect with how it would feel to be in that role. The role may be very familiar or very foreign, but have the person try to get a sense of how his or her body would feel, the energy they would carry, the way the person in that role would sit, see themselves, others, and the world. Then have the person describe the experience speaking in the role, still in the physical position associated with that role. For example, in the abuser role, the experience may feel powerful and tense in the body, with the person feeling bigger than they actually are, sitting up tall, leaning forward aggressively, and scowling. In the victim role, the body, mind and energy may feel diminished, collapsing in the chair, cowering. In the rescuer role there may be a feeling of a different kind of power, and an urgency, with the person leaning, open-armed towards the victim, or attempting to get between the abuser and victim. In the observer role, there's usually a feeling of awareness of the trap in the system of those three roles, with each person limited and caught in a dynamic that won't work. The person in the exercise is likely to identify the aspects of the roles familiar to him or her either from personal experience or from observing others.

For the individual, this exercise can help identify the roles played in the family, and how those roles have been internalized. With dissociative people, the roles may be played by different parts of the person, so it is important to see if the person can share the experience with other parts of the self. For instance, a part that best knows the abuser may share that experience, while a rescuer part shares the feeling of being in that position, and the one who carries the role of victim shares their sense of self, connection to body and to others, and world view. Last of all, the person connects with being able to be the observer as much as possible, to step outside the triangle of interwoven roles and bring new perspective to the person.

This exercise can also be used with groups, such as groups of interns, graduate school students, clinicians working with trauma survivors, or colleagues in a study or consultation group. Break up into groups of four. Each person has the chance to be in each role, getting into the physical position that role would take, and feeling the feelings, identifying who was in those roles in the abusive situation, and how the psyche continues those roles within their own mind. Finally, how the other person and the therapist is experienced and perceived from that role.

Roles: Victim, Perpetrator, Rescuer, and Consciousness (Outside the System)

Teach people to identify with consciousness, and be able to observe those other roles going on in their own internal dialogue.

The observer is the actual self, unencumbered by roles. This is where the person's true power resides. Consciousness can change the structure of the brain. It's that connection within. This is the "I" that says, "I can't stand this anymore" and wants change. When people dis-identify from roles, and identify with that "I", then they can connect with their true power and step away from destructive roles.

For the therapists, the exercise does two things, exposes them to their own processes, enabling them to know themselves better, and also allow them to both identify the experience the client is having and how the client is communicating their feelings and needs, pulling for old responses that won't satisfy.

This exercise can be used to heighten the intern or student's ability to feel and use the transference and countertransference, working with it to move beyond it in therapy.

Role Driven Relationships

Trauma survivors often live in constant fear of abandonment, rejection, and annihilation. Many hold a profound sense of shame and a core belief that if other people saw the 'real' them, then they would be abused and ostracized. This fear of authenticity leads the survivor to adopt prescribed and proscribed roles of relating.

Role driven behaviors and relationships offer a false sense of safety. Survivors who grow up in hostile and unpredictable environments accommodate to the chaos by developing many ways of relating, a whole stockpile of ways to get needs met and stay alive. Liotti (1992) and others have written about the inability of the child living in a dysfunctional, disorganized, and abusive family to predict which aspect of the caretaker may appear at any given moment. The inability to make such predictions, the loss of a stable, overarching consistency in the home leads to the child developing multiple models of how to build a relationship. To simplify and better organize this chaotic experience, the survivor relies on role driven relationship patterns. Roles limit the behaviors and relational patterns and create some degree of stability. Further, the role driven behavior acts as a mask, hiding the authentic self of the client behind a prescribed set of characteristics and actions.

Unfortunately, there are drawbacks and limits to this strategy. Growth requires some ability to tolerate shifts and changes, to be open to something new. In those open places, people feel vulnerable. When the environment is not safe, vulnerability feels exceptionally dangerous. In addition, roles as defined in dysfunctional families fit together to create the only kind of stability those people know. Within the dysfunctional family system, the abuser and the compliant others seek to maintain a homeostasis, knowing any kind of change may upset everything. The family needs the client to play given parts, to accept certain behaviors. The parents want the child to meet their needs, to not challenge the dysfunctional paradigms, to not question the ways and means of dysfunction. The child grows up not knowing any other way to relate.

In some dysfunctional systems, roles are set up for other reasons, many much more serious. Extreme roles can be found in dangerous systems, and are almost always found in criminal systems. In these situations, people are used as objects and their behavior is conditioned by the people in power, with severe and sometimes life-threatening repercussions if the behavior doesn't satisfy those in charge.

Role driven behaviors and role driven means of relating exacerbate the client's struggle with externalized locus of control (which will be discussed shortly). The client chooses the role that will best fit the perceived demands of the other, regardless of how well it reflects the client's authentic self. Having to disown and disavow their feelings, wishes and needs in order to 'be' the role results in resentments, internalized conflicts, depression, and despair. These intrapsychic dynamics in turn fuel acting out and self-harm behaviors are very familiar to those who deal with traumatized clients and clients with histories of dysfunctional and abusive childhoods. Further, these same issues manifest in myriad different ways, complicating interpersonal relationships as well as the therapeutic relationship.

Stockholm Syndrome

An additional problem complicating the trauma survivor's life may be the manifestation of Stockholm Syndrome. This relational paradigm, named after a 1973 bank robbery gone wrong, describes another dynamic aspect of a victim's connection to an abuser.

In cases of Stockholm Syndrome, there are certain conditions present. The victim is dependent upon the abuser for survival. The perpetrator may control access to food and water, and limit the survivor's ability to sleep. In the case of the original bank robbery, the assailants had guns and threatened to shoot the hostages. The victims are isolated and cut off from other means of support while their needs can only be met through the abuser. Food, clothing, shelter, and any kind of potential protection (even from the abuser himself or herself) can only be gained through the will of the abuser.

In order to survive, the victim bonds to the abuser, adopting the abuser's perceptions and beliefs, believing the abuser's rhetoric. As a survival strategy, this dynamic works very well. So much so that in hostage situations, hostage negotiators will encourage this bonding between victims and assailants in order to increase the odds of survival even though this may lead to the hostages being less useful in subsequent prosecution. One could look at Patricia

Hearst/Tanya as an extreme example of Stockholm Syndrome. If rescued from the situation, the attachment may have become so strong over time, that the victim may attempt to return to the abuser, defend the abuser, and (in some cases) victims have even married one of the people who abused them.

Another aspect of Stockholm Syndrome when it extends beyond the actual event, may be an attempt to justify the emotional sacrifice of the situation in order to preserve a sense of meaning, a kind of reaction to the cognitive dissonance of allying with the aggressor.

In dissociative people, having a part of the self be able to bond to the perpetrator helps other parts remain separate and helps the person survive the situation and preserve a sense of self. Other parts of the self may help hold some of the overwhelming experiences or the multiple, conflicting emotional reactions to the event. As the reactions and thoughts may be unsafe to express in the moment, having dissociative parts of self enables the person to manage otherwise unmanageable experiences. Because one or more parts took on the task of complying with the abuser's demands, other parts were able to avoid those traumas, so the parts involved with the perpetrator protected the rest of the self from feeling the attack in the same way as the military protects civilians. For the parts that do bond with the abuser, it works best if they find a way to genuinely connect in a positive way, which is not a genuine reflection of the whole person's relationship to the abuser. It's simply a way to try to survive a horrible situation.

Suggestions

Acknowledge the wisdom of the instinct to bond with the perpetrator. Help the person appreciate the ability to do that. That the bonded part experienced in aligning with the perpetrator is helpful information in understanding the context of the abuse—what was motivating the abuser. In looking at that, the person may be better able to know that the abuse was not personal, but an acting out of the perpetrator's own internal struggles. Hopefully, survivors can remove themselves from the relationship with the abuser, knowing that they were never truly seen as separate people but as a part of the abuser's inner drama. With distance and safety, the survivor may still hold compassion for the abuser, having a sense of that person's woundedness while also having strong emotional boundaries to prevent further entrapment. Playing into someone else's disturbed drama does not help either person heal.

Acknowledge the links between the part(s) who bonded or complied and the part(s) that resisted, rejected, or avoided the perpetrators' demands. Explore when and how the bonded part of self came to be manifested in the sequence of the traumatic event. What part of self was being manifested prior to that 'switch'? What happens when the bonded part feels the anger, resentment, or terror held by the prior part? Note that the client needs to have sufficient ego strength, internal resources, and internal cooperation to attempt this integrative task.

Psychoeducation about Stockholm Syndrome and how people react in hostage and prisoner situations is very helpful to offsetting shame and internal blame. Another model is the comic description of how volunteers are selected for dangerous missions. The sergeant calls for a volunteer to step forward. One unsuspecting soul stands still, not choosing to volunteer. However, the rest of the squadron steps back leaving our hapless hero unwittingly "volunteering". This model reflects that there was not a conscious choice. Rather "everyone else" leaves and one part of self finds themselves in the thick of a firefight doing what has to be done in order to survive.

These suggestions also work well when working with angry and aggressive alters. The internalization of the abuser may be seen as a parallel process to Stockholm Syndrome.

7 Foundational Issues—Conceptual Issues in Therapy

Locus of Control: Internal and External

> A bird sitting on a tree
> is not afraid
> of the branch breaking,
> because its trust
> is not on the branch,
> but on its wings.
>
> Anon

The bird in the poem has trust in its own power to fly. That's an image that corresponds to an internal locus of control, the feeling of being able to trust oneself, to initiate and have power to direct one's own behavior, and life.

Locus of control refers to the perception of who has authority in a relationship. People with an internal locus of control feel that they can have an effect on what happens to them. They feel their own authority, and they have personal power and the ability to use it when necessary. In contrast, people with an external locus of control feel that the power rests in those outside of them, and in order to get their needs met, to lessen the chance of getting hurt, or to just survive, they must do what the other person requires or expects of them. They have no feeling of personal power.

To determine whether a person has an internal or external locus of control, consider addressing the following questions:

Who's in charge of your life? Who has the power to create change? People with an internal locus of control believe that they are able to create change in their own life. People who have an externalized locus of control believe that the ability to direct their life lies in forces outside of their control, within other people.

The familiar plea of the person with an external locus of control is, "Just tell me what to do". As discussed earlier, role driven behaviors and role based models of relating contribute to an externalized locus of control. Continuing to engage in role driven behaviors maintains that externalized locus of control. Thus, victims may stay in the victim role because they have developed an external locus of control; doing whatever they are told to do by the person

DOI: 10.4324/9781003217541-8

perceived to be in charge. This dynamic is most often an adaptation to a relationship in which the survivor could either do what they were old or be punished or abandoned. Complying offered a better chance at survival, so it was necessary to learn to pay attention to the person in power. Over time, any stirrings from within—the internal sense of self -were lost.

When people with this dynamic come into therapy, they may appear to be model clients. They will do anything they're asked to do, and even try to anticipate the therapist's wishes. However, for the therapist, it feels like the client is not truly there. There's no genuine discussion of what may work best for the client, no disagreement or alternative suggestions given by the client, no push back to anything. These clients may have been so thoroughly conditioned to do what they were told; they have no idea of what they may actually want for themselves.

People are conditioned to live within the environment within which they have been born and raised. Conditioning is a kind of learned behavior that teaches the person to automatically respond and react in ways deemed acceptable to the people raising the child or to other people in a position of power over the child. Conditioning may be as simple as learning to automatically say, "Please", and "Thank you" in social exchanges. It can also go to the extreme, becoming severely controlling. Labeled by some as "mind control", the extreme forms of conditioning attempt to lock the person into behaviors that are detrimental to health and sanity. Severe conditioning is often found in situations of organized abuse, such as sex trafficking and pornography rings, and criminal gangs and organizations. In these extreme situations, human beings are used, seen as commodities, and dehumanized, often through brutal means. They are conditioned to feel powerless and subservient. If they do not comply, they are often beaten, raped, or killed. If they manage to escape, they carry a lot of terror, pain, and rage. Breaking down their conditioning takes time and patience, with repeated exercises in confronting the conditioning with conscious thought and planned behavior, until the conditioning is extinguished. The treatment for these people may include systematic desensitization of various kinds.

In dissociative systems, the conditioning may include triggers to access certain parts of the self that have been trained by the perpetrators for some specific use, such as sexual alters to use for sex or pornography. This is an extreme form of external locus of control. The person as a whole may not even be aware of that conditioned part, or may know about it and attempt to disown it because of the behavior associated with it. The internal split and avoidance of these parts of the self may be seen as evidence of how far the person has been pushed to behave in ways not natural to the self. Integrating parts of the self that were conditioned to behave in extreme ways will include the acceptance of the fact that human beings are very adaptable and will do almost anything to survive, even at times when they deeply wish they could just die.

In some cases, the parts of the self that have emerged or been created to deal with the worst abuse remain in executive control of the whole person, keeping the more vulnerable parts of self unavailable. They may present this way because they still perceive themselves to be in danger, and that may be true, so they present as the person who has control, mirroring the external control they experienced in abusive situations. This is probably the only version of internal locus of control they can create. They may also be carrying so much intense pain that they need to stay in a protective mode in order to feel that they can survive. People in prison, war zones, dangerous cults, or other unsafe situations may need their tough exterior in that context, making their growth and healing more difficult.

Confusion about locus of control often grows out of the disturbed relationships and paradoxical messages the child experiences while being abused. The child has no power, no ability to change events, yet the child is often blamed for the abuse. From the child's egocentric perspective, they are responsible. The untenable message is, "I control you, and you control me". To further complicate and confuse the issue, responsibility is separated from power. The one in power is not being responsible, and the one who is made responsible has no power.

The dynamic becomes even more conflicted because the child resents and dislikes being controlled (abused) and all that entails. The child seeks to reject and undermine that sense of being controlled, yet lacks any clear or functional model to do so. Honest overt attempts to assert the self are met with greater abuse and rejection. The child is left resorting to rage and aggression (a frequent means of establishing and manifesting control in dysfunctional families) or turning to forms of manipulation. The problem with using overt, aggressive strategies is the abusive parent is often too powerful, and to square off against the perpetrator is tantamount to suicide. Thus, the trauma survivor frequently develops a range of covert, manipulative tactics to undermine other people's power and to get needs met. It is important to note that these tactics are not employed out of an attempt to be oppositional. Rather, they are used as the best way to protect the psyche and to get needs met. There were no better alternatives available.

Unfortunately, these strategies of either being controlling and abusive or submissive and manipulative, play havoc in relationships. The people most likely to join our clients in relationships within those parameters are themselves dysfunctional and/or dangerous. These skewed relationships are rife with mixed messages and random attempts at undermining their partner's voice, and serve to exacerbate a tenuous and precarious connection. The resulting blow-ups and string of failed relationships serves to further define our clients as difficult, unlovable, and shame-filled.

Another dynamic that makes the situation more painful is the need for the person being abused to avoid feeling completely powerless in the situation, even if they were. They are often blamed for the abuse, and they will frequently take responsibility for it rather than face the reality of having no power at all. This is an attempt to maintain the illusion of being able to effect change, to have some kind of agency or personal power. Often the only actual power they had was to survive, and it is helpful to comment on that dynamic. To point out that even if they had wished to die, their bodies chose to live, is a powerful and profound observation.

The most frequent model for how power is manifested in dysfunctional families is the "power over" model or "power = control over others". The perpetrator dominates and controls the victim, establishing the power hierarchy within the relationship. This model reflects and supports the externalized locus of control paradigm discussed earlier.

This model is essentially a "zero sum" game in which whatever is gained by one side is lost by the other. Within this framework the perpetrator is the winner and the victim is the loser. Losing means giving up one's wants and wishes. Losing requires giving up mastery and the ability to direct one's destiny. Losing means surrendering one's will, and adopting an external locus of control.

With a history of losing, the trauma survivor approaches relationships with expectations of being controlled and losing, of not having a voice, of not being an equal partner. The unspoken wish is to not lose. However, the only way within this paradigm to be the winner would be to be the abusive one in control. To win, the survivor must become the perpetrator and enact the dynamics of the abusive relationship, employing the tactics and techniques of perpetration used against them. Again, it is critical to remember that the clients engage in this pattern of behaviors and strategies because this was the only viable model they know. They have a limited number of tools available in their tool box. Further, they have first-hand experiences that validate how well these abusive, domineering actions seem to work to capture another person.

An interesting paradox to note in the discussion of the Power Over model is that the focus is on winning by dominating and imposing one's will on another. Yet the very act of dominating another destroys the fabric of any relationship and thus the winner loses.

People who have grown up with an external locus of control expect to be controlled by others, or in reacting to that, they may attempt to be the one in control. They have no experience of working within themselves, acknowledging their own power, or having genuine interactions with others who also have an internal locus of control and a sense of their own agency.

In any relationship, the survivor is assessing which role(s) they will play. When the opportunity presents itself, the survivor may manifest in the perpetrator role, the controlling, domineering, powerful, abuser. When the situation reads as precarious or uncertain, they may fall back to the voiceless, shame-filled, passive victim. When the trauma victim has DID, they often have several self-states that manifest as either perpetrator or victim. Further, this dynamic of perpetrator vs victim is played out internally as well.

This alternating between different roles plays havoc in most relationships and as noted previously, leads to on-going interpersonal failure as well as repeated re-victimization. In the therapeutic relationship, such behavior results in unflattering and unhelpful labels that exacerbate the client's sense of shame and failure. Expectations for the client to behave in "appropriate: ways reflecting respect and mutuality without first clarifying and modeling such behaviors becomes a set-up for increased shame and estrangement. Expectations for the client to give up the entrenched and seemingly essential survival skills after being introduced to pro-social relational behaviors is wishful thinking. Gentle, persistent practice and re-direction is needed to help the survivor to learn, experiment with, and ultimately rely on healthy alternatives.

In order to teach and model healthy expressions of power and authority, the therapist needs to understand the difference between rational and irrational forms of power and authority. Erich Fromm, in "To Have or To Be" makes the differentiation clear when he states, "Rational authority is based on competence, and it helps the person who leans on it to grow. Irrational authority is based on power, and serves to exploit the person subjected to it" (Fromm, 1988).

It is easy to see how survivors have been subjected to irrational power, and confused about how to develop their own sense of authority in the world without becoming like their abusers. Helping clients learn the difference between authority that helps and power that inhibits makes it clear that their healing and becoming empowered won't result in them being like their abusers, but distinctly unlike their abusers. Therapists, in sharing their knowledge and supporting the client's self-discovery and growth, are also modeling rational authority, so the client learns about this important part of life through new knowledge and experience in the therapeutic setting.

In discussing concepts of power and control with clients, in addition to exploring the destructive and dysfunctional aspects of the Power Over Others model, it is helpful to offer an alternative model for how one manifests and expresses and experiences a sense of power. One such alternative is the "Shared Power" or "Power With Others" model. This is a collaboration-based model, reflecting that the synthesis of two (or more) working together can create a *gestalt* that is greater than what an individual might do alone. This is a way to use rational authority, using power in an empowering way. An example would be an orchestra wherein all the musicians layer and interweave the notes, melody, harmony, and counter-melody to create something greater than an individual performer alone.

Collaborative Modeling of Rational Authority

A key component of the Collaborative model, rational authority, is how the participants create something together. Whereas the Power Over model, irrational authority, is based on winning and dominating another, the act of mutually creating something leads to a sense of mastery, competence, and an experience of healthy collaboration. What follows are guidelines for structuring homework assignments to facilitate the development of an internalized locus of control.

In therapy, be mindful about giving too many directions to the client, when a question or conversation might be more effective at engaging with the person. Tasks and homework assignments need to include open-ended options, such as giving suggestions and then saying, "See if you can find a way to express what just came up in a way that feels right to you". The client with an external locus of control will try to anticipate what mode of expression will best please the therapist, so it may help to add a message that conveys a challenge to please the self, apart from the therapist. A positive double bind might be to let the client know that you, the therapist, will be happy seeing him or her find what is personally pleasing to him or her, so pleasing the therapist turns into doing something genuinely pleasing to the self, "I'm really interested to see what pleases you, what options you choose to take".

Another important instruction is to give permission to the client to modify the assignment. Clients who modify assignments tend to get better faster. As clients rework and reshape the assignment into something that more closely meets their immediate needs and limitations, they are taking a more active and collaborative role in the treatment process. Working with each client to learn how the changes were important and how they were of greater benefit to the client is additional therapeutic material for understanding the client's needs and goals.

When the client apparently alters the assignment to effectively water it down, the clinician is encouraged to explore the positive move to create safety. How these modifications provide safety, and why safety in that clinical corner is critical are vital clues to facilitate careful pacing of the therapeutic process.

Be aware of the client who feels overly compliant. Challenge the client to come up with other possible ideas or responses. Qualify statements made to the client, leaving room for interpretations that are different from those of the therapist. Offer alternative ways of seeing or doing things, leaving it open for the client to choose, or to create something else. Focus on the process, not the final decision. Teach the client how to consider different alternatives, seeing the strengths and weaknesses of each and eventually choosing the one that seems best for the client. The therapist can help with this process, adding to both positive and negative sides of each choice and encouraging the client to stay with the ambiguity for a while before settling on something to try. Analogies, such as being fitted for glasses or contacts, may be useful. The eye doctor will ask, "is this better or worse?" over and over, with different variables, and it's up to the patient to respond with what seems most clear. Teaching the client to observe and evaluate how different techniques, homework assignments, or structure of the therapeutic sessions feel can help develop an internal sense of self.

For some of these people, it may help to start with the basics. Just as children learn what they like by experimenting, these people may need to learn to experiment. For instance, the client may go online, pick something, a shirt or other item, and then choose a color, whichever one looks most attractive at that moment. Buying isn't necessary—it's not to own it or to show anyone, just to practice picking up things the way a child would pick up the colored item that caught his/her/their attention. Other ways to discover what is liked can be to look through a menu or cookbook and pick things that sound good, or sing, play an instrument, write, dance, or paint, only for the experience of it, not to show anyone else. This is all time spent being curious about the self, out of sight or control of others, in an effort to find out something that feels internally true.

Hypothetical questions can be very helpful, such as, "What would you choose if no one was looking? What would you write, draw, play, or sing if no one would know? What job or career would you choose if you would automatically have the expertise to do it? How might you be different if you were born into a healthy family?" Questions such as these can open the mind to hear inner desires, talents, and wisdom that a person's actual environment has silenced.

Learning to Interact Authentically

Asking for emotional needs to be met requires vulnerability, and people who have been abused are wounded in that area. It's much more difficult for them to ask, even if they have the capacity to do so. Recall our earlier story of the client who sorted and hid her Christmas presents. Knowledge of her likes (and dislikes) gave the person who abused her power.

Giving the client emotional space may help create sufficient safety to express their thoughts and feelings. Asking them what they would ask for if they could ask is one way of making the request hypothetical, providing a bit of emotional distance. They may still say they don't know. If they say that, ask what they would say if they did know. Then, if they still say, "I don't know", ask them to guess. The last step would be to ask what they imagine they would say if they could, if for no other reason than to humor you. That usually lightens the mood, and makes the request so far removed that it no longer feels threatening. Still, it's been said, and that makes a difference. Having been said, there can be a discussion when it becomes safe enough to talk about.

The Rules

There are spoken and unspoken rules in the culture of abuse. Part of healing is identifying those rules and challenging them with strength and kindness. Those rules are often held in place with shame and violence. Even when the abuser is no longer present, people may shame or hurt themselves if a rule has been broken. To break those rules and try another way of relating takes a great deal of courage, and trust in the helper. Stating all of that out loud can be helpful. Then, planning how to take care of the self after breaking an out-dated rule is also important. Finding a safe way to acknowledge freeing the self from a debilitating rule can reinforce the achievement and allow the person to feel pride, a powerful antidote to the experience of shame.

Some Typical Rules from an Abusive Culture

Don't talk
Don't feel
Don't know
Don't be vulnerable
Don't think of yourself
Don't love anyone
Don't love anything
Don't hope
Do whatever other people want you to do
Never say "no"

In a Healing Environment, People are Taught

Talk
Feel
Know
Be vulnerable
Think of yourself
Love people
Love animals, the planet, etc.
Hope
Do what you want to do
Say no when that is what's right for you.

Moving from the first list to the second typically stirs feelings of being selfish and self-centered. Actually, moving in the direction from selfless towards self-care, the person is moving in the direction of "selfish" —but they're highly unlikely to become selfish. If they make it halfway, that's perfect, that's the place of appropriate self-care. The therapist may help by letting the person know that if he or she ever starts behaving selfishly, the therapist will say something. Meanwhile, the client can ask the therapist, "Am I being selfish?", and the therapist will say, "What do you think?" and help the client process what it feels like to take healthy care of the self, and what it may feel like to go past that point and do something that starts to feel selfish. This interchange can help the client learn, from the inside, the difference between self-care and selfishness - they actually feel different inside and in a relationship.

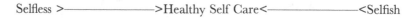

Selfless >————————>Healthy Self Care<————————<Selfish

Having too little sense of self, the focus on developing the self may feel wrong. There's no sense of balance inside, being aware of both self and other, and navigating the needs of both. It's a gray area, and most survivors of abuse are unfamiliar and very uncomfortable in gray areas. All or nothing and either/or scenarios are more comfortable, even though they don't work well at all. Someone or something always gets left out in the either/or format. However, negotiating to have both people's needs met requires skills many abuse survivors have never had the opportunity to learn. That doesn't mean they can't learn them. People who learn these skills consciously may end up being able to use them better than those who have been able to take them for granted.

The other problem inherent in breaking old rules is the emotional impact that becomes conscious when an old rule is identified and removed. Grief for all that did not happen, anger at the impact of the old rule, are two of the common reactions to letting go of old ways of being. People may also berate themselves for not breaking disabling rules earlier. That is often the emergence of another old rule, the demand that a person know what they don't know before having had a chance to learn. Small children who are punished for not being able to read, or cook, or take care of adults learn that they are supposed to know what they've never had a chance to learn. Their not knowing leads to punishment, helplessness, and shame. In recovery, that same pattern may emerge as anger against the self for not knowing what there was never the opportunity to learn. That is simply unfair to the person. No one is supposed to know what they've never had the chance to learn. That reality may be very difficult for a survivor to take in.

Trauma clients enter adult relationships seeking clues as to who their new partner wishes them to be. Open-ended and well-meaning statements such as "just be yourself" strike fear and terror into their hearts. There is no reference point for "yourself". They are certain that any statement that isn't in sync with and in response to the other will be wrong and punishment and shame will surely follow.

In Chapter 6, we discussed the tendency of dysfunctional families to push children into specific roles to maintain the family homeostasis. We further noted that children attempting to connect with and manage the multiple, conflicting demands of disorganized parents, developed multiple, conflicting roles or ways of being (and not being) themselves (Liotti, 1984). Clients often refer to this as if they learned to wear many different masks. No one has actually seen the real, authentic person. Worse, they themselves don't know their own authentic self. As noted above, they have not been allowed to express their own needs, wishes, feelings, etc. They were not allowed to have their own dreams. They have had to subjugate their sense of self to the abusive other in order to survive. This survival skill has become an on-going way of life.

The Relationship between Self Expression and Sense of Self

The concept of Self is critical to appreciating and understanding many levels and nuances of the impact of on-going trauma, the power of roles and rules, and the complexities of treatment. Van der Hart, Nijenhuis, and Steele (2006) refer to the Self as an organizing construct, an ongoing process of continually creating a comprehensive and congruent gestalt out of the events, emotions, thoughts, and behaviors that make up our daily lives. As noted above, Liotti posits that children organize their emerging sense of self (or selves) in response to the demands (consistent or disorganized) of their caretakers

Stolorow (2015) describes a phenomenological context for understanding the process whereby emotional experiences, and the structures that organize them, arise within a relational or "intersubjective" framework. He goes on to note that recurring patterns lead to principles which can be also referred to as cognitive-emotional schema or "meaning structures". He suggests that the principles are pre-reflective, a normally unconscious substrate by which behavior and experience is organized.

"These intersubjectively derived, prereflective organizing principles are the basic building blocks of personality development, and their totality constitutes one's character" (Stolorow, 2015).

The ability of the growing child to express needs, wants, and wishes, to describe and give voice to their daily experiences and have those reflected in the subsequent attuned response of a good enough caregiver, helps the child develop their authentic sense of self. If the developing self is constrained into mirroring only the beliefs and values of the abusive caretakers, if the child is organized to meet the needs of the parent and to deny having their own needs and wishes, then there can be no authentic self. Instead, there arises a false self (or series of false selves) in service to the abusive and controlling other.

The acknowledgement and acceptance of the child's independent wishes, wants, and behaviors, separate and distinct from the parents' set of personality constructs, is critical. To have these differences met with an unconditional, transcendent sense of love further strengthens and reinforces the child's growing sense of self. Inherent to this process is the acceptance of the child's oppositional behaviors, cognitions, and different ways of being-in-the-world.

These oppositional behaviors manifest when the child recognizes what they don't like as well as recognizing what they do like. Owning a sense of what is "Not Me" is as necessary as identifying what is "Me". The child's emerging sense of boundaries and their ability to set and maintain these boundaries is vital.

In dysfunctional families, the inability to say "no" and the inability to define and maintain clear interpersonal boundaries complicates this dynamic. A critical developmental part of adolescence is the oppositional phase. Up to this point, the child was happy to identify as part of the family and in relation to their parents or caretakers. During this developmental period, the teenager separates in significant ways from parental dictates and expectations. Manner of dress, behavioral affectations, musical choices, and a host of other elements representing their sense of self are shifted from parent-approved modalities to ones designed to distinguish the child as their own person separate from the parent. While the initial move may be to identify with a specific peer group or social norm, the key point is the move to disengage and distance the child from the previously held definitions of self as the start of a process to better define who they are.

In reasonably healthy families, while this time in the teenager's (and parents') life is filled with *sturm und drang*, changes are acknowledged, in some ways accepted, and ultimately worked through. All that is accomplished with an overarching sense of on-going love and unconditional acceptance.

"I might not love what you are doing, how you dress, and that godawful music you listen to, but I will always love you" (Glazier, 1968, private communication).

Unfortunately, in the dysfunctional families our clients grew up in, any deviation from the demands of the abusive parent(s) was met with intolerance, physical and emotional abuse, and/or the withdrawal of affection and support. Connection with outside peer groups is discouraged, robbing the teenager of sources of support and the space to try out new ways of being.

Suggestions

Prepare the person for the backlash they are likely to experience when breaking old, harmful rules. Ask them what they think they might feel when they break a rule. Sometimes they know there will be a backlash, and sometimes they don't. Going back to how the rule was learned will help identify the possible backlash. "If you didn't do what you were told, what would happen to you?" is a question that can evoke the emotional impact of breaking the rule. The person may have been physically, emotionally, or sexually abused, evoking pain, shame, and feelings of abandonment. Letting go of that rule as an adult is likely to bring back the anticipation of those same feelings. Knowing that can help, especially when there is a plan for how to deal with those emotional memories. The best plans usually come from the client, tapping into an intuitive sense of what may help.

Some possible plans could be to schedule a therapy appointment soon after trying something new that would break a dysfunctional rule. Or, scheduling a telephone check-in with the therapist soon after.

Other plans could involve supportive people accompanying the person, or meeting before and/or after an experience that would likely trigger a backlash.

When the trigger is not likely to be too overwhelming, the person can plan to do extra self-care before and after, such as visiting a park or sacred place, having a good meal, journaling, doing art or playing a musical instrument, scheduling a massage, warm bath, or finding something pleasant or uplifting to watch or read.

For clients with Dissociative Identity Disorder, the backlash experienced from the breaking of old family rules may trigger internal conflicts and reprisals. The need for internal collaboration and communication is essential. Discussing what possible reprisals would have taken place in the old abusive relationships needs to be carefully explored. Permission to "test" the validity of these old rules must be carefully negotiated. Engaging both scared parts of self as well as critical and aggressive alters is crucial. Allowing for smaller steps and providing the client with options to stop the rule breaking process provide additional levels of safety.

Learning to live authentically happens with the help of a healthy, respectful relationship, beginning with the attunement that comes from collaborative experiences. This is the experience of rational authority building competence and the experience of sharing power with the other person.

Collaborative Goal Setting

The earliest moment of potential change occurs when the therapist and client first begin to speak about the decision to work together. Creating a collaborative endeavor begins as the therapist authentically asks the client to define the goals for treatment and to share their decision for seeking therapy. Engaging the client in a discussion of what the client wants and what the therapist can and cannot give or do creates a framework of collaboration and shared power.

For some clients, the invitation to collaborate in goal setting may feel like a trap. For them, giving up information is giving away power. Their experience is that what they share can and will be used against them. Some clients may be scared to state their needs in a direct and open fashion for fear of being ridiculed or shamed. Some may feel uncertain or confused from having multiple, conflicting ideas of what they need or want. Some may come seeking the therapist to fix them and tell them what to do and how to be. Some may want to tell the therapist how to do therapy, micromanaging the minutiae of the therapeutic engagement.

The therapist needs to define the treatment as a collaborative process where power and control are shared. How that is manifested, what that looks and feels like needs to be carefully described. Further, the client will need to be invited and reminded to engage in this shared process on multiple occasions, throughout the therapy.

Some simple yet powerful guidelines may be useful. Letting the client know that they can control the depth and the flow of shared material is important. Knowing that the client can call a halt to the session or ask for a time out with a word or a gesture is tremendously empowering. Asking the client what issues and topics they wish to address at the start of the session reinforces their role as a collaborator in the journey. Inviting feedback as to their experience of the therapy process and the quality of the therapeutic relationship acknowledges and validates them as a partner in the process.

In order to do these things, the therapist and client will need to set up the signals they will use to stop the process, and engage in a conversation about the process itself. To be able to talk about what's being discussed helps both people take a step back and evaluate the therapy as it progresses. Signals can also be used as a way to practice pacing the therapy so that it will remain in the person's Window of Tolerance (more on pacing later on in this chapter).

The subjects to be covered in therapy are also things that can be discussed. Clients can learn their own personal ways of approaching therapy by noticing whether they tend to avoid difficult subjects or push themselves into them. One person who found herself practicing how to avoid difficult subjects in therapy learned to start her sessions stating the subjects she wished to avoid. She would enter the office and say, "Today I do not want to talk about sex." For her, this was a humorous way to put that subject on the table for that day's work, because it cued the therapist to ask her why she wished to avoid that subject. Another client would come into therapy wanting to delve into horrible memories of abuse, as if to purge them from her system. She had serious health problems and very little support at home, so the therapist needed to remind her how that approach resulted in her having flashbacks at home, alone. Together, they would choose a part of the memory to work on, keeping it within the client's ability to manage.

Another extremely helpful thing to do to manage therapy collaboratively is to have regular check-ins about how the therapy is progressing. This gives the client a chance to reflect on their goals, how it's been to work towards those goals, and whether there needs to be any adjustment in how the work is being done. In order to do this, clients have to check in with themselves, and that helps to develop a sense of what is working and not working for them, as individuals. The more they learn about themselves, the better they become at noticing what is helpful, and what preferences they may have about how to work with themselves. All of this contributes to becoming more authentic. The therapist creating room for the client's self-reflection supports that process.

How Is This Done When The Person Is Dissociative?

When dealing with a dissociative client, the therapist needs to keep the whole person in mind at all times. So, when creating goals, the therapist might ask the person to check inside to see if it feels ok to pursue this goal. The client may hear a voice from an internal part of the self, or just get the sense of the goal being acceptable or not. The exercise in considering what's inside is the important part. The therapist and client can then create a sign or word to alert them if the therapy is approaching the limit of the person's ability to tolerate strong feelings. The person can answer yes by raising his or her right index finger, or no by raising the left index finger

With dissociative people, the therapist's respect for all aspects of the client, known and unknown, provides the foundation for the client to accept the whole self, even while still fragmented. This process models what the dissociative person needs to learn to do inside, to listen, consider what's best to do for the whole person, and give it a try. Evaluating the results will give the person a chance to listen to all of the reactions they may have and learn to work with those. This will translate into the beginnings of being able to deal with mixed feelings and ambiguity when the person integrates. The external collaboration with the therapist models what is needed internally.

Honoring the need to stop, or slow down actually helps the therapy to proceed. Stopping allows the person to go further the next time without dissociating. Also, the constant give and take, and checking in, is extremely important to keep the therapy and the relationship on an even keel.

Saying "No" Experiment: "At This Moment, It Just Doesn't Feel Right."

A powerful activity to facilitate the challenging of old, dysfunctional rules is the "Saying *NO* Experiment". This activity is promoted as an experiment rather than an assignment or exercise. When engaging with the client in an experiment, the therapist and patient become collaborators in the gathering and assessing of data. The therapist is removed from the role of expert imparting wisdom and thereby "telling" the client what to do and how to be. The very nature of the scientific method, to gather data, test a theory, and ultimately, let the data tell the story, helps the client develop a critical thinking mindset to challenge old injunctions. Clients are encouraged to think for themselves and to draw their own conclusions.

In keeping with the cautions noted above, the client is encouraged to start small. Care is taken to engage as many dissociative aspects of self to agree to observe the process and to later join in the discussion and analysis of the gathered data. Objections, reservations, and fears are acknowledged and accounted for in setting up the experiment prior to engaging in the "field testing".

The heart of the experiment is for the client to say "No" to a request for a small favor from a friend or colleague. The client need only do one actual field test in the time between sessions. They can select any small favor as they feel ready to take on the challenge. A key element of this activity as an experiment lies in shifting the focus of the client's attention to the reactions and responses of the person asking the favor and then being told "No". The therapist may note that the client may feel a great deal of anxiety as to what the peer's response will be and that as the purpose is to gather data, the challenge is to watch and observe the reaction, not to prejudice the outcome by saying anything or giving in too quickly.

Frequently, the peer will simply accept the "No" and move on to ask someone else. In which case, the data demonstrates that saying "No" does not carry the same negative consequences from their childhood in the dysfunctional and abusive household.

Occasionally, the peer will ask the client, "Why not?" This simple question often triggers guilt and fear in the client and leads to collapse with compliance and the loss of boundaries. The therapist should note that, at best, the question is a simple request for information. However, the therapist should also discuss the frequent manipulation that occurs when the person making the request attempts to undermine the client's attempt at boundary setting. The manipulation takes the form of asking "Why not?" with the implication that if the client cannot adequately justify a rationale for saying "No", then they are beholden to submit to the request.

To deal with this challenge and facilitate the continuation of the experiment, the client is given the following carefully scripted response, "I don't know. At this moment, it just doesn't feel right."

There are two essential elements embedded in that statement. The phrase, "it just doesn't feel right", shifts the rationale for saying "No" from a logical reason that could be argued with to an emotional state that need not be explained any further and need not make any sense at all. The initial phrase, "I don't know", further reinforces the rationale as an intangible, unexplainable, "Teflon" argument. Drawing from Assertiveness Training, the client is coached to repeat, if necessary, this rationale in the face of repeated questioning on the part of the person making the request. If the person making the request challenges the client, claiming their reason doesn't make any sense, the client is instructed to agree with that observation, noting that it is a feeling state and repeating the line, "At this moment, it just doesn't feel right."

It is important to note that the first half of the line, "At this moment" is the escape clause. As previously noted, the client should have the option to end the experiment early if they choose. Should the client feel unsafe, overwhelmed, or in danger of dissociating, they can ask for a brief break such as a moment to go to the bathroom. After taking a few minutes to practice calming and grounding exercises, the client can return to the peer and observe that feelings are funny and that feelings come and go. That the moment where it didn't feel ok has passed, and they are now open to their peer's request. The client is encouraged to save this option as a last resort measure, but they can employ it at their discretion.

Following up with the client in subsequent sessions offers the therapist and client the opportunity to explore differences (and possibly similarities) in the interpersonal dynamics of the client's past and present relationships. The client's responses and reactions to the experiment as well as the observations of the peers' reactions are important elements of on-going discussion. In a larger perspective, the client is engaged in developing critical thinking skills that facilitate the ability to challenge many other critical beliefs learned in response to the dysfunction and abuse of childhood experiences.

For clients with Dissociative Identity Disorder, the heart of the experiment is the same as described above. The differences lie in the initial exploration of the client's fears and reservations. Attention must be paid to how the client compartmentalizes aspects of self, fear, resentment, compliance, into alter self-states. Communication and collaboration among self-states is critical to ensure that all parts understand the nature and intent of the data gathering experimental process. Further, enlisting those parts most fearful to not immediately sabotage or shut down the experiment is essential.

Similarly, in the post experimental discussion of the gathered data, having an open discussion among the different self-states is vital. How each self-state accounts for and understands the experience is a rich and robust source of therapeutic material. Discussing the process of the experiment, whether there was cooperation and collaboration or confusion and interference is invaluable.

Redirection Experiment

Another powerful activity to help clients experience setting boundaries and asserting themselves is the "Redirection" experiment. Again, this activity is undertaken as an experiment with the key to gathering data and then drawing a conclusion based on what the data shows.

The initial setup asks the client to identify three restaurants local to their home or work where they can be sure to find something they like on the menu. The prices should be equivalent across all three restaurants.

When invited to join peers for a meal out, the client is instructed to be non-committal as to what they would prefer to eat. They are to stand back and let the others decide. Once a decision has been made, they are encouraged to speak up, saying that they just realized that they would prefer eating at a different establishment. Having three available options allows them some flexibility and to select something other than what the group has chosen.

The goal is not as much to change the group's decision as it is to observe the reaction to a request for change. Are they ostracized, rejected, or ridiculed as was the course of events in their family of origin? Is their request honored and accepted? Is their request noted and the basis for a bit more discussion before the group settles on a final selection? Is the client welcomed into the decision making process or shamed and ignored?

Again, the client is warned that they will probably experience a certain amount of anxiety as they run through this protocol. Their focus needs to be on the reactions of the others around them rather than on their internal process. This may take a certain amount of coaching and practice before using this "experiment".

For clients with DID, it can help to decide which part of the system will do the experiment. Other parts may observe from inside or go to whatever safe place has been created inside to protect parts of the self from situations they may not be ready to handle.

It is also possible for some dissociative people to have a part or parts give support from inside to the presenting person who has decided to try this experiment. That may take the form of another part giving energetic support from inside, or figuratively standing behind the person, backing them up.

Alexithymia and Playing Charades

One of the characteristics of trauma survivors is a difficulty in talking about the trauma. Some of that is due to the neurological effects of trauma, such as the lessening of blood supply to Broca's and Wernicke's Areas (critical language centers in the brain) during traumatic events. Other causes may be the difficulty of speaking about the intolerable experience, or keeping the secret because of threats or a perceived loss of attachments. Still, the need to communicate, to be seen, is strong, and experiences are shared, even when the verbal outlets are stifled or silenced.

Alexithymia is the condition wherein the client has difficulty identifying feelings and correspondingly difficulty expressing feelings. However, a person cannot not feel. Persons with alexithymia are, sadly, profoundly unaware of their internal process. Clayton (2004) noted a connection between alexithymia and somatoform dissociation.

Clients with alexithymia will often appear blunted or flat, when asked as to what they are feeling, they report not feeling much of anything. Occasionally, they will deny feeling anything while tears are rolling down their cheeks or they are clenching and unclenching their fists. When the emotions build to a breaking point they explode in an unmanageable and out-of-control "affect storm".

Bear in mind how clients growing up in dysfunctional or abusive families are taught to ignore their feelings or are given messages distorting their awareness and invalidating their internal experiences. What does it mean to the battered or sexually abused child, crying that their Daddy doesn't love them when the enabling Mother says, "Of course your Daddy loves you and he would never hurt you."?

When there are no words, behavior speaks. Like a game of Charades, the person communicates the unspeakable through actions, often demonstrating the trauma, or aspects of it, in the relationship with caregivers or therapists. "Acting out" is a familiar issue with trauma survivors, frustrating both the survivor and the caregiver. Survivors are frequently shamed for their behavior, the assumption being that they could and should control themselves. However, when behavior is the only way in which the person can communicate, when no other and better way is offered, then the choice is between continuing to attempt to share what's happened or being shut down, with no way to continue emotional growth.

Transference is the secret language of the abused and countertransference is the means by which we hear the unspeakable.

In Charades, people act out and the observers watch intently, trying to understand what is being shared, and, eventually, finding the words that match the behavior. At that point, the game ends. The same dynamic often happens in treatment, with the survivor unconsciously acting out aspects of the abuse until someone sees clearly enough to put words to what was unspeakable. At that point, the acting out behavior diminishes or stops completely. People don't enjoy acting out. It's upsetting for both the person caught up in it and the other person who is trying to help. The feeling of mastery that comes with being able to verbally express what happened is liberating and empowering. When, as Ross said, "the problem is not the problem", clients and therapists can spend a great deal of time learning how to identify the actual problem. This can be frustrating for all involved. However, when the true problem is identified, there is a sense of relief and hope. The client feels seen and heard. The therapist no longer feels confused and stymied. The behavior makes sense in a new way. Just like all the gestures and mimes, done in a game of charades suddenly become clear, when the underlying communication is recognized, the behavior of the client can be seen for what it was - an attempt to communicate what could not be said.

For example, a client may not show up for a session, or call far past the agreed upon time to notify the therapist before being charged for the session. When the client is billed for the missed session, he or she becomes upset. The client wants the therapist to cancel the bill, even though he or she signed an agreement at the start of therapy and was told the office policies by the therapist. The therapist is put in the position of saying the bill needs to be paid, and is then characterized as not caring, only caring about the money, not the client. If the therapist waives the fee, the contract has been violated, and the safe container of the therapy has been damaged. It's a classic lose-lose dilemma, a situation that is probably familiar to the client. Perhaps the client was taught that caring meant sacrifice, that in order to be acceptable, he or she had to put personal needs and feelings aside and give to the abuser whatever the abuser wanted. There was no reciprocity or respect for the client in the past. Bringing that experience into therapy, the client's missed appointment becomes a challenge for the therapist to prove he or she cares for the client by sacrificing the fee. Once therapists find themselves in the re-enactment of "prove to me that you care", they will need to step back, label the process, talk clearly about what's going on, and confront the impossibility of ever succeeding in caring enough to meet the client's lifetime of unmet needs. The client will then need to work on the loss of that wish to have the therapist fill the emptiness inside, and deal with their upset and deep grief.

Suggestions

When asked what they are feeling, the client with alexithymia might respond, "I don't know what to say". To help, start by tuning into and developing an internal somatic awareness. Possible areas to focus on include attending to where they experience tension in their bodies or somatic state changes from relaxed to tense. Helping them focus on periods of hyper or hypo arousal and the somatic components of those states. Noticing the muscle tension that corresponds to being angry or sad. A helpful question is to ask, "What is it like to be in your body?". Even more fundamental is to take a body inventory noticing what the client is aware of as you attend to different large muscle groups.

To facilitate the development of affective language, one can use a diagram of different facial expressions and note the feelings corresponding to each look. Simple tactics include asking the client to use the word "I" instead of "you" to facilitate greater ownership of their experiences. Asking the client to try on a sentence; giving them a phrase to say reflecting the affective state that they appear to be in and then inquiring as to if that resonates or fits with their experience. Additionally, using art or journaling to encourage the client to track their affective states and emotional responses between sessions is helpful.

Transference and Countertransference:

One of the most effective ways of understanding what is being communicated through the behavior of the person is to pay attention to the transference and countertransference in and between sessions. Transference refers to behaviors and attitudes that the client transfers from earlier relationships onto the therapist and therapeutic relationship. As stated previously: "Transference is the secret language of the abused and countertransference is the means by which we hear the unspeakable."

Everybody has transferences. They are emotionally economical, when they work well. We transfer our experiences with authorities, like our parents, onto authorities in current life. If we had positive relationships with our parents, we are likely to work well with authorities as adults. If, however, our relationships with original parental authorities were harmful, frightening, and downright dangerous, we are likely to have difficulty relating to authorities in the present.

Countertransference refers to the therapist's response to the client's transference. For instance, if the client transfers a negative experience from a parent onto the therapist, the therapist may react in a negative way, reinforcing the negative transference. If the therapist catches the potential countertransference, he or she can look at that potential negative reaction and learn something about the client's experience with his or her abusive parent and childhood experience.

In the "prove to me that you care" example above, the client would be transferring the experience of being with a parent that didn't care onto the therapist, along with unmet needs and possibly anger. The therapist, if they tried to care enough to satisfy the client, would end up worn out and hopeless, experiencing the client's side of the old relationship. Or, the therapist could shame and blame the client for needing too much, replicating the attitude of the neglectful parent. If therapists use the awareness gained from within while in the interaction with the client, they can reflect on it, bringing it to consciousness, giving it words that will help the client identify it and begin to work on it. In this situation, the therapist might say, "I hear the unmet needs you carry from having parents who were never able to meet them. I'm tempted to try, but I know that would fail because you are no longer a child, and I am not your parent. That's sad and upsetting—for both of us. I also don't want to replicate what your parents did and give you nothing. That would just be more of the same. So, I will give you what feels right for me to give to you, and I know that will not be enough to fill that emptiness left by your parents. What we can do is identify the things you need, and how it feels to not have had those met for all of these years. I may be able to model some of them for you, and then you can practice giving them to yourself and finding people in the world who could appropriately give you more. All of that together can make a big difference." Over time, this approach will help the person recognize unmet needs, the feelings of upset and anger about them, and will also learn ways to heal and have needs met appropriately from self and others.

Suggestions

Addressing the behavior with curiosity, noticing repeating patterns and wondering aloud what those patterns may be helping the survivor express can be a non-shaming way to collaboratively look at problematic behavior. If the assumption is that the behavior speaks some part of a truth that needs to be seen, heard, and dealt with, then it is more likely that the survivor will be willing to become self-observant, more mindful of their own behavior, and more open to learning other ways to communicate what has been available only through acting out.

Clients often feel very bad about their acting out. Taking that feeling of "bad" and teaching the person to "Be A Detective" may help them shift from self-blame to a more helpful stance of curiosity about their own behavior.

Examining how the behavior may have been helpful is one way to think about how the behavior has been helpful in the past. The behavior may have served to bring people close, to create a barrier to vulnerability, or to engage with people and still remain defended. Acting out may be a way to avoid something that feels more threatening, like facing the truth of what happened. It may also feel more familiar, another crisis like all the others, awful but predictable, ostensibly more manageable if the crisis is created by the survivor.

Crises do pull in other people. With acting out, the survivor is connecting, through crisis, in a way that is a combination of safe and dangerous. The familiarity of being in crisis mode may be oddly safe for the survivor, keeping them away from more difficult feelings or harder truths. It may also provide a very effective diversion from the feeling of threat that often accompanies growing intimacy—even when that intimacy is safe, or particularly when that intimacy is safe.

Another way to examine the effect of the behavior is to see what emotions and dynamics are being brought into the relationship. Those are often the emotions and dynamics of the traumatic situation, re-enacted unconsciously. Often, it's the therapist who has the knowledge needed to step back and reflect on the dynamic between therapist and client and identify how old unhelpful patterns may be emerging. Sometimes, the client automatically identifies the feeling of a re-enactment by saying things like, "This always happens to me", "You're just like my mother" (or father), "Everybody always treats me like this", and other statements that reveal the familiarity of the pattern to the client. The therapist can look at these statements as a gift, because they provide a way for both therapist and client to talk about their relationship, and that alone makes their relationship different than past ones.

Erotic Transference

One of the most challenging dynamics that emerges in the client-therapist relationship is an erotic transference. The client becomes preoccupied with the therapist, and that can emerge as seeing the therapist as special, looking towards the therapist with longing, a need to be seen as special, or, sometimes, a proclamation of love for the therapist. This may be a way for the client to express the longing for intimacy stemming from a childhood where that intimate connection was absent (Chefetz, 1997).

The declaration of love, or the seductive pull for "specialness", puts the therapist and the therapy in a very uncomfortable position. How can the therapist address this issue with respect for the depth of the emotions and needs of the client while still retaining appropriate boundaries and keeping the therapy on track?

Notice the power of the fantasy, and how that might tie into both a history of unmet emotional need, and a current desire to connect with a person who actually sees and seems to care for them. Both of those emotional realities involve a deep need for personal connection and intimacy. The fantasy of having the therapist fill those needs may be understandable, and the reality of the therapist being unavailable may be what allows those feelings to be expressed. The therapist will need to hold the appropriate boundaries firmly, and with kindness, taking the time to explore the needs that went unmet in childhood, and support the person beginning to care for their own wounded self, and growing to a place where they can connect with an available adult to create the kind of relationship that first emerges in the fantasy of being with the therapist.

Maintaining the dignity of the client through this process is crucial. The emotions involved often come from the person's heart in ways they may not have experienced prior to this, and that vulnerability needs to be valued and protected as much as possible while simultaneously dealing with the disappointment involved in the reality of the unavailability of the therapist. This dance is similar to the good object/bad object experience of early childhood. First, the therapist is fantasized as the Good Object. However, the therapist is actually not available, making the therapist the Bad Object. If the therapist can remain present, consistent, reliable, and kind, the client may be able to integrate both the desire and love for the therapist and the reality of the therapist not giving them all that they want and need, and come away with an experience of earned secure attachment with a Good-enough Object.

In situations where an erotic transference emerges, it is very helpful for the therapist to seek supervision and/or consultation. Most often, what the therapist hears about is the potential awful consequences—ethics complaints, and loss of license being right up at the top of the list. Other consequences to the therapist may come from disruption or loss of existing relationships, and the impact of that on immediate families.

What about the impact on the client of acting out this kind of transference? If the client "succeeds" in forming a special relationship with the therapist, or ends up in a sexual relationship with the therapist, how does that impact the psychological growth of the client? The therapist, once removed from that role, would no longer be completely focused on the needs of the client. The relationship would, of necessity, be different, and may not fulfill the fantasies of either person. In an effort to "save" the client, and be that special person for the client, the therapist will have failed to help the client do the deeper work necessary to find an appropriate partner outside of the therapy room.

When the therapist is able to work with the client, addressing the erotic transference as a reality to be dealt with in session, unpacked, worked through, and used as an avenue for growth, the client learns to relate at a different level, with greater emotional depth and authenticity. One client reported that the work done on this issue with the therapist changed the way he related to others, including potential partners. He was able to connect at a much deeper and emotionally satisfying level, and he met and married, sending the therapist a note of gratitude for the work they'd done together.

Erotic transferences touch into the vulnerability of both the client and the therapist. Navigating the relationship requires great care, and, hopefully, excellent support.

Suggestions

Gently remind the client that the relationship they have is unusual, and one of the things that is clear is that there are clear boundaries. There cannot be a personal relationship of the kind the person longs for between the two of them. Appreciate the client being able to speak about those feelings, and let the client know that this is an important topic. As you work with the person, notice what the fantasy is, what wishes or needs does the fantasy address? What kind of relationships has the person had in the past, and what is the quality of any current relationship? A fantasy is usually very pleasant, often idealized, and can provide an escape from the person's less-than-ideal reality. Does this fantasy fill that need? What about the potential for disappointment? Having a strong erotic transference can become a distraction from deep work that needs to be done, and provide an escape from loneliness or other challenging emotions. It could also be a kind of set-up, longing for someone who is not available, and, therefore, not getting one's needs met may be a pattern in the person's life.

Notice any discrepancies in how you are treating this person. Are you changing your boundaries in any way, and if so, why? Are you giving this person more attention, time, or an unusually low fee?

Does this person begin to stand out in your mind as exceptional, needing and wanting more from you than other clients? If so, why? Is this a reflection of a particularly stressful time, or is it a pattern of needing and wanting something more from you than is normally part of a therapeutic relationship?

Notice if you are being perceived as exceptional and special, and, if so, how that is impacting how you think and feel about the client. Notice if you're being drawn into a "dance of specialness" with the client. Take a mental and emotional step back and look at that. Think about the client and how this dynamic may be communicating a longing for specialness that was never fulfilled for the client. If this fits, begin to gently address this in therapy - how the longing is normal, and the wish to have a relationship now that will fill in that historical "missing piece" will not work. The work is about recognizing and grieving the loss, and working on healthy relationships with people outside of therapy. The therapist is there as a guide and support, but not as someone to fill an unmet need of that type.

Talk with a supervisor or consultant. They can help you identify the dynamics of the relationship, and where and how boundaries need to be gently or firmly held.

8 Foundational Issues— Therapeutic Strategies

Working with Memory

Managing memories is adapted from Richard Bandler's ideas on the use of Neuro-Linguistic Programming (Bandler, 1985). What follows is an exercise used to teach clients new ways of thinking about and managing intrusive flashbacks. Prior to engaging the client in the exercise, describe the exercise, and ask their permission to work together on this. Additionally, start with simple, fun, or at least emotionally neutral events to avoid triggering intense emotional reactions and dissociative defenses.

The Playing with Memories Exercise

The therapist describes the following actions as he acts them out. (Please follow along in your imagination.)

Table 8.1 Managing Flashbacks Exercise

Therapist Says:	Action:
I am now standing up out of my chair.	Therapist stands up.
I am rubbing my head and patting my stomach.	Therapist rubs head and pats stomach.
I am now hopping to the side.	Therapist takes 3 or 4 hops sideways.
I am now making the "Bronx Cheer".	Therapist makes "raspberry-phbbbbbt" sound.
I am now done.	Therapist takes a bow and returns to his chair.

After completing the above activity and resuming his seat, the therapist asks the client if they can recall the therapist standing up, going through the silly motions, making the silly noises, taking the bow, and then sitting down. When the client answers affirmatively, the observation is made that they are sharing a memory, as the therapist is now sitting in their chair. Further, they now have a memory that they can learn to 'play with'.

DOI: 10.4324/9781003217541-9

Playing with the memory involves trying a number of interesting manipulations including but not limited to:

- Making the visual images brighter, darker, bigger, or smaller,
- Running the visual images faster, slower, or even backwards
- Making the sound (both the narration and/or the "Bronx cheer") louder, quieter, or muted.

Most clients can manage these playful manipulations as these are variations on dissociative processes by taking parts of the experience and "playing" with them. The client is proactively directing the dissociative process.

Some therapists may not be in a place where silly examples would be possible. They can easily find simple, random sequences of events that will work for them, with a flow of events that can be used as examples, such as getting up, going to the door, looking out, turning around, coming back and sitting. Whatever is used, it should have a sequence of events that can be referred to in a similar manner as the silly example used. No matter what the sequence of events, maintaining a running commentary is a necessary component as the client needs to practice altering the pace of the event, as well as the volume and other auditory components of the memory.

Another element to discuss in employing this exercise is in observing the temporal flow of the events. In an earlier section we observed how different alter personalities/ego states/aspects of self manage different parts of traumatic events. Problems arise when only a few parts of the event are accessible to the presenting aspect of self.

Using the shared, silly memory as a template, the therapist and client can explore together how it would feel if they were stuck only able to recall a small segment and the need for different parts to share their respective components in order to make sense of an event. Further, the client can learn to ask for that part of self who knows how a given traumatic event ended to share the conclusion as means to bring stability and closure to an intrusive flashback.

A few notes of caution. The client should observe several different emotionally neutral events and then practice manipulating them to gain a sense of mastery of these techniques. The therapist should also observe that these interventions are not solutions but stop-gaps to help reduce distress. Further, no intervention will work every time and, in every situation, therefore developing a collection of intervention strategies is a prudent course. Finally, in the beginning, when the client is in early stages of therapy and/or experiences intense intrusions, they most likely will not have the presence of mind to step back and employ the intervention single-handedly. Rather, they will need an outside resource (therapist or support person) to walk them through the storm.

The Divide And Conquer Storage Technique

With any attempt to teach the client to 'put away' a memory, utilizing symbols that are familiar and client friendly is essential. Therefore, the therapist needs to invite the client to define and describe the storage container or device. Some examples include Tupperware, film canisters, and file cabinets. One client even wrapped the memories in gift boxes complete with ribbons and bows, valuing them as future gifts to herself.

However, there are some guidelines that are helpful to keep in mind.

The container needs to be able to be reopened at some later date. The goal is to gain time and distance from the intrusive flashback. It is important to bear in mind that the intrusive images, feelings, or flashbacks are memories that contain valuable information that one part of self is trying to share with another. Attempts to permanently banish the memory will be met with resistance and undermined. Such a move will exacerbate internal conflict between the desire to know and integrate the traumatic material and the desire to avoid the overwhelming emotional pain and distress.

Containers will 'leak'. The memories will need to be re-packed from time to time. Saying this up front is an important point, lest the client feel like a failure when the inevitable leakage occurs. The leakage is tied to the on-going need to understand and process the traumatic event.

Once the client has identified a storage device, a helpful strategy is to teach the client to put away the memory in bits and pieces rather than as a whole. Earlier, in Chapter 2, we noted the component model of dissociation. That conceptual model posited that events were experienced as different components; behaviors, affect, sensations, and knowledge. Teaching the client to put away the sights, then the sounds, then the physical feelings, and finally the emotions allows the client to break the experience into manageable chunks that can be more easily processed. As this intervention parallels the client's existing dissociative processes, this strategy has a greater chance of working to help the client to focus and take proactive control of their dissociative defenses.

Managing the Trauma Material within a Dissociative System

When the client is dissociative, it's helpful to teach him, her, or them how to ask for help inside to slow down the flood of traumatic material, or to divide it up amongst parts of the self to make it more manageable. A lot of these techniques involve hypnosis, another reason to study hypnotic interventions and strategies

For instance, a dissociative client may have parts that hold onto the belief that the trauma should be expressed as fast as possible in order to get through it. The therapist can teach those parts that pushing for speed results in the whole system becoming overwhelmed, necessitating more time spent in stabilizing the client, and prolonging the healing. Remember, the saying in the field is, "The slower you go, the faster you get there" (Kluft, 1993). Once the parts that are overly eager learn to slow down and pace themselves, the therapy actually goes faster.

Each person and each dissociative system is different, so it is very important to work collaboratively with each client to discover what approaches work best for each individual.

Memory

There has been a lot of questions and research done about memory in the past several decades. When people come into therapy to deal with past traumas, they are dealing with the reality and complexity of memory. People don't record their experiences in the same manner that our electronic devices record them. People's experiences are far richer and more complicated, impacted by the events, the emotions involved in all of the people, the developmental stage the person is in, the culture of the people, the relationship between the people involved, the presence or absence of alcohol, drugs, any other consciousness-altering substance or situation, and the individual's own resources or lack of resources. The mind records what is relevant to that person in that situation. The externals may be fairly easy to identify—they are labeled as assault, rape, abandonment, war, natural disaster, or witnessing horrifying events. Memory is encoded not only in the brain, but also in the body, and traumatic memory is recorded differently than non-traumatic memory.

In non-traumatic memory, the event is experienced at a level that is comprehensible enough to be noticed by all the senses involved, processed through the hippocampus and stored in the brain, accessible to conscious recall. In traumatic memory, the experience overwhelms the system, isn't integrated by the hippocampus, and is stored in pieces in the brain and body.

In working with traumatized people, it takes patience to connect the various parts of the memory, and some aspects of it may not be retrieved. People need to know enough to comprehend the impact of the trauma and work through the effects that remain as best they can.

There may be times when a memory is clear, and there may be times when a memory turns out to be more than was first expected. For instance, someone may remember being assaulted, and, at first, have a picture and sense that it happened in the basement of the church. Later, that person may visit the church and discover that it doesn't have a basement. Confused, that person may walk around town and freeze before another building close-by, flooded with memories of the assault having happened there. That building matches the memory. Later, the person remembers that the abuser was a church member. Two things about the memory, who abused them and where it happened originally felt like they belonged together differently than they did. In other instances, what may at first seem to be one memory turns out to be two very similar ones remembered together.

When working with memory, the therapist needs to allow for confusion and uncertainty, working with what comes up, knowing it may change over time.

It's common for survivors to ask the therapist if he or she believes them when they share memories of trauma. If the client feels credible, the therapist can say something like, "I believe you are trying to tell me the truth, as much as you know it at this time." The therapist cannot substantiate the client's abuse or trauma unless that person has come through a system (like the court system) in which records of the abuse have been taken. However, the therapist can usually tell if the person is being sincere in recounting the abuse as best they can remember it. Occasionally, the therapist will feel something feels "off". In that case, saying something like, "I'm taking in what you have to say, and I'm having a hard time connecting with it. I don't know why, but if I look like I'm trying to make sense of this, I am. Please tell me more." On rare occasions, that "off" feeling persists, and that would be a good reason to do a comprehensive assessment.

It is essential to note that the details of the memory are not the most important thing. The essence of memory work is not about recapturing the details but getting enough information about how it impacted the person in the past and in the present.

Given the plasticity and vagaries of memory, and given the therapist is not in a position to adequately determine the exact historical accuracy of memories presented by the client, a more helpful and useful avenue to explore focuses on the meaning of the event as understood by the client. What did the little child come to understand about themselves, their parents, and other important people in the world? What did the child learn about the nature of relationships and how people treat each other? What plans, defenses, coping strategies arose as the child attempted to manage overwhelming abuse and neglect?

These 'life lessons' become the underlying basis for cognitive schema that informs and guides current behaviors in our clients. That their behavior seems maladaptive, manipulative, and dysfunctional to us may be more a reflection that we are not looking at the behaviors through the same lens that our clients employ. Their behaviors, when viewed through that lens, now makes sense as the unprotected child's valiant attempt to control the uncontrollable. Without an appreciation of the essential pro-survival nature of these apparently maladaptive behaviors, we cannot engage the client in a meaningful discussion focusing on change. We will be characterized as another well-meaning person who does really get the extent of terror, shame, and abuse our clients live with on a daily basis.

Ordeal Mode

Pacing the therapy to help the person stay within their window of tolerance, and allows the person to stay in the process without feeling out of control, either hyperactivated or hypo-activated. This sounds like an obviously helpful thing, but many survivors resist stopping and taking any kind of break.

For some, that is the result of being in Ordeal mode, a replication of the old reality that once the traumatic event started, there was no stopping it until it was over. In the past, the person had no power to stop, and the only way out was for it to be over. In therapy, these clients dive in and don't want to stop until the whole memory is out. They have no sense of how that affects their body. Their sense of needing to stop has been overrun so often that they no longer feel the signals within that say "enough, stop". As one client said, "There were no coffee breaks during the abuse." In that environment, feeling the need to stop just adds to the torment, so that feeling is lost, or dissociated. Regaining the connection to the body, and learning to honor the internal sense of "enough" can be relearned, and practicing pacing is one way to do that.

Ordeal mode shows up as a "let's get this over with as fast as possible" approach to therapy, with the client or their alters pushing to do trauma work far too fast for anyone to be able to manage all of the emotions and the physical impact of the traumatic events while still functioning in their life. As these people decompensate, they may still think that the best way to deal with their overwhelm is to push through it and keep going. This is a reflection of their traumatic experience, the need to get to the end of it believing that will bring relief and they'll be done.

Ordeal mode doesn't work. It replicates the trauma and wears down the person's physical and mental health. When clients learn the value of pacing the process, they begin to experience how much more is learned by going slowly, all the skills that are developed, mentally, emotionally, and physically, that make the rest of their healing and their life far healthier and more manageable.

When There Isn't Enough Time

One of the common current dilemmas in therapy is the client with needs for long-term therapy and the mental health system with demands for limited sessions. The awareness that there is little therapy time available may contribute to clients wanting to dive in and get through as much as possible while they have a therapist or counselor. The opposite can also be true, with clients not fully engaging in therapy because they know it will end too soon.

In these situations, it's best to outline what can be done in the amount of sessions available, and what resources the client may be able to access beyond the limited therapy sessions. Creating both a treatment plan for therapy, and a roadmap for healing can be helpful, giving the client a sense of what can be accomplished in sessions, and how to proceed with healing when sessions have run out. The roadmap may include an outline of the basic process of therapy, such as an explanation of the three stages of stabilization, trauma processing, and integration, with skills to be learned and tasks to do in each stage. While the three stages are usually described in a linear fashion, they actually happen organically, with movement circling through the stages repeatedly at different levels of healing. Also included in the roadmap should be resources available in the community, such as hotlines, groups, exercise and recreational opportunities, places for meditation or religious practices, and resources available through the internet. The roadmap offers some answers to the question, "How do I get from here to there?"

When limited sessions are used to formulate a roadmap for recovery, they can provide both hope and a practical plan. It is also helpful to add emergency plans—what to do when things don't work at any stage of the plan. Providing "Plan B, C, and D" can be reassuring and profoundly helpful if "Plan A" doesn't work. As much as possible, give people things they can also do on their own, so they can feel in charge of themselves and progress even if the outside resources are erratic or unavailable.

In general, a roadmap to healing would include a process of identifying issues and resources that would be helpful to address those issues. For example, review the process that has started—recognizing that there's a problem or issue, defining it, seeing it in the context of the person's life and history, and identifying personal goals. Next, outline what the next steps in healing are likely to be—dealing with practical and emotional challenges, locating appropriate available support. Then, set approximate goals—to join a support group, to deal with social, housing, financial, or work issues that are impacting the person's health. Set goals that are within the person's ability to achieve, making them small enough to move forward and build confidence. Let the person know that this is a plan—to get the big picture, begin with whatever small step feels possible, and then continue, knowing that over time, their ability to take bigger steps will improve. Discuss some way in which the person can feel rewarded for their efforts, something within their ability to do for themselves. That may be anything that represents a personal acknowledgment of progress—making a note in a journal, playing their favorite song, wearing their best sweater, checking something off of their list, telling their friend or support person, etc.

It is not unusual for people caught in this situation to protest that it isn't fair, and not what it should be. They are usually correct, and should know that. However, while it might not be fair, it is what it is, and the person needs to do the best they can with it. At some point, there may be a way to make the system more responsive, so that it does feel fair. Encourage everyone to move in that direction while not waiting for things to be better before taking positive action in their own lives.

Pacing

In trauma therapy, learning what pacing is and why it's important is crucial prior to engaging in memory work. Once the concept of pacing is understood, it needs to be demonstrated and practiced in session by working with memories that are relatively mild. The client can choose a memory, talk about it with the therapist to make sure it's sufficiently low-intensity to be able to stop fairly easily. Then the therapist explains what they will do when they stop the client's narrative.

The therapist then listens to the client talk about the trauma, waiting for the intensity to begin to shift and move towards the limit of the person's window of tolerance. Before the client reaches their limit, the therapist tells them to stop. Then they can do any of the things they have learned that bring the client back into a stable place, including breathing exercises, grounding exercises, sensorimotor or EMDR techniques, tapping, or any number of other ways for the person to return to center.

Once the client is centered, they can return to the trauma narrative and continue to speak about it. As emotions become intense, the therapist again monitors and, as needed, stops the client. The therapist and client then evaluate this experience of pacing to see what worked best, and how it felt to the client. After several practice sessions like this, the therapist and client can approach more intense emotional material and keep it within the client's window of tolerance, allowing them to move through it to a place where it's a memory of something that actually feels in the past.

When dealing with all intense emotions, it's important to stay within the person's window of tolerance, whether the feeling being expressed is anger, terror, grief, or shame. Learning when to stop, and how to stabilize are skills necessary in therapy, and all of life. People from highly traumatizing backgrounds may not have these skills and be appropriately afraid to tap into feelings for fear of losing control and not being able to get it back. Intense emotions may push the limits or even exceed the 'window' for short periods of time. Clients who have developed good emotional regulation skills can stretch a bit and for that brief period of time, allow themselves to experience emotions beyond what they usually tolerate. As they become more secure in their ability to return to a stable place, they may allow themselves to vent safely, cry

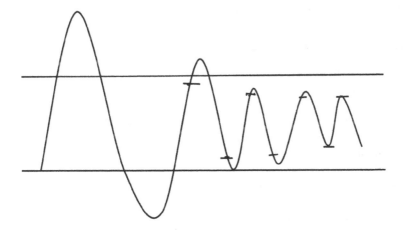

Figure 8.1 Window of Tolerance Stabilization

deeply, scream when going down the roller coaster, or laugh whole-heartedly with tears streaming down their faces. Their emotions don't scare them. They are free.

Pacing—What to Say

First, as soon as possible, educate the person about the need to pace the process. Use normal language, such as, "When upsetting things happen (or use whatever terms they're using for their upset or trauma), it's helpful to go through them slowly, taking things one step at a time, with breaks in between."

Then describe the breaks—time to check in physically, to breathe, bring yourself fully into the present, let your nervous system relax.

Practice: using something that may be mildly upsetting or annoying, have the client talk about the incident, with the plan in mind that one of you will initiate a break on purpose, use the grounding tools you're practicing, and then return to the subject.

Analogy: this is like putting the traumatic event onto a screen and giving the person the remote control. When the action becomes too intense, the person hits "pause", gets up and leaves to do something calming. When returning, there is the option to hit "play" and return to the recorded event, or turn the screen off. The event is still stored and accessible. The person does not have to watch the whole thing through at one time. The goal is that over time, enough of the event will have been seen and understood so that it is no longer intruding on the person's life.

The beauty of the movie analogy is that it is an easy way to explain how to work with memories. Like the movie, memories can start, run all the way to the end, and then replay, over and over. Or, they can be stopped, rewound, and played at slow speed to pick up important details. Then they can be fast-forwarded over things already known, or too disturbing to stay with, slowing down to pick up another piece that can be seen and taken in.

How to Take a Break—Grounding Exercises

The following is a list of grounding exercises that can help clients re-group and re-ground.

Breathe—exhale slowly, or just breathe regularly and consciously.
Put your feet on the ground, tap or stomp them alternately.
Get up and walk around.
Stand up and stretch.
Notice the colors in the room. Slowly identify five things that are yellow, or red, etc., describing each one.
Listen—what do you hear?
Take a whiff of peppermint, or Rescue Remedy, or another strong scent chosen by the client.

Feel your body in the chair, the weight against the seat and frame. Shift around and see how that feels.

Share what you had for breakfast or lunch.

What did you notice on your way to the office?

What's in your pockets, backpack, or purse?

Sing or recite something known to be calming to the client.

Toss a ball back and forth, or an orange, an eraser, anything easily and safely tossed back and forth.

All grounding exercises involve doing things that bring the person more in contact with the immediate environment, physically and mentally. They are concrete or relate directly to concrete things connected to the five senses.

Trance

People in dissociative states are in trance. In trance, the right brain is very powerful, and helpful images can become tools for healing. If the client feels "lost" in their own mind or memory, sometimes using the imagination can bring them back. Training in hypnosis is extremely valuable with this population. With clients who have been conditioned through hypnosis, or have been abused with hypnosis being part of the abuse, it is essential that the therapist be very knowledgeable about hypnosis, and if using it, only use it with permission from the whole person, as much as that is possible. If anything in the process doesn't feel right to either client or therapist, stop and process what's going on before deciding whether to continue or not.

If you want to use a visualization or a healing image with a client, if possible, have the client choose the image. Example: imagine lowering a ladder or a rope into a dark place, so the person can see and, in their imagination, find a way out of the dark and back into the light. People often use imagery to contain things. It is said that Napoleon would imagine stuffing his troubles into drawers in a large chest of drawers, shut the drawers tight, and then was able to fall asleep (Chandler, 2009).

If you are guiding a visualization, leave openings for the client to either follow what you're saying or do something different, whichever works best for the client. Phrases like, "you may, or you may not", or, "there may be something else, or not". There's always permission to follow one's own intuitive path.

When using hypnosis, or dealing with someone who spontaneously goes into deep trance, it is extremely important to do whatever possible to bring them out of trance before leaving the session. One tool for that is the Howard Alertness Scale.

The Howard Alertness Scale (HAS) (2017) asks the subject (a) to attend to his or her experience of certain sensations and perceptions before the induction of hypnosis and (b) to make a global estimate of baseline alertness, reported on a ten-point Likert-type scale ranging from 1 (very low alertness) to 10 (very high alertness). After dehypnosis, the subject is asked to rate his or her sense of alertness compared to the benchmarked experiences. Baseline assessments can be administered in just over a minute; follow-up estimates take only seconds (Kluft, 2012).

Part II
Complicating Factors

9   Challenging Behaviors

Intrusive Flashbacks; Self-Harm Suicidality; Organized Sadistic Abuse; External Locus of Control; The Window of Tolerance; LGBTQ; Sexuality; Gender Identity

Flashbacks

In the three-staged treatment of trauma, the first stage is stabilization, and therapists are taught to put off trauma processing until stabilization has been achieved. This is a worthy goal, but clients are not necessarily able to contain their trauma, and it can leak out beyond their control, resulting in flashbacks, sometimes while in session.

Flashbacks are experiences or reliving past events. While intrusive thoughts are common for trauma survivors, most of those resolve on their own within a month, and that experience is normal. When intrusive thoughts last longer than about a month, they are usually the result of neurological processes, an overactive amygdala fear system. Dissociative flashbacks are also neurologically based, a result of hypnotizability and highly sensitive sensory cortices, and can be described as a kind of hallucination (Dell & O'Neill, 2009, p. 784). As Beere (as cited in Dell & O'Neill, 2009, p. 281) explained, dissociative clients may be having more flashbacks than are noticeable by either therapist or client. These small flashbacks may be ignored, such a part of daily experience that they are automatically avoided. They do, however, have an effect on the person's nervous system and ability to be fully present.

Flashbacks may be visual, auditory, olfactory, sensory, or involve all of the senses. They are triggered involuntarily, and can't be controlled by the will alone. They're overwhelming, frequently embarrassing, and sometimes dangerous. In complex trauma, the person is overwhelmed with the experience from the past. In someone with a dissociative disorder, a part of the person may go into a flashback, while another part is pushed away, sometimes able to observe, and sometimes not. Grace described her experience like this:

> One day, I saw a man who triggered a panic attack in me. I started having nightmares, flashbacks and intrusive memories of a traumatic

DOI: 10.4324/9781003217541-11

event that happened many years before. I could see a teenage girl in my mind and felt her presence. She looked like I did many years ago. She started sharing her thoughts, feelings and memories with me. She was able to take complete control of my body, but I could see through her eyes and knew what was happening. This is what it was like for me to discover I had an alter personality and Dissociative Identity Disorder.

(Ciszkowski, in press)

When clients are having frequent flashbacks, they need to begin to identify what sets them off, the triggers in their thoughts, feelings, relationships, and environment. When and where do they usually occur? When and where do they seldom occur? Over time, people begin to see the situations in which they are most vulnerable to having flashbacks, and they can start to make steps towards having some ability to impact the frequency and possible intensity of them.

Triggers for flashbacks are often thought of as concrete events, sights, sounds or smells. Stephanie Dallam (2012) observes that there can be relational triggers based on qualities of the relationship between the client and others. Often these relational triggers are based on power differences between client and other, reflecting a similar status between clients and the person(s) who abused them. For example, people who have been abused by authorities in the past often feel triggered when needing to relate to authorities in the present. The position of authority and the activity may combine to produce a particularly intense trigger, such as a doctor giving a woman who has been sexually abused a gynecological exam, or a dentist needing to work in the mouth of someone who was orally raped.

Suggestions

When a person has a flashback in session, the first thing to do is to ensure they are as safe as possible. If they go into a memory and shift into using present tense about an historical event rather than past, be ready to step in if necessary, reminding them that what they're currently experiencing is a past event. It's over. They are having a memory. They are in your office, having a memory, but they are currently safe. The trauma/event is over. Your voice will be the connection to the present, so even if they are not responding right away, keep talking in a calm and reassuring voice. If you have to do anything—call someone for help or move around the room—narrate your action as you perform them so that everything you do is labeled correctly by you and doesn't become part of their internal trauma.

If the person's eyes are closed, ask the person to open them. It may take some time for that to happen. Keep at it. "Open your eyes, even if you can only open them a little and peek, open your eyes. It will help to open your eyes, open your eyes, peek out, open them a bit further, notice the rug, a little further, look around a bit. When you can, look up until you can see me. It's ok here, you're in my office and it's safe here. Go ahead, open your eyes."

Talk to the person in a steady, calm voice. Use your voice to connect with them. Say their name, say yours, and tell them to follow your voice until they can find themselves back in the room with you. Ask them to look at you and say your name. Then help them ground with where they are - in your office, on this day, at this hour, where they came from, where they will return, and any details that may help connect them with the present, like the new shoes or backpack they wore into the office. Let them know this is a flashback, and that they are in your office. "(Say person's name) You're having a flashback. It's a memory. I'm (say your name), and you're here in my office. It's a memory. You're here, safe, with me in my office. It will be ok. The memory will pass. Take a peek and see where you are. It's ok here..." Your voice, calm and kind, can be an avenue out of the flashback. Having the person open their eyes, even a little, can be very grounding, evidence that what you are saying is correct.

Other grounding techniques that may help:

Give them water to drink.

Have the client hold ice, or a cold water bottle on the inside of the wrist or on the neck.

Notice their breathing. They may slow their breathing or almost stop breathing. To wake them up, have them inhale regularly, and exhale quickly and with force. Or it may feel more appropriate to coach the client to breathe slowly and deeply, and breathe along with them. When in doubt, choose to ask the client to breathe regularly with you, intentionally keeping the breathing at a normal pace.

Have the client sniff a strong scent, chosen beforehand, that has a powerful grounding effect on the client. Be sure to discuss this specific technique with the client before employing it. Some people are very sensitive to fragrances. Some fragrances are triggers in themselves.

Give the client something to grab on to—the sides of the chair, a tennis ball, a pillow or stuffed animal—allowing the person to make physical contact with something stable and safe.

Have the client focus on the feeling of the body being held, by the floor, or chair, or whatever is currently supporting the client.

As said before, have the client open their eyes, even a little. Eyes closed intensifies the flashback. If they have their eyes closed, tell them to open them enough to see where they are. If they have a hard time doing this, reassure them with a calm voice that it's ok to be here, they are in a chair in your office (describe things to them that they would normally see or notice), and continue to ask them to look, or peek, until they are able to open their eyes and make contact.

If the client's eyes are open and they are still intensely involved in the flashback, slowly move into their line of vision, making sure to stay more than an arm's length away, and talk to the person, calmly (as above), asking the client to look at you. If the client was looking at you, and then went into a flashback, they may have stopped seeing you at that moment, and are seeing something or someone from the past. Calmly remind the person where they are, and who you are. Sometimes it helps to say something like, "Let yourself see that it's me, and become aware that you're having a flashback. The flashback will pass. You're in my office, nothing bad is happening now. It's just me over here, (say your name). Breathe, feeling your hands in your lap, notice that you're sitting on a chair, there's some music playing, it's warm, your eyes are looking towards me, let them see me. It's just me, (name). It will be ok." "Will be ok" recognizes that it's not ok at the moment, and that's an important distinction to make. It may take a while to bring someone back, so be patient, and don't make any fast moves.

If you need to move, for any reason, narrate what you're doing and why. "I'm going to stand up slowly and go over to the chair to get a pillow for you to hold. I'm picking the blue one, and I'm bringing it back for you. Here it is, just reach out a little and take it, and I'll go back and sit in my chair. If you can't reach out, that's ok, I'll just put it here where you can reach it, and now I'm going back to my chair." The narration helps the client in two ways; your voice is a soothing presence that helps contain the effects of the flashback, and your narration keeps the reality of what you're doing clear so that your movement doesn't play into the flashback.

If you are trained in hypnosis—which is a powerful tool with traumatized and dissociative people—you may use that to bring the person out of the flashback. Something as simple as saying to put the action on a big screen, slow it down, hit the pause button, and then turn it off can give the client the ability to stop the flashback. That kind of intervention can also give the client a tool to use in the future.

With clients who have DID, it's often possible to ask other parts of the system to help, either by stopping the flashback, or by gently removing that part of the self from the old event. In some cases, the system may have learned to act like good care-takers, so when a part of the system falls into a flashback, another part of the system may step in, like a parent who sees a child frightened by a scary movie. The caregiver would step in, turn off the "movie", and comfort the "child".

People with DID frequently use trance logic, the ability to suspend critical thinking and allow what would normally be impossible or contradictory to exist in imagination. So, it's possible for them to use unlikely or even impossible resources, like time travel, going into the flashback from current time and rescuing the younger person they were, bringing them back into the present. Or, they might speed up time, moving through the old scene and be out of it in minutes rather than hours or longer.

Recall Exercise in Managing Memory

Even if you're not aware of a dissociative person's whole system, you can ask for help from inside. You could say something like, "check inside to see if there is energy to help (client's name) come back to the present, or a way to give them enough distance from what's happening to be able to hear me so I can help". It's also possible to ask for the memory to slow down and stop for now, or ask parts of the self to take some of the overwhelming affect and help it disperse so the client can return. Having dissociative parts cooperate to take small amounts of the overwhelming feeling empowers the system. Having parts or self-states contribute their strength is also empowering. These are ways to access the strengths the client has within and practice using them to become more capable of remaining present.

When working with a dissociative person, it is helpful to hear what has worked for that person in the past to pull out of flashbacks or trance states. It's also helpful to talk with aspects of the self to see how they might be able to help when confronted with flashbacks.

If a flashback feels imminent during a session, the therapist can help prevent an escalation by saying things like, "Keep your eyes open, look at me, breathe with me (slowly). Feel your feet on the floor, notice the music from the radio, feel the sun on your shoulder, give yourself a hug, tell me what you had for breakfast. It might help to stand up slowly, stretch, then stand in a power stance and feel your own strength (etc.)".

The "power stance" is standing tall, head held high, hands on hips, elbows out, and legs and feet in a wide stance. Holding that position for even a short period of time can help the person regain a feeling of presence and strength. Continue to talk to the person through the grounding tools that have been taught and found helpful to this person.

How to Prevent or Limit Flashbacks

The overall goal is to practice defusing and calming potential flashbacks so that full blown flashbacks no longer occur. In general, this involves choosing the smallest trigger available and using systematic desensitization techniques. This takes time and patience, time enough to calm the nervous system and work with the parts of the trauma that fuel the flashbacks.

Help the client learn when and how flashbacks happen. Flashbacks are frequently triggered by something in the environment. Sounds, scents, certain behaviors, and emotional situations, can all set off flashbacks. It's empowering for the client to become a kind of detective, taking notes about what things happen right before flashbacks. What precedes the flashbacks? Note both the external situations and the internal clues so that the flashbacks begin to make sense. It was well known in the 1980s that helicopters flying overhead could easily trigger Vietnam veterans. Currently, war veterans are outspoken about the effects of unexpected fireworks around the fourth of July. The sound and vibrations trigger being back in the war. Those triggers are very clear. Many triggers are not so easily discovered.

Some triggers may have to do with people, some with the time of year, or a geographical location. Smells are often a very strong trigger, causing an instantaneous reaction. If rituals were part of the abuse, or closely associated with it, as in clergy or cult abuse, even benign rituals may be triggering. In some cases, certain words or phrases may trigger people. Those words or phrases may have been used by the abuser either intentionally as in hypnotic suggestions or unintentionally as in language or phrases particular to that person. Although it may seem contradictory, it can also be a trigger to have everything go well, because that's when the abuser would be most likely to strike, resenting the peace and joy of others.

In some cases, as was stated earlier, the triggers are relational, replicating a relational dynamic that was present in the abuse. One of the most common of those is the replication of power over the person, such as in the position of being a patient in the care of a doctor or dentist. In both of those situations, the client may feel helpless before someone with power, who is also someone they need. In addition, medical or dental procedures may be uncomfortable or feel invasive, making the triggers more intense. In these cases, it is helpful to find a physician or dentist who is trauma-informed and will help the client feel an equal partner through whatever procedures they may need.

Becoming curious and investigating one's own behavior can be very empowering. It can also provide increasing amounts of information about situations, physical and/or emotional, that trigger flashbacks, allowing the client to devise ways to manage the triggers and stay on top of potential reactions.

Teach people that a flashback is like a malfunctioning fire alarm, going off when there is no fire. The person has the ability to learn to be increasingly able to identify the emergence of flashbacks and calm the body, so that, over time, flashbacks lessen and then stop happening. The person learning about flashbacks is the first step in stopping them. Knowledge alone, however, won't immediately work because the flashbacks are automatic reactions, and it takes time to calm those to the point of having conscious control over them. Slowing down when things begin to get intense, using stabilization and grounding techniques, and asking for support can all help the person diminish the intensity and duration of flashbacks.

When the person has enough knowledge about the flashbacks and what triggers them, therapy can begin to focus on defusing those triggers, taking the smallest ones first and working up to the major triggers. In this way, the skills learned in working with small triggers helps the person deal with the ones that are most powerful. The use of grounding tools, pacing, reinforcing appropriate positive beliefs and other resources helps the person stay present and learn how to tolerate and deal with the emotions and events that have come through flashbacks. Over time, the person learns how to have a coherent narrative about the event in the flashback, able to talk about it with the appropriate feelings. Being able to do that is evidence of the memory being integrated. Before that step has been taken, the memory may have been related without emotion, or come through flashbacks without the narrative. Being able to tell the story, complete with the emotions being identified and informing how the story is told, indicates that the person is speaking from a place where the memory is within the Window of Tolerance.

In addition to exploring when flashbacks tend to happen (triggers), it's also very useful to notice if the person has ever managed to avoid or stop flashbacks. How did they manage that? While preventing flashbacks may seem like a positive thing, there are times when the cure may be worse than the symptom. Some people stop flashbacks with self-harm or other potentially dangerous activity.

Most clients are not in constant flashbacks, so it can be very helpful to track when there is an absence of flashbacks for any length of time, noticing the conditions in which there was a calm period. Time of day, presence or absence of other people, more or less physical activity, obvious reminders of the trauma or complete absence of reminders, more or less recreation, spiritual connections, physical health or illness, etc., are all things that vary in a person's life and may impact the frequency of flashbacks.

For clients with DID, another consideration is the use of flashbacks to control intrapsychic processes. When the client is in a profound state of conflict, torn between knowing and not knowing about their abuse history or other untenable emotions or thoughts; they may find that intrusive flashbacks may work in lieu of more obvious self-harm behaviors in distracting the self and the therapist from addressing the fearful issue. Similarly, exploring the role of the flashback in the context of the client's significant interpersonal relationships, both in and out of therapy, may prove insightful.

Sometimes therapists treating trauma may expect their clients to be able to put away or banish intrusive flashbacks through cognitive techniques. While those can be helpful to a certain extent, to help put the brakes on cognitive patterns that may automatically slide into flashbacks, flashbacks are, by definition, involuntary, so any expectation of control is likely to fail, creating more distress and a profound sense of powerlessness. This sense of powerlessness replicates the feelings of helplessness in the original trauma and reinforces a feeling of lack of mastery.

Also, blanket attempts to banish the flashbacks are frequently doomed to failure. While it is preferable to handle traumatic experiences in the second stage of therapy, as was said previously, that may not be possible, and the inability to prevent a flashback is evidence of its strength, and not evidence of the client not trying to cooperate. The intensity of the experience may be too big. The event is part of their history and can't be undone or banished. Further, if the therapist is too direct, even though well meaning, this will also reinforce the sense of powerlessness and create a dependency.

In the midst of dealing with flashbacks, pay attention to what they contain. That is all information about what happened to the person and how the person reacted to the experience, including beliefs and feelings that need attention, or, as in Grace's experience mentioned earlier, the awareness of parts of the self that had been dissociated (Ciszkowski, in press). In the midst of flashbacks may be expressions of shame, helplessness, responsibility, grief, or rage. Those unprocessed feelings or issues may be impacting the person's reactions in present life, making current life more difficult than it needs to be. Working through the trauma that initially presents in flashbacks takes the emotional energy out of it. When the work is done, the person can remember the trauma and realize the effects of it in a way that is informative rather than disruptive. There may be intense sorrow or upset about what happened, but it becomes manageable and no longer interferes with the person's current life and relationships in a damaging way.

Self-Harm

Compelling, and deeply disturbing, self-harm often strains the relationship between therapist and client. The therapist may feel upset, angry, disappointed, and helpless. (Which probably mirrors some of the feelings the client is having at the time.) These normal reactions may or may not be helpful in the therapy. Before sharing any reactions, it's helpful to discover why clients hurt themselves.

There are many reasons people self-harm, and there are many forms of self-harm, including cutting, eating disorders, substance abuse, purposely placing oneself in harmful situations, and massive self-neglect. These behaviors, in general, are an attempt to pull the person back into their Window of Tolerance when no other ways to do this are known, or don't work quickly enough. If the person is hyper-aroused, the self-harm may feel calming. If the person is hypo-aroused, the self-harm may be activating and feel like a 'waking up' experience. Self-harm can also be a way to displace emotions, such as taking anger out on one's own body rather than confronting the rage inside or expressing it to a dangerous abuser.

In a recent study done by the TOP DD group, Nester and colleagues (2022) found that greater emotion dysregulation was associated with greater dissociative symptoms and self-injury among the TOP DD patients. Thus, focusing on improving emotion regulation and grounding in treatment may help stabilize self-injury. In addition, the researchers learned that it is particularly difficult for individuals with dissociative disorders to stay engaged in goal-directed tasks when they are distressed. People with dissociative symptoms also have very high levels of not being aware of, or accepting of, their emotions. Their level of emotion dysregulation is very high, even compared to other clinical groups.

> Analyses revealed emotion dysregulation was associated with heightened dissociative symptoms and greater endorsement of self-injury in the past six months. Further, patients with a history of self-injury in the past six months reported more severe emotion dysregulation and dissociation than those without recent self-injury. As a group, DD patients reported the greatest difficulty engaging in goal-directed activities when distressed, followed by lack of emotional awareness and nonacceptance of emotional

experiences. DD patients demonstrated similar patterns of emotion dys-regulation difficulties irrespective of recent self-injury status.

(Nester et al., 2022)

There are many, many reasons for self-harm, and in order to address it well, the therapist needs to work with the client to discover what functions the self-harm serves. Some possible reasons might be:

To stop the feelings.
To be able to feel.
To transfer the emotional hurt into physical pain, which may feel easier to address.
To see the hurt outside, to know it to be real.
To get others to be able to see how bad it hurts inside by showing it on the outside.
To release endorphins through cutting, which provide an immediate (and very temporary) relief.
To express how much the body and all its feelings are hated.
To punish the self—feeling responsible for the abuse or shamed by its effects.
To connect with being alive—"I bleed, therefore, I live," or by pushing the self into hyperarousal.
To prevent something worse from happening—like choosing self-harm rather than suicide.

Another recent study by Nester, et al. (2022) identified six themes for self-injury, each with subthemes: (1) trauma-related cues, (2) emotion dysregulation, (3) stressors, (4) psychiatric and physical health symptoms, (5) dissociative experiences, and (6) ineffective coping attempts. Participants reported that they were able to identify their reasons for self-injuring sometimes (60.26%) or almost always (28.85%), with only 3.20% unable to identify any reasons for their self-injury.

Some people use self-harm to stop feelings that are intolerable. With cutting, the harm shifts the energy into physical pain and the need to care for the wound. It's a distraction, a temporary one, and while it may seem to work in the short term, it only adds to the harm done to the person. Self-harm through eating disorders and substance abuse serves the same function, temporary relief from disturbing feelings.

There are also times when a person is hypo-aroused and feels so numb, they no longer feel anything. That can be alarming, and may provoke the person into harming the self in order to feel something real. Going into hyperarousal through putting oneself in dangerous situations, using substances to push the body into alert states, or cutting the body to wake it up are all ways to attempt to feel and get back into the person's window of tolerance.

Transferring emotional pain onto the body is fairly common. Physical pain seems to make more sense and feels more manageable to some people than facing their emotional pain. It's outside, observable, and obviously real. Cutting, provoking violence, and some eating disorders can be used for this. Combined with making the pain physical, other people can see it, and thus know the person is experiencing pain. This may be the only way that their hurt and suffering can be communicated. Moving from emotional to physical, pain that feels a step away from heart and soul, is now observable to others, very real, and an obvious wound may bring an acceptable form of help to the person.

Ask people who engage in self-harm, and they will often say that self-harm is helpful. It brings immediate relief. The body, when hurt, floods the system with natural chemicals that ease pain. It's fast and effective, and very short-lived. Still, it's something that people turn to when there doesn't seem to be any other way to relieve the torment they feel. Substance abuse and eating disorders also have a short-term effect that feels temporarily helpful.

People who have been repeatedly abused may end up with a great deal of self-hatred. This is especially true for those who have been sexually abused and conditioned to be sexually responsive in abusive situations. The hatred of the body for responding in those situations may be expressed through deliberately hurting the body, starving it, bloating it, allowing it to be abused by others, or even trying to cut parts out, re-enacting the sadistic sexuality they were forced to experience. The rage and shame in these re-enactments is heart-breaking, more so when the self-harm is condemned by professionals thus adding to the shaming of the person. In these situations, the person may also be punishing the body for responding when that is not what the person wanted to experience.

With these people, especially with sexual abuse survivors, it is helpful to teach them how the abuser used their normal body reactions to make them experience things they would never have chosen. An analogy would be to experience someone jamming a piece of chocolate cake in another person's mouth, blocking airways and causing the person to panic or faint. In the midst of all of that trauma, the person's taste buds would register "chocolate = sweet". That simply means the person's taste buds are working the way they're supposed to work, there's nothing wrong with them. What's wrong is the whole experience of violence and cutting off someone's air supply, and that was the sole responsibility of the abuser.

There are also times when people become so numb that they no longer seem to feel anything. They begin to wonder what's wrong with them, and miss the simple ability to feel anything. Some of those people may try self-harm or use drugs or violence as a way to trigger feeling and as proof that they are alive. If they bleed, then that means they really are alive. These people are living in hypo-aroused states, below their window of tolerance, and are struggling to find their way back to being able to feel. *"Dolore, ergo sum."*

When asked about the cause for the self-harm, some people may say that it was the best alternative they could think of at the time. It was an alternative to suicide. That's good news and bad news. It's good because the person managed to stay alive, and it's bad because the person was hurt, again. In the big picture, however, it's better they did that rather than killing themselves, so the message may be, "I'm so glad you're still here, and so sorry you felt you needed to hurt yourself in order to stay." That statement would be followed by an exploration of what happened and the identification or creation of other things to do to stay alive and not need to self-harm in the future.

In general, self-harm is an attempt to modulate affect. The feelings are too strong, or too absent, and the person is attempting to stabilize. Teaching self-soothing techniques helps in the long run. However, self-soothing techniques take longer than self-harm, so the client needs to be willing to use the new techniques and tolerate the amount of time it takes for them to work.

Self-soothing may involve gentle, supportive self-talk, reassuring oneself that there's no danger present, no need to flee, no need to carry the pain or rage quite so strongly right now. Breathing intentionally, slowly and deeply, calms the body. Slowing down in general is helpful, allowing the person to become more present and in the moment, away from overwhelming feelings from the past or fears of the future. Writing in a journal, drawing, playing music, talking with a supportive friend or someone on a helpline, holding one's pet, having something to eat or drink that's healthy, taking a soft shower or warm bath, are some ways to self soothe. As clients heal, their list of self-soothing activities grows longer, and their trust in their ability to manage emotions increases.

When first trying self-soothing techniques, they may resemble the self-harm. Journal entries may be about wanting to hurt oneself or filled with self-condemnation. Drawing may involve red markers on the arms where the harm would usually happen, or pictures of drugs, alcohol or violence. This is progress, and needs to be supported. It's better than actual physical harm, and it represents the person's ability to shift his or her behavior in a positive direction. Small steps count.

Frequently, people have been abused repeatedly, and they learn that the abuse doesn't end until they are hurt, badly. That's what they learned, over and over. Self-harm may be the only way they know how to end an abuse cycle. Remember the story about the client who became highly agitated, and asked, begged, her therapist to hit her. That was how that abuse ended when she was a child - the adult hit her and it was over. In therapy, she was not hit, but was helped by her therapist to calm down without harm. It was only after she had become calm that she was able to appreciate the therapist's refusal to hurt her.

At the time she was pleading to be hit, she truly believed that was the only way to stop her overwhelmed, intolerable experience. Afterwards, when she was stable again, she could see and appreciate that she could be helped to calm down without abuse. There was a better way, and people hurting her was not ok. The next step in this process would be for the client to learn how to soothe herself when upset, modeling after how her therapist behaved, and become better able to initiate that kind of care from the inside.

Self-harm may also evoke something in the therapist that needs to be seen and heard. For instance, some self-harm can horrify the therapist. What can the therapist do with that experience?

First of all, the focus needs to remain on the client, but that doesn't mean that the therapist can't, at some point, talk about the reactions that kind of self-harm evokes and wonder about it. If the self-harm was horrifying, the therapist may be able to connect with the client about things the client saw that were shocking or horrifying, and help the client deal with that experience. What happened? How did the client deal with the situation, and why might that be coming up through self-harm at this point in time?

Less serious self-harm may draw the therapist closer and evoke concern. That dynamic may mimic a client's history of never getting any attention unless he or she was physically hurt. Some clients may come into session with serious self-harm and want to ignore it. Where did that come from? Were their obvious wounds ignored? Is that what they learned—to ignore their need for help when hurt?

In effect, self-harm can hold a therapist hostage. It demands attention, and may prove for some to be the only way they know how to keep the therapist (or anyone) close and engaged. To the therapist, it feels like the person is insisting on their attention, and that element of the dynamic stands out from all the other issues that may be part of the self-harm.

While all self-harm requires attention, there's a different feeling in situations where it is being used to hold on to the therapist. It may represent a re-enactment, an experience in the client of being held hostage by someone who threatened to hurt or kill themselves if the client left. Alternatively, the use of self-harm, or threats of self-harm, may be the only "safe" way for a client to draw the therapist, or other potential caregiver, close. Directly asking for attention, time, or a demonstration of concern may feel too risky. The client may feel desperate and needy, struggling against boundaries and limits to external contact. For these people, talking about safety may be alarming. As Brand, et al. (2022) explain, "For individuals who may have never known safety, the idea of 'getting safe' can feel entirely inconceivable, and 'getting safer' can seem like a trick and/or feel impossible."

Exploring the relational dynamic is key. Gentle and genuine curiosity examining the possible emotional and interpersonal aspects of the moment without accusing or shaming the client shifts the focus from a "cat and mouse" covert power struggle to a collaborative search for authentic needs and healthier solutions. Important questions to consider include asking if the client ever felt trapped, helpless, or powerless. Also important is to investigate if the client has ever felt invisible as if significant people in their life ignored them and didn't really understand how badly our clients needed someone to respond to them. It is helpful for the therapist to reframe the behavior from "attention-seeking" to "connection-seeking".

With some clients, especially with dissociative clients, forms of self-harm may replicate the abuse. Binging and purging may be a re-enactment of having been forced to eat or swallow something awful. If there is a history of that kind of abuse in the person's background, then the behavior may be signaling distress in that area, or with the alter who was present for that abuse.

Cutting and substance abuse may also replicate previous abuses of that kind and be the only way a dissociated part or memory can communicate that abuse to the therapist. In some dissociative systems, protective alters may trigger self-harm episodes to slow or stop the therapy when it feels threatening for any reason. The self-harm in those incidents may replicate the punishment given to the person for speaking, telling the truth, trusting, or believing he or she can become free. Exploring the client's inner world in a collaborative way, asking for reasons for the self-harm, and seeing if and how that might be communicating something can help the client learn to use words and other methods of communication that don't further harm the person.

Eventually, when clients find more direct, useful ways to express themselves, care for themselves, connect and receive help from others, the self-harm stops.

Ongoing Abuse

There are also situations where people are caught up in long-term abusive situations, and return repeatedly to their abusers to be abused again and again. The situation may be a severely dysfunctional family or relationship, a dangerous cult, or ongoing incest. While the person's going back to an abusive situation is a form of self harm, it is different in that it is an ingrained pattern of behavior that may be sustained with the belief that it is necessary, that the person will be harmed more by not returning on their own. Also, in the case of on-going incest, when sexual abuse becomes an integral part of a person's childhood years, the result is a conditioned sexualized attachment, reinforced with shame and fear (Middleton, 2013). Disengaging from this pattern takes a long time, often extending past the time of the abuser's death, with patient work to build the person's inner and outer resources, strengthening the person to the point where they may have the ability to leave the abuser. People abused in this manner are often DID, and at high risk of serious self-harm and suicidal behavior. Most hear their perpetrator's voice in their head, as an introject or aspect of self. In dissociative systems, the parts that take the abuse need to remain in place until the person has the ability to not return. When the parts of the system that are being abused come into the therapeutic process, they lose the ability to manage the abuse, and it's not a good idea to lose that ability for self-preservation until the on-going abuse can be stopped. Steve Frankel calls these parts that manage the abuse that cannot be avoided 'heroic' for managing the unmanageable while the person is still trapped (Steve Frankel, personal communication). That approach helps with internal acceptance of parts created to help the person survive, and helps those parts feel a little grace for all they endure.

Some people are also connected with groups that are not their family but powerful enough to force them by threats or manipulation to continue to return and be used and abused repeatedly. These may be people who are being used in prostitution or pornography rings run by a range of perpetrators, from a few semi-organized people to large, well-organized criminal groups. Helping people in these situations discover resources from within and from outside can create a pathway for them that can lead them out of their devastating circumstances. People will need to keep their defenses in place until they are no longer necessary.

Organized perpetrator groups seek to control what a person may know, what they may feel, and who they can bond with (Hassan, 1988). If an organized group can establish a level of control in those domains, especially in terms or where the person feels accepted and understood, then the client is further enmeshed in the abusive relationship while fearful and uncertain that any other option truly exists. In these situations, the quality and strength of the therapeutic relationship will be tested. The therapist will need to demonstrate that the client can be understood and appreciated outside of the demands and constraints imposed by the abusive group.

Working With Survivors of Organized Abuse: Patterns and Challenges

People whose abuse has been deliberate, often planned in order to use the person for power or financial gain, have a particularly difficult healing path. The intentionality of the abuse, the torturous conditioning that can sometimes begin in very early childhood and persist for decades, makes the survivors', and the clinicians', work long-term and intense. The brutal conditioning needs to be identified and addressed while, at the same time, new ways of thinking, and responding, need to be learned and practiced. People with this kind of experience are often dissociative because they have been trained to use dissociation, and it's not unusual to discover that drugs were a part of that conditioning experience, making resistance impossible. In organized abuse, the conditioning is aimed at training the person to do whatever is required while often also being conditioned to present "normally" in public, keeping the abuse well hidden. Rituals are used to reinforce the power of the conditioning.

It is not uncommon for organized, extreme abuse to include rituals. Rituals are intentional experiences with shared group meaning. Normally, they are used in social groups to mark the high and low points of life and all the significant steps between—birth, death, transitions of age, marriage, commitment to the community, acknowledgment of status or accomplishment, etc. They serve to highlight an experience, make it significant to the whole group. When they work well, they are powerful events for healing and group cohesion. When they are used abusively, the damage is felt on all levels, personal, existential, and communal. When they are also kept secret, they isolate and further disempower the person.

At some point in the healing process, people will need to learn to reclaim rituals, healthy rituals, by creating events that have meaning for them, bringing in friends and supportive people to re-experience the power of meaningful, supportive rituals. When rituals are reclaimed, profound healing can happen, to the individual and to all who participate.

It's a long journey, however, from devastation to freedom. There are so many obstacles to overcome, lessons to learn or relearn, all kinds of thoughts, feelings, and beliefs to release, and so many new ones to experience. From a distance, this looks like the hero's journey, similar in so many ways to classic myth and archetypal symbols. Up close, it's a daily challenge—to live, to just put one foot in front of the other, to choose over and over and over again to keep going. There is nothing romantic in the reality of healing from this level of abuse and torture, and yet people do emerge from darkness to light, from fragmentation to wholeness, and they are often called inspirational to those who know them.

How Do They Do That?

There are many theoretical approaches to dealing with trauma survivors. They are all helpful, to a point. However, when the survivor has had to deal with organized, extreme abuse there are issues and dynamics that go beyond what most therapists are taught.

There are specific issues and patterns common to survivors of organized and ritual abuse, and there are ways to deal with them, empowering both the therapist and the survivor.

The Ordeal

The pattern of enduring until the end, powerless to stop what's happening. In organized abuse, once the event has begun, there's no stopping, for anything or anyone. People learn early on that they will have to endure until it's over. Their natural desire to stop is ignored or punished. Over time, it's silenced. Survivors can no longer tell when they've had enough and need to stop. In fact, stopping usually provokes fear. In therapy, survivors just want to get it over with, be done with it, and the only way they know how to do that is to white-knuckle it to the end. In fact, they have often found ways to get to the end faster. Self-harm is one of those ways. If the belief is that the pain will only end when they are hurt really badly, then they may hurt themselves really badly as a way of ending the event. There are also clients who will seek some kind of sexual release because that was the signal that the event had reached its end.

In working with this dynamic, the therapist works to teach clients to stop, breathe, take a break, and pace themselves. If clients understand the reason to learn this behavior, they will almost always do everything possible to learn this new behavior. It is difficult to learn to slow down, but, eventually, it offers so much relief.

The Double Bind

Abusive conditioning puts people in a lose-lose position. Resisting the abuser is not an option, and going through with it is deeply traumatizing. There is no negotiation. People feel pulled apart emotionally, not able to move in either direction, knowing there's horror on both sides and resisting the feeling of choosing.

Stepping out of that bind involves stopping either/or, all or nothing thinking. Current events seldom replicate the 'no exit' reality of the abuse, although they are often perceived to do just that. Clients need to learn there actually is another path, and to choose that path. The process usually involves stepping out of the bind completely, refusing either of the two impossible options given. The most well-known example of this cutting through of a double bind comes from the legend of the Gordian Knot. In Gordium, in Turkey, in 333, Alexander the Great solved the problem of the Gordian Knot. It was believed that whoever untied the Gordian knot would rule all of Asia: Alexander the Great is said to have undone the knot by slashing through it with a sword.

In organized and extreme abuse, the option of stepping out of the bind was not there. It's important for survivors to realize that the double bind was intentional, a deliberate manipulation to evoke feelings of powerlessness and shame.

Having had the experience of no way out, the reality of the ability to choose is lost. Compliance is automatic.

A kind of Gordian knot solution was demonstrated very simply in a master's program. The professor was setting up an exercise for the class to experience. Even though there was a sense that this would be a "gotcha" kind of experience, most students were complying, except one guy. He just stepped aside and said, "no", he chose not to participate, a polite and effective refusal, given nicely, with a smile. He sat off to the side and watched everyone else being set up and put in uncomfortable emotional positions.

Stories like that, role plays in session, brainstorming about ways to step outside the confines of a double bind all help expand the options for survivors and empower them.

The Illusion of Choice

The severely limited options typically given in organized abuse are not what the survivor actually wanted. The word "choice" is often used when no choice actually exists. Teaching what a genuine choice really is—the ability to say "no" without being attacked or abandoned—is an integral part of this work. The word 'choice' when used where there were so few options, and an absence of any option that would be acceptable is the same as no real choice being given. Because people truly want to have the power to choose, they will often believe they are making a choice when they are only being given the chance to select from two horrible situations. This is how the double bind manifests—no matter what people decide, they will suffer. The word 'choice' normally involves the option of saying "no". In this case it doesn't, but the person is still treated as if it does and put in a position of feeling responsible for things they could not avoid.

In working with the issue of choice, it's important to preserve the person's actual power to make choices. Underlying a lot of what happens in organized abuse is a deep choice to live. Often the choice to live is not conscious—consciously people may want to die more than anything. Still, the body/mind/psyche/soul chooses life. Life holds hope, hope for a future that will bring healing.

Whatever the superficial choice made by the survivor in the abusive situation, there will be an underlying choice for life that is powerful. I've even heard this emerge when the survivor chose what would have appeared to be a self-sacrifice in order to help another person live. That's still a choice for life. Likewise, the wish for death in these situations is often a realization that what is happening isn't about life at all, an awareness of how profoundly wrong the whole situation is, with death seeming to be the only choice that says "I refuse to be a part of this".

The Classic Set-up

The classic set-up is an expectation that people should know what they have not had the chance to learn, and then be humiliated, blamed and shamed for not knowing. This is very common with people abused as children. At some point, before, during, or after the abuse, the children are told they must have known what would happen, and therefore, they have actually chosen to do whatever happened and are responsible for it.

Another main hook in all of this is that the survivor may have a part of themselves that does know what happens, but that part is dissociated and not available at the beginning. When this happens, the survivor has some sense of the abuser being right in saying they would know what's going to happen, and that makes the setup even worse. The survivor knew, but didn't know, and no matter what was known or not known, the abuse was inevitable. The feeling of "I should have known" just makes it all worse, causing people to feel far more responsible for their abuse than they were.

The Deliberate Targeting of any Attachment

If you love it, it will die. A lot of survivors already have attachment wounds, and when the abusers target anything the person loves, whether that's a person, pet, or even an inanimate treasure, it makes the attachment wound worse. The fact that people come into therapy and try to connect is heroic. Taking the risk to care means facing the fear of loss.

All those interactions in which the client anticipates a negative response from the therapist, and all of those fearful anticipations of the therapist leaving, stem from the fear of abandonment and horrible loss.

What follows from this attachment wound is usually a pervasive terror of abandonment. When you, the therapist, go on vacation, it's often felt as if you'd died. That's how devastating it can be for the client. Years ago, having become aware of this dynamic, a therapist went a year without a vacation. She couldn't bear the thought of putting her clients in that horrible situation. It felt as if she was hurting them when she did. As you can imagine, that didn't work. As intensely painful as it is, both therapist and client need to acknowledge that reality of loss, grief, feelings of abandonment and fear that comes with separation and allow it to heal naturally over time as the therapist comes back and re-engages with the client. It does get better.

The other part of this is that if clients connect with the therapist, they may immediately feel the therapist has been put at risk. Their connection equals risk. Clients have said they needed to terminate because they thought that their perpetrators would target their therapist. They wanted to leave to protect the therapist. Some even brought gifts of pepper spray to the therapist, wanting her to promise to be vigilant at certain times because they have been so terrified that their work with her would end in disaster.

Sometimes, perpetrators will call and leave messages for a therapist. Rarely, very rarely, they might do something else, like sit in the car, outside the office, knowing the client would see them and be triggered by their presence.

Still, there are times when perpetrators do prove to be more than an annoyance, so therapists should listen to what their clients are saying about possible threats, and do the appropriately cautious things to stay safe. That's just the smart thing for the therapist to do, and it models how to handle this kind of thing for the client.

Training in External Locus of Control

Whatever anyone else says, goes. This dynamic erodes a person's ability to hear their own sense of what they want or need. They become blind and deaf to themselves, looking only to others to determine their behavior.

Encouraging people to listen to their own intuition is helpful, but they may have no idea what their intuition is, and that learning is a gradual process of identifying, sometimes after the fact, the clues given from inside about what feels 'right'. In a dissociative system, there sometimes may be parts of the self better able to connect with intuition. People usually know what parts have that capacity—their "inner self helper", "wise one", or "spirit guide". Or, they may have a system where that inner connection is a function that is not specifically carried by any one internal person or persons.

Often this kind of learning is like the client being a detective, going back over situations to look for clues. As they do this, they may run into the "I should have known" trap, so it's important to continually remind them that it's not fair to expect anyone to know what he or she has not yet learned. Fairness is an innate sense in all mammals, so to identify something as fair or unfair helps connect with innate wisdom.

Therapists and support people can also help by identifying potential choices and allowing clients to make decisions for themselves. This is much easier said than done. Survivors will continually revert to old decision-making patterns, not by choice, but by ingrained torturous training. After years of therapy, it's not unusual for a client to ask, "what do you want me to do?", a question that reflects an external locus of control. Every time that happens, or any other old pattern emerges, it's another chance to empower people to make their own choices. So, don't take the easy way out and answer a question like that. Take the long, scenic route, and have clients come up with an authentic answer from their own inner wisdom.

Karpman's Triangle

Karpman's Triangle describes the dynamics of the Abuser, Victim, and Rescuer. As mentioned in Chapter 6, this is a system familiar to everyone working with people who have been abused. This is the way people learned to relate, and this is also how survivors continue to relate to themselves and to everyone around them. It's the cause of a lot of stress, pain, and frustration. Survivors often have no idea and no experience of any other way to relate. For many, stepping out of the triangle is the first step towards freedom.

In organized abuse situations, the roles of perpetrator, victim, and rescuer are extreme, and survivors are often put in a position where they feel all three at once. No wonder there's so much splitting associated with this kind of abuse. Victims are forced to hurt the one they want to rescue. There is no saying, "no". The survivor has the experiences of being victimized, and is often forced to feel like an abuser, whether that is accurate or not. Sometimes there's a rescuer in the picture, a person who genuinely tries to help, or someone whose rescuing is just another set up. Sometimes the survivor manages to rescue someone in some way, and is then further victimized. There are all kinds of scenarios, but they are all locked into these fundamental roles.

In therapy, the roles play out in the survivor, and in the relationship with the therapist. Many survivor clients come into therapy looking for rescue. They feel victimized and some of them identify as victims. Some come with the split reality of being a victim and an abuser. Many spend a great deal of time rescuing other people, and animals, who need help.

Therapists may find themselves wanting to rescue the client. Or, at times, become aware of abusive kinds of thoughts or feelings towards the client. There are also those times when the therapist may feel victimized by the client.

These are all manifestations of the power of those three roles, and how they trap people into re-enactments.

There is a way out, and it is powerful. Consciousness is the key. When people become aware of the roles they have been trained to play, and realize that they do not need to be in any of those roles, a profound change can begin to happen. The feelings and impulses continue to be there, but the person can choose to notice them and not act on them. The roles begin to be seen as roles, not as the person's identity.

The Trauma Bond

Why is it hard to break away from those who hurt you? This is a question that comes up frequently in therapy, whether it's spoken or not. Survivors can and do go back to their abusers for a lot of reasons. Some of that may be programming/conditioning. Even if it is a programming kind of conditioning, there's usually an underlying reason that makes that conditioning stronger than it needs to be.

It's all about attachment and survival. Severe abuse quite often happens when the person is a child, a dependent, immature child. Children being victimized still need the person who's harming them in order to live—physically and emotionally.

When the child is hurt, there's a natural drive to seek comfort from the parent. When the parent is the abuser, which is too often the case, seeking comfort becomes dangerous. The child is caught between the need for the parent and the fear of the parent. There's also the deep need of the child to be seen by the parent. Some professionals are now saying that it's the profound invalidation of the trauma that comes when the child's reality is not seen that makes the trauma stick as tenaciously as it does.

Theological, Alogical, Mind Traps

In some organized abuse, especially in abuse that includes rituals, theology is misused to harm victims. One very common practice is telling children that God hates them, that they belong to the devil, etc., reinforced with ritual and torture so that the child feels awful to the point of not feeling human or worthy of anyone's love, much less God's. The absence of rescue by God is used as "proof" that God has abandoned the child.

This is a "you feel bad because you are bad" trap.

One of the main problems with this is that children are almost always incapable of thinking of any other reason why they are being hurt. "If I feel bad, I must be bad", is simple, concrete thinking. It makes sense. The ability to think that feeling bad is because something bad has happened, and it has nothing to do with the person's worth requires more maturity and mental development than most child victims have. They're not sufficiently mature to understand that kind of reality.

Also, if something bad happens because the child is bad, then the child can assume that with personal change, they can become better, and then bad things won't happen. It's the illusion of control, the hope for a way to make the suffering stop. This kind of thinking preserves the feeling of personal power, even if it's not the truth in the situation.

The Use/Misuse of Magical Thinking

People abused in these settings are taught to attribute power that doesn't exist to their abusers through the use of hypnotic trance states, suggestions, and commands to perpetuate control when abusers are gone.

For children, magical thinking is normal, and that is abused in these settings. Monsters and devils are real, and, therefore, any other creature or magical power might also be real—that's what the children are taught. Reality checking in this area is terrifying, especially to young parts in a dissociative system. Patient teaching helps. Also, the use of the trance state to counteract the old messages is very, very powerful—know what you're doing before you try it, and talk with the client about what you're doing before you do it so that it's collaborative.

Conditioned Paranoia

Children are literal thinkers. In abusive situations, adults can and do take advantage of that. When an adult says, "I know what you're thinking", it's probably true at that time and place. It's really easy to see the expression on a child's face and identify the thoughts and feelings behind it. Normally, this ease in reading a child's emotional state is used by healthy parents to help the child—to learn the names of emotions and how they might be expressed, like the mother in the mall mentioned earlier. In extreme abuse situations, this ability to know the child's state of mind is another thing that is used against the child, to establish control, and instill fear, to the point of paranoia. When an abuser says, "I know what you're thinking", and then adds, "And I'll always know what you're thinking, no matter where you are, forever", the child has no way of understanding that kind of omniscience is impossible. This is another example of reality tied to unreality that disempowers the survivor, potentially forever.

Breaking down the message, identifying what was true then, and what was not true then or ever, is a difficult process. The mental ability to do that doesn't emerge until adolescence, and some people never seem to get that capability.

Double Messages

In abusive situations, words and behavior often conflict. Often the words used may sound positive, while the behavior is the complete opposite. People may be told they are very special and then raped or tortured. Abuse may be coupled with words about love or status. Or, on the opposite side, loving behavior may be labeled as weak or bad. The confusion between words and behavior further disempowers the person, setting mind and emotion against itself.

Working through double messages takes time, but the process is actually quite simple. A worksheet suggested below can be used to demonstrate one way to do this process.

Using Beliefs to Prolong Control

Programming, conditioning, learned behavior, learned helplessness, etc. are all about the mind telling the person to do, or not do, something. There is no feeling of choice, the person feels out of control of their own mind. Minds can heal from this—neuroplasticity of the mind, the mind's ability to create new connections and divert itself from old ones causing them to shrink is documented by brain scans taken of people before and after therapy.

One of the things that keeps old conditioning in place is the belief that it is permanent. It's not. The mind can heal, and will heal, according to the beliefs of the person. The most powerful thing a person has is their consciousness.

It's been said, "The person with the most consciousness, and clearest intent, has the most power." This is true with survivors—the development of consciousness and the ever-increasing clarity of the intention to heal, the knowledge of what health is like, combined with the accumulated experiences of enjoying healthy relationships with self and others, will transform the mind, the brain, and the life.

All of these patterns bind the survivor to the trauma. As powerful as they often are, with time, work, clear intention, and consciousness, they can all be overcome.

Suggestions

"Words and Behavior" Exercise: words and behavior are supposed to go together and make sense. In abusive situations, they often don't. This is an exercise to help people sort out what's being said and what's being done to see if the words and behavior actually match.

No matter what is said, the behavior will speak the truth of the situation or relationship.

For those people who may return to an abusive situation or be forced back, finding a safe house or other secure place for them is optimal. When that is not available, or the person will not agree to go to one of these places, then

Table 9.1 'Words and Behavior' Exercise

Step 1. Recording what was said and done	
What the abuser said	What the abuser did
Step 2. Taking it apart to make sense of it	
What the abuser said	Behavior that matches the abuser's words
What the abuser did	Words that match the abuser's behavior

the work becomes one of damage control. Focus on building the internal resources necessary to make the move away from the destructive family or group as soon as that becomes possible. This usually takes a lot of time because of the severity of the abuse and the survival adaptations the person has needed to create in order to live. Noticing any improvement will help. Building on things that help the person move in the direction of health will help.

Acknowledging real danger and difficulty will soften some of the loneliness of this situation, and will open the discussion of what can be done. It's important that the therapist not join the person in feeling powerless. Continuously look for solutions, steps forward, what can be done internally, in therapy, and in the community. Hold hope when the person cannot find any within, and keep working at it.

Suicidality

The most severe form of self-harm is suicidal behavior. Too often, when suicidal feelings are expressed, the therapy virtually stops. Sometimes, when the threat is imminent and serious, that's necessary and appropriate. The client needs to be alive and safe enough to engage in therapy. Often, however, clients have suicidal feelings that need to be expressed and heard so that actual suicide can be prevented.

When suicidal thoughts and feelings emerge in therapy, it is necessary to do a suicide assessment immediately. Although that may seem obvious, there are times when that first step is skipped. Therapists may miss that step because they have heard the client express suicidal thoughts so often that they no longer take them seriously, or clients may express suicidal thoughts or feelings in such a vague manner that the therapist may not pick up on the severity of what's going on. For instance, a client may say something like, "I won't be here for very long". He may be referring very subtly to his desire to die. His therapist may assume what he said was in reference to there being only a few minutes left in the session, missing the hint that was too tenuous to catch. In between those extremes are numerous other situations in which the therapist and client miss directly confronting the potential suicidal threat.

Suicidal thoughts, feelings, and attempts can come to people with many different diagnoses. There are, however, some populations where the risk is alarmingly high.

It is fairly well known, and documented, clients with complex PTSD and Dissociation have a high level of suicide risk. The presence of non-suicidal self-injury (NSSI), suicide attempts (SA), and suicidal ideation (SI) in these clients is a constant challenge to both clients and therapists. Scanning the literature, the topic emerged in several areas of this field.

Statistics

"Dissociative disorders and PTSD are consistently associated with increased NSSI and SA/SI" (Ford & Gomez, 2015). In psychiatry, "each type of trauma and dissociation contributed to suicide attempts and self-mutilation, but dissociation was the most powerful" (Zoroglu et al., 2003). In social work, the reality of mental health professionals having to deal with the suicide of a client stands in stark contrast with the lack of training in how to deal with this kind of event, professionally and personally.

> The results indicate that 55% of social workers will experience at least one client suicide attempt and 31% will experience a client suicide completion during the course of their career. Additionally, less than 50% of the social workers surveyed received previous training or education about client suicide in their MSW programs
>
> (Sanders, Jacobson, &Ting, 2008)

For patients with DID, research done by Webermann, et al., found that 78% self-injure, and up to 86% attempt suicide. Within mixed psychiatric treatment samples, a DD diagnosis has strongly predicted multiple suicide attempts and completed suicides (Webermann et al., 2016).

These findings point to dissociation and depression severity as important correlates of NSSI and suicidality in patients with dissociative disorders and have implications for self-harm prevention and treatment

There are many reasons for people to have suicidal thoughts and feelings. Some common ones are:

- Wanting to escape from intolerable feelings and situations
- Feeling like a burden to family and friends
- Needing to feel some control over their life
- Self-soothing function of knowing there's a way out
- Fantasy of making others finally see the impact of their behavior and feel appropriate guilt and remorse
- Attempting to see if anyone really cares
- An attachment cry—like the child screaming in the crib, hoping someone will come and help
- An automatic, conditioned response to any attempt to break away from the control of the abuser, or abusive group
- A signal that life as they have known it does need to die, so they can live

Trauma is often a strong contributing factor to suicidal thoughts, feelings, and behaviors, whether that be an accumulation of microaggressions, assaults, or, for some people, tortuous interpersonal or war related abuse.

There are many roads that can lead a person to consider suicide, including:

- Depression
- Despair
- Isolation, loss
- Pain—chronic physical and/or emotional pain
- Shame—a deep hatred or rejection of the self
- Moral injury—they have seen or done something that has hurt others. This is actually a sign that the person has a good moral sense. They feel anguish because they have the ability to feel with others, and they have the sense of what is right or wrong. For these people, it is helpful to find ways to "give back", to put back into the world in ways that help others survive and heal
- Deeply ingrained beliefs—certain behaviors or conditions result in expulsion from the person's family or group, and they may be expected to suicide. Think of the cultures where shame is supposed to be taken care of by committing suicide. People who are dissociative, with PTSD, DID, or DDNOS may have places/people inside who are actively suicidal, and they are not consistently aware of these feelings or plans. Self-harm and suicidal behavior for these people may be out of their consciousness and their ability to contain.
- And, sometimes, people hold on to suicide as a possible choice because they have never had any other way to feel control over their life. For them, it's used like an "exit" possibility, something they could choose to do when there are too few, or no, other ways in which they have control over their lives. People who have been trafficked will sometimes hold onto suicidal thoughts and plans for this reason.

It is not uncommon for people to experience several of these at once—such as a feeling of failure leading to despair, dropping the person into depression, causing others to back away and leave the person alone. Or, being involved in something that felt deeply "wrong", causing a moral injury, shame, and the feeling of not deserving to live.

For some clients, saying they feel suicidal may be a way, perhaps the only way, that they know how to let the therapist know they are in trouble and need the therapist to know that this is very important. Anything less may not feel adequate to the level of distress the person is experiencing. Also, anything less may come with a history of being ignored or dismissed, so the person has learned to say "I'm suicidal" in order to be taken seriously. Unfortunately, if they use this strategy too frequently, it may lose its power to call attention to serious issues, and put the person in the position of feeling a need to escalate in order to be heard.

When suicidal feelings function to help people to feel in charge of their own lives, they may never use it, but just knowing it's there is often what enables them to stay.

Quote from Former Client Identifying as 'Bliss':

...for the six years that this was my reality. It was dark and you were simply there and asked nothing of me—demanded nothing of me. You did not require that I give up my feeling of wanting to die. I mean, after all, it was all that I had—it was the only thing I felt I had been left with was control over whether I lived or died because every other ounce of control had been stripped of me. So, I clung to it with all I had. It was all I knew until I knew something different. It took about six years of having someone significant, you, show up and not turn away no matter how dark I was—no matter how dark it was. Seeing possibility in the eyes and heart of that constant someone is what saved me. Eventually, I could branch out and find some light for myself on my own, slowly. I believe it is the love from others who are willing that makes the healing possible.

(Bliss, personal communication, 2020)

Sometimes, things happen during those necessary years, things outside of therapy, outside of the client's or therapist's ability to prevent. There was a chronically suicidal client once who was being seen by an excellent, caring therapist. His suicidality was intense, and he frequently said he wanted to kill himself. Once, when he was out in the world, he said that again, and a friend, someone who had heard it before, many times, got frustrated and said to either stop saying that or just do it. He did it, he shot himself. That person's therapist was stunned and devastated. It's likely that the person who was understandably frustrated felt even worse. In that situation, it was the client's responsibility to tell the friend that saying he wanted to die was a way to release some of those feelings so he could live. If he couldn't speak that truth, there was nothing left for him. Hearing that, it would be highly unlikely that his friend would have said what he said, and that man may have lived through that crisis.

People may consider suicide as a way to have some control over their lives, a way out of unremitting pain, physical and/or emotional, or sometimes when they feel like a burden to the people around them. Take note of comments like, "they'd be better off without me."

So, how does the therapist know what the suicidal message means? That requires unpacking it, finding out the person's history with this issue, asking inside the system for help in understanding it, and acknowledging that this message may mean many things to create some curiosity about it within the person. The more the person can unpack the suicidal package, the more power they will have in communicating what's felt and needed, and the better able they will become in getting genuine needs seen and met as much as possible and stay alive.

That said, no one can ever know their client completely, or successfully predict what that client may do. No one.

There are also many levels of suicidal ideation. There are ideas of suicide that come and go, intrusive ideas of suicide, and persistent ideas of suicide.

The threat level of the suicidal thinking also varies. Asking about any potential plans is one part of a suicide assessment. If there is a plan, how potentially lethal is it? The client saying he was suicidal, with a gun within reach was in imminent danger. Having access to weapons, especially loaded guns, makes suicide possible in one, impulsive, moment. Other people may be behaving in a suicidal manner much more slowly, by neglecting their health in serious ways, failing to take necessary medications, taking too many medications. Hoarding medications to accumulate a lethal amount is a serious risk.

Wanting to escape from intolerable feelings and situations is actually a normal reaction - people try to get away from pain. When the pain is unavoidable, as in dealing with life-long trauma and betrayal, and chronic emotional duress, the client may see no other means to get away except by dying. In these cases, therapists may naturally want to offer hope and options, which can be helpful. The part of this experience that is often overlooked or given too little time is the actual despair of the client.

Before being able to grasp any hope offered, the person needs to be heard. This can be very difficult for the therapist who may be afraid that by hearing the depth of despair in the client, they may be making the situation worse. There is a difference between hearing the despair, and colluding with it. One client expressed that difference by telling her therapist that when she was drowning, she didn't want the therapist to jump in with her and drown, too. She wanted the therapist to stand on solid ground, throw her a life preserver, and help her get to shore. To hear the despair can result in the client no longer feeling alone with their pain, and that is helpful. The client first needs to be heard. Then the client may be open to accepting change, to reaching out for help. Then the therapist can intervene in a way that will slow or stop the client's downward spiral.

Feeling like a burden to family and friends leaves people feeling like those they love would be better off if they were gone. They see the stress their problems cause others, and assume everything would be better without them. The first impulse of most therapists is to reassure them of their value, and they do need to hear that. The other part of the process is to understand the situation and the perceived stress of the person's family and friends. The person's perception may be accurate, or it may be exaggerated. When it's accurate, it's an indication that the family and friends need help. If it's an exaggeration, it may be seen as worse than it is because the client genuinely wants to participate in life far beyond their present capability and projects that disappointment and frustration onto other people, assuming they feel the same.

Needing to feel some control over life may be behind some suicidal behavior when that seems to be the only sense of control currently available to the person. "I can always leave" gives a sense of having an option when no other options are available. Knowing that suicide is possible may retain a sense of power that is available nowhere else in the person's life.

Very similar to needing to feel in control of one's life is using suicidal thoughts as a way to self-soothe. In this case, knowing it's possible to die at will can make living more acceptable. There's a feeling of choice given to the person, "I could die, but not now. I choose to live." Having the feeling of choice is empowering, and that can help the person live.

The next two reasons are also similar. Suicidal feelings and behaviors may emerge out of a fantasy of making others finally see the impact of their behavior and feel appropriate guilt and remorse. "When they come to my funeral, they'll see that they really did hurt me, and then they'll feel bad about that." This is a wish to be seen by the people who caused their pain. It's a fantasy, and needs to be labeled as such. It may help to talk about the fantasy, and the probable reality, and identify the wish behind the fantasy, and the grief and upset still current in reality. It may also help to use a Solution Focused therapy technique and imagine what it would be like if the abusers were miraculously healed for a few minutes and could truly see and acknowledge the person and the harm they'd caused. What would they say to the client? How would it feel to finally hear that?

Going through that exercise may provide some sense of satisfaction. However, the idealized wish for acceptance and acknowledgement from abusive family members is unlikely to happen. A significant struggle is in helping the client acknowledge that their family or the people who abused them will not, cannot, and will never love them. Processing the grief arising from recognizing this tragic state of affairs becomes an essential part of healing.

Having suicidal thoughts and feelings can also be a way to check and see if anyone cares. Does it matter to others whether this person lives or dies? For people who have been ignored, or treated as objects, this may be the only way they can ask people if they matter. Sadly, for some trauma survivors, this may be the only context in which people do respond, and their response may be the only thing that allows the person to continue to live.

When infants are left alone too long, they cry. Their cries escalate into desperate levels attempting to reach people who will respond. That is an attachment cry, and that kind of emotional outcry is also heard in many forms in adults. Suicidal thoughts and feelings may at times function like attachment cries, becoming more extreme in the hope that someone will hear and come to help.

There are also times when suicidal thoughts or feelings may be an expression of the desire for a new life, an expression of a kind of death that would free the person to live a more satisfying life. Once an older monk approached the Dalai Lama asking the Dalai Lama if it was possible for him, as an older monk, to start a particularly difficult spiritual path. The Dalai Lama told him no, that path was very demanding and meant for younger monks. The old monk went away and killed himself, in hopes of being reincarnated and then able to pursue the more difficult spiritual path (Dalai Lama, 1998).

The old monk, in this case, literally chose death in order to have a more advanced life. (This is also an example of how even the Dalai Lama, a very wise person, may say something that he later regrets.) While he did this in a literal way, others may have suicidal thoughts and feelings that come from a similar motivation, to be free from this life as it's being lived and able to engage in life in another way that would be preferred for some reason. Their suicidal talk is more of a metaphor for how they feel about the way their life is going.

The therapist can examine this possibility by asking. "Are you thinking about killing yourself, or are you saying something else?" Another useful avenue of exploration is to ask how suicide might improve the person's life; what problem will they not have to deal with, what emotion will they not have to feel? The person using suicidality as a coping mechanism will normally respond with something that indicates conflicted feelings; a desire to live in tension with uncertainty as to how to resolve the problems confronting them.

Suicide Assessment

Suicide assessments include asking about suicidal thoughts and feelings, and the presence of a plan. Men are more likely to suicide than women. Alcohol increases the risk. Previous suicide attempts increase the risk. Being alone, feeling like a burden, illness, recent loss, and other difficult current situations can increase a person's suicidal thoughts and feelings, and therefore, increase their suicidal risk.

The deadliness of the plan is also very important. "I want to die..." with no plan, raises concern and should be examined fully, while "I plan to kill myself, and I have the gun and bullets," demands immediate, comprehensive intervention. There are all kinds of variations, and each one needs focused attention. Never take a suicide threat lightly. Make a habit of asking about suicidal feeling and potential threats with clients who feel at risk in any way.

Ask about the person's history with suicidal feelings and behavior. If there is a lengthy history, how intense has it been, and how potentially lethal? It is well known that the best predictor of future behavior is past behavior, so if the client has a history of severe suicidality, with dangerous attempts, more caution will need to be taken, and more vigilant attention to the status of suicidal thought and feelings. In this context, it can be helpful to try to identify the triggers that prompted the suicide attempts, and also notice what is happening in the person's life and psyche when suicidality is lower, or not present.

When a person has a history of suicide attempts, it is important to check in regularly about the status of their suicidality. Some people develop a way of rating their risk, from low to high, or from imminent to future, and all the gradations between. Creating a way to talk about the current suicidal risk helps both client and therapist keep track of the level of that threat.

To minimize safety risks, clinicians should regularly assess patients' safety and symptom severity; teach symptom management techniques; as well as explore barriers to implementation, such as demoralization, shame, and negative beliefs related to childhood maltreatment and depression, e.g., "Nothing helps," "I don't deserve to feel better" (Howell, 2011).

Complications—Sometimes People are Dissociative:

While there are many ways to assess for suicidal feelings and plans, there is an extra complication when working with people who dissociate. First, they may not have access to their own suicidal feelings, and plans. Second, they may default to suicidal thoughts and feelings for many reasons, known and unknown. Some suicidal responses have been conditioned, and some may be the result of the person preferring to die rather than feel, know, confront, a reality too difficult to tolerate. Some mistakenly believe that killing "the body" won't result in their own death.

This leaves the therapists with several challenges. Are there suicidal thoughts, feelings, and plans within the person's dissociative system? And if there are, how will you know? It's possible that your client who attempts suicide did so from a place inside that wasn't in therapy with you. It's possible that the client's ANP wasn't aware of the suicide plan. It's possible that something triggered the client that was unforeseen by you or the client. There are many ways in which people who dissociate have learned to not know what they know.

Some Clues: For this, like many things, knowing past behavior and patterns is the first, and most easily accessed way to determine how suicidal your client may be.

1   Chronic hospitalizations for serious suicide attempts puts the client in the highest risk group.
2   Hospitalizations for suicidal feelings are at a second level of risk.
3   Having suicidal thoughts and feelings without a history of needing extra help, while still serious, is a bit lower on the risk scale. Saying this, however, doesn't mean that any suicidal ideation doesn't need to be explored (Pisani, Murrie, & Silverman, 2016).

Unpacking the Message

Suicidal thoughts, feelings, and plans, if any, need to be unpacked. What do they mean? How serious are they?

- Finding out the person's history with this issue
- Asking inside the system for help in understanding. Talk through on a regular basis
- Acknowledging that this message may mean many things to create some curiosity about it within the person

Pisani, Murrie, and Silverman (2016) present a more nuanced model for teaching and communicating suicide risk assessments. They state:

> Psychiatrists-in-training typically learn that assessments of suicide risk should culminate in a probability judgment expresses, as "low, "moderate," or

"high." This way of formulating risk has predominated in psychiatric education and practice, despite little evidence for its validity, reliability or utility. We present a model for teaching and communicating suicide risk assessments without categorical predictions.

Instead, Pisani, Murrie, and Silverman (2016) propose risk formulations which synthesize data into four distinct judgments to directly inform intervention plans:

1   risk status (the patient's risk relative to a specified subpopulations), PTSD, DID and DD are high risk subpopulations.
2   risk state (the patient's risk compared to baseline or other specified time points), Is the client's suicidal intensity rising, stable, or falling?
3   available resources from which the patient can draw in crisis, Other professional support, friends, safe family, community groups, 24 hour call lines, etc.
4   foreseeable changes that may exacerbate risk. Loss of housing, benefits, job. People leaving, pets dying, health issues, etc.

Learning New Behavior

Identify reasons for suicidal feelings and behaviors and plan for other ways to express those needs and feelings. Alongside that exercise, create a list of things that connect the person to life - people, spiritual connections, nature, life goals, etc. When a person is suicidal, they often cannot access those things, but if they've written them down, or recorded themselves listing the reasons they have to live, they may be able to connect with their own life-giving resources.

Make a list of people to call when in trouble. The list is best when it's long and includes people who can hear and be supportive without feeling overly burdened, and also includes 24-hour hotlines.

Make a list of things to do for the self prior to any suicidal acting out—preventive measures. These may include all of the person's grounding tools, and ways to connect with supportive people, nature, animals, etc.

Agree to contact appropriate people to ask for help when overwhelmed. Many people put off asking for help until they are desperate, and then they feel like they're asking too much of others and hesitate to reach out. If they can practice reaching out earlier, it will be easier on themselves and everyone else. It will also work faster and prevent crises.

Suggestions

So, what do you do if you think someone may be suicidal? First of all, ask them. If you think that may feel intrusive, or leave you feeling foolish, consider how much easier those emotions are to deal with than what you would experience at this person's funeral. Ask because you care. Ask because it matters.

Ask them how they feel, ask what's going on.

If you know they've been traumatized, then remember that suicidal thoughts and feelings may be a result of that trauma. Being alive may be especially challenging for the person who will need to learn how to deal with all the intense emotions and physical results of the trauma. That takes time.

In working with partners, spouses, family members, friends, and support people, make sure they all have emergency numbers to call. Seek out resources for the client and their support system. There are suicide hotlines open all day and night. There are also ways to text for help. There is an organization dedicated to working with suicidality—suicidology.org—where you can find resources in English and Spanish, for all kinds of populations. Look through that site (https://suicidology.org/).

- Put emergency numbers on everyone's phone. Arrange for regular check-ins
- Locate professional help in your area, even if the person is currently unwilling to go
- Look at what your city, county, province has available for emergency interventions and help
- If the person is seriously suicidal, don't leave them alone—make sure someone is there until the crisis passes, or the person can find professional help
- If you're supporting a person who has been chronically suicidal, and suddenly that person seems fine, seems to be feeling good again, and is giving away items of sentimental or monetary value, be alarmed. That sudden "I'm much better now. Here, I know you've always liked this" scenario may be evidence that the person's struggle to live is over and they have decided to die. They feel relieved. They are in serious danger

With suicidal people, no one actually has control, but everyone has influence. Use the influence you have. Your presence, your caring, your practical and emotional support all have influence.

Make sure you take care of yourself. This level of emotional intensity is exhausting, so your self-care needs to be excellent. Also, engage as many people in supporting the suicidal person as you can. Human beings need other human beings. We are communal creatures, and when one of us is in trouble, all of us need to gather around and offer our help, our support, and our love.

Sexuality

Many trauma survivors have been sexually abused. That abuse affects the person's experience of their own body, and impacts relationships in subtle or major ways. Part of healing from sexual trauma involves being able to address sexual issues in therapy.

Some of the consequences of sexual abuse may be:

- Self-harm through sex
- Avoidance of sex
- Using sex as a primary way of connecting, (only value, way of attaching)
- Attempting to control others through sex, using sex as power
- Transference and countertransference in therapy in relation to sexual issues
- Specifically sexualized parts or alters in dissociative system
- Interaction of client's sexualized behavior and therapist's vulnerabilities

Self-harm Through Sex

When sex has been abusive, it often evokes shame, that feeling of being bad. It's not uncommon for people to have very conflicting feelings about their bodies and sexuality when they have been sexually abused. Some people hate their bodies for being sexual, for having genitals that others would hurt, or for feeling any kind of arousal in situations that were fundamentally awful. Often this misplaced sense of self-hate comes out through sexualized self-harm—hurting the genitals, or engaging in sex with violent people, re-enacting the original abuse or aspects of it. When sex has been linked with pain, that connection may be very difficult to break. Worse, some survivors are conditioned to become aroused in frightening and/or painful interactions. When the physical conditioning is added to the shame and self-hatred commonly experienced by sexual abuse victims, acting out those dynamics through harmful sexual experiences may become a regular pattern of behavior. Stephen Porges (2021) has described how sexual abuse, the combination of arousal and defense mechanisms, causes the body's polyvagal system to wire together in an unnatural manner. Normally, when sexually aroused, the body also relaxes, so there is arousal and relaxation experienced at the same time. Most people know this as the 'weak in the knees' feeling in the presence of the person they love and sexually desire. Emily Nogoski (2018) has written and talked about the difference between arousal and desire, underlining the separateness of those two states described by Porges.

Other times, people react by avoiding sex as much as they possibly can. This may include physical self-neglect as a means of disengaging from the body (or those parts of the body) where the harm occurred. These clients dress and behave in ways to discourage any sexual attention. They have great difficulty addressing sexual issues in therapy. When they become sexually aroused, they panic or dissociate, unable to tolerate those feelings.

When people have been repeatedly used for sex, they may develop an identity that is based on their sexuality, as if sex were the only thing they had to offer another person. When others, like their therapist, refuse to engage with them sexually, they are at a loss to know how to relate, and may have no idea that they have any value beyond being objects to be used. The loss of identity and roles that have been used for a lifetime can leave the person feeling exposed and extremely vulnerable. When sexuality has been the only avenue for connection and the only way in which a person could experience being worthy, the loss of that mode of relating equals the loss of relating at all.

In a situation where a person has little or no power, whatever ability they do have to influence others will be used. If sex was the only thing that could be used to influence others, then the person might recognize that and learn to use it in a roundabout way to get things that were not available through direct means. This gets labeled "manipulative", and it's unfortunate that the word has such negative connotations. In most cases, people choose manipulative ways to get needs met when direct ways are dangerous or not available. Sex is powerful and possibly the only aspect of life in which the person may have felt any power. If the person learned that the only way to feel any personal power is through sex, then that avenue will be used. They do not feel and are unaware of the power available through their minds, hearts, creativity, talents, and potential for truly connecting with other people.

For some people, sex becomes an identity. Their whole presentation in the world is sexualized, as if that were the most important thing about them. When that occurs, it's usually because that has been their experience. One particularly gorgeous woman came in for therapy and related a history of betrayals and molestations. It seemed as though every person who came close to her attempted to molest or seduce her. Eventually, harassed for her beauty, like the heroine in the Italian movie "Malena", she gave in and set up her own sex-service business. In therapy, she expected judgment for what she did for a living. However, her therapist did not judge her at all, but asked to hear her story. Tears came to the woman's eyes, and her hardened exterior vanished. The therapist's acceptance of her as a person, and desire to see her as she experienced herself brought down the defensive shell she had created to protect herself.

With dissociative people, there are often sexualized parts of the system, created to manage inappropriate sexual relationships. They may be "Daddy's girl", or names that are more blatantly sexual and derogatory. These parts of the person may emerge at any time, but their timing is always significant for some reason. They may be triggered by something in their own environment or in the relationship with the therapist. Perhaps there's warmth or connection, and to that part of the dissociative system, that's a signal for sex. Or, maybe things are getting too real, and the sexual part comes out to be done with this interaction because no one ever cares beyond the sex. People are trying to get the best they can out of interactions with others while keeping themselves as safe as possible. With dissociative people, that means the therapist may encounter several parts of the system in intense situations, including sexual parts who are doing whatever they believe their jobs to be—to divert attention, engage the person, assert control, or just do what they've been trained to do.

The probability of the therapist encountering sexualized behavior or an alter personality who uses such behavior to get needs met is exceedingly high. Accordingly, the clinician is encouraged to be prepared with a range of gentle and clear means of clarifying the therapeutic boundary and shifting the focus onto the meaning of the event. Great care must be taken at this moment to address the client in a safe and non-shaming manner. Authentic curiosity as to the goal of the behavior and the internal experience of the client in the moment facilitates open discussion. The therapist's concern for genuinely helping the client, expressed as care for the client, can be paired with the need for safe and clear boundaries.

Sexual boundary violations usually occur when the therapist is vulnerable or emotionally compromised in some way. Vulnerability can come in many forms, from being excessively lonely, struggling with loss or illness, or needing affirmation, affection, or power. It is the therapist's responsibility to be mindful of their own vulnerability and getting emotional and sexual needs taken care of appropriately outside of therapy. In situations where clients have been sexualized through their abuse, it is helpful to have regular professional supervision, consultation, or other support to monitor and maintain therapeutic boundaries.

Sexual Arousal in the Therapeutic Setting

Erotic transference talks about a wide range of deep and vulnerable emotional and physical reactions and responses in therapy. There has been some material written about that and some discussion in training. There is less written, or said, about sexual arousal in the therapeutic setting. What is stated regularly is that sexual contact between therapist and client is unethical, illegal, and can cause the therapist to lose their license, and the client to suffer harm. So, "don't do it" is the message.

Knowing that sexual arousal is not to be acted on with clients is one very important piece of information. It doesn't, however, help much in figuring out what's going on and what to do with this very uncomfortable reality. What therapists are seldom taught, and which clients also need to learn, is that arousal and desire are different. People can be physiologically aroused without having any desire to act on that arousal. Also, people can have the experience of desire without arousal. With survivors of sexual assault, an experience of arousal can be devastating, as if the body was betraying the person. Perpetrators may deliberately arouse their victim, and then tell the victim that means the person wanted the abuse. No, it doesn't mean that at all. Arousal is a physical reaction to stimulation of some kind. Desire is the person's felt wish to engage. Sometimes, the desire is there, but arousal is not. In marriage counseling, couples are helped to identify that as a physical aspect that just needs some extra attention, and doesn't mean that the person isn't wanting to be intimate. Arousal and desire are two separate experiences.

In therapy, especially when the client is needing to deal with sexual issues or recover from sexual abuse, quite a bit of time is spent talking about sex. In that context, people may become sexually aroused. It is very important at that point not to add meaning to that experience. Just notice it, and do what you do to calm your nervous system. In the therapy session, it may be time to take a short break. Pause, do some grounding, have a drink of water, and take a break from the subject. With sexual abuse survivors, it is helpful to do some psychoeducation about this subject as early as seems appropriate, so that it will not be a surprise, and there will already be ways to understand and work with that kind of situation.

For the therapist, it may help to notice the arousal for a couple of reasons. First, obviously, it's a personal experience that may be unnerving in this situation. Second, it may be part of a transference, countertransference experience, and the sooner that is recognized, the better. If the situation does seem to contain a lot of transference, and subsequent countertransference, it can help to pause and ask, "what's going on right now? Is this familiar in any way?" Bringing curiosity into the situation can help to bring the rational mind back in charge without invoking shame.

Emily Nagoski's work can be helpful both for the client who needs to know that arousal didn't mean "they wanted it", or "they enjoyed it". It simply means that the body is reacting to stimulus. Desire has more to do with the emotional experience, and the pleasure of that experience. The same is true for the therapist—there may be arousal when there is some kind of stimulus (Nagoski, 2018). (See https://www.ted.com/talks/emily_nagoski_the_truth_a bout_unwanted_arousal?language=en.)

That, however, does not mean the therapist has any desire to be sexual with the client. In fact, the therapist's reaction to any arousal may cause the therapist to distance from the client, and the therapist needs to be aware that their distancing can be perceived as rejection, triggering shame or other devaluing emotions in the client.

Suggestions

Begin to notice if there is a discrepancy or a congruence to the systems of arousal and desire. For example, if someone does a great job of describing slicing into a big, juicy lemon, the listener may experience salivation. That's arousal. Does the person want a lemon? Not necessarily. If not, then there is a discrepancy between the arousal system and the system of desire. If the person would dearly love to have that lemon slice, then there is a congruence between arousal and desire.

In the therapy office, in the moment of realizing a sense of arousal, it helps to have some internal resources in place. Imagine a two-way mirror on the wall, with supervisors watching the session. What helpful and supportive things would those supervisors be saying? What suggestions would they have about how to navigate this situation in a way that would be helpful to the client?

Talk with a supervisor or consultant. Look into the dynamics in the relationship with the client, and into whatever way you may be vulnerable at this point in time. If you become aware of vulnerabilities in yourself, begin to take care of those in your personal life in whatever way is appropriate.

If you find the situation is not resolving, or is getting more intense and potentially hazardous, consider what might be needed to get back on track (with the support of supervisors or consultants), or, if that does not seem feasible, how to properly refer the client.

Seek your own therapy. It will be a great support through this, and a chance to learn a lot about yourself that will benefit you as a person and as a therapist.

Be prepared to talk about sex and relationships with sexually abused people. As soon as possible, tell them that it will be a subject of conversation at some point. That doesn't mean you need to start having those conversations about it right away, but letting the client know this is a topic that needs to be discussed, and will be discussed at the appropriate time, opens the door to having the discussion when the time is right.

When clients become seductive, it can help to let them know you recognize what they're doing, and while they may be good at that, you wonder why they've needed to learn that, and how it has both helped and harmed them in their lives. This is a way to keep the professional distance in place while not shaming the client. It also is the beginning of putting language to the behavior and discovering its purpose and meaning, and that will help teach and empower the client to learn how to have a close relationship that does not require sexual services.

If the client becomes too assertive, pushing for a sexual relationship, it can help to let them know that their being sexual is seen and recognized, but will not be acted on in this relationship, because it would keep them from experiencing things other people know but, unfortunately, they never had the chance to learn. To engage in sexual contact would be more of the same, and would not help them discover anything new and better. For the protection of both client and therapist, sessions may be videotaped (with appropriate signed permission), or held in a room with a one-way mirror and a supervisor on the other side, monitoring and supporting the therapy.

It is important to make the boundaries clear without rejection or shame. Equally essential is identifying and acknowledging how the bid for sexualized contact fulfills some important, relational purpose. Validating that need without replaying the abusive dynamics but instead offering appropriate connectedness and therapeutic interactions empowers the client and the dissociated sexualized aspects of self to grow.

When working with sexual issues with a client who is in a marriage or intimate relationship with a committed partner, sexual issues will need to be addressed. It is not uncommon for the sexualized parts of a person, dissociated or not, to be taking care of the sexual aspects of the person's relationships. In those cases, the person may be performing sex rather than engaging in it with the partner or spouse. If that's the case, there may be little or no actual intimacy in the sexual relationship for the survivor. The survivor may not even be aware that sexual intimacy is possible. For those people, or alters in a dissociative system, sexuality needs to be learned from a fresh perspective. One facet involves the client learning to feel pleasure in the body in non-sexual ways. Another element is to learn to experience emotional intimacy with their partner, again without shifting into sexual activity. Then moving slowly to being able to feel closeness and physical pleasure when with the other person. In dissociative systems, the part designated for sex will be the last part engaged in this process in order to help that part learn slowly from the rest of the system and prevent an automatic shift into conditioned sexual performance.

Issues with Gender

In dealing with issues around gender, and gender identity, it can be helpful to separate biology from gender roles. There are several components that make up a person's sexual experience. The first is biology—was the person born with male or female genitalia? The second involves the level of sexual interest. Interest in being sexual varies over time, and also varies from person to person. Some people have a high level of interest in sex, while others have a low level, and if charted, the population would probably form a bell curve in regard to sexual interest. The next component is sexual attraction—is the person attracted to the opposite sex, the same sex, or both? And, finally, there's the issue of gender roles. How do people fit in their society's way of conceptualizing gender? The simplest gender role division is binary, man or woman, as defined by any particular culture. This is not universal, with some cultures having more than two gender designations. Indigenous people in North America often had a third gender, "two spirit", and in Hawaii, the māhū make up a third gender. The descriptions of gender roles vary widely from one culture to another, and also shift over time.

It is helpful to be able to identify which of these aspects of sexuality may be of concern to clients. Starting with biological sex gives people the chance examine how they may experience themselves sexually, in terms of whether they feel 'at home' in their bodies, or not, in terms of their sexual biology. Some people feel they are in the wrong body, physically. This experience is more fundamental than not wanting to be in the body that was abused, which is a form of dis-identifying with the abuse. Some people with complex PTSD and dissociative disorders also have issues with their bodies feeling "wrong", not the right biological body for them. Especially with people who have DID, it can be challenging to sort out how pervasive the experience is for them. Are they talking about a fundamental, underlying issue of their biological sex feeling wrong for them, having issues related to not wanting to be in the body because of the trauma, gender role issues, or a combination of any or all of these?

Sexual attraction is a separate issue. People may be attracted to the opposite sex, the same sex, or both. It can get very complicated when a person is born biologically female, identify as male, and be attracted to males. Or, a person born male, may identify as female, and be attracted to females, males, or both. Sexual attraction is definitely a separate issue. Some people may have issues with too much or too little sexual interest, feeling their sexual energy somehow doesn't match what might feel right to them. This may have physical origins, or, at times, it could be the impact of trauma linking sexual arousal with abuse, connecting the polyvagal system in such a way to link arousal with the sympathetic nervous system rather than the parasympathetic nervous system, so the person becomes aroused in situations that are stressful and not so much when they are safe and relaxed.

Gender role issues refer to the person not feeling comfortable with the roles assigned to them because of their sexual biology. Gender roles are social constructs, and they vary, sometimes greatly, from one culture or setting to another, and they evolve over time within cultures. People can feel fine in the sex of their biological body and have little or no connection with the gender role their environment attaches to that sex. They may identify more strongly with another gender role, or not identify with any of the gender roles around them.

When people are not feeling comfortable in their body, or in the gender role assigned to them, they will have more and varied challenges to face. They may be unable to be who they feel they truly are. They may not be seen, or seen too seldom by too few other people. Micro and macro aggressions are common for people who don't fit society's roles and rules. Violence and even death are very real threats.

If these people are also severe trauma survivors, their sexual and gender role challenges add to all that they carry, and also add to the potential for self-harm and suicidality, and the difficulty in finding appropriate psychological and physical care. For example, almost a quarter (23.4%) of high school students identifying as lesbian, gay, or bisexual reported attempting suicide in the prior 12 months. This rate is nearly four times higher than the rate reported among heterosexual students (6.4%) (Ivey-Stephenson et al., 2019).

Sex, Gender, Trauma, and Dissociation

When people have issues with sexual identity, gender roles, trauma, and dissociation, it takes a great deal of time and patience to help them sort out all of the internal and external factors that impact them at all levels—being in the body that they have, dealing with the abuse they've experienced, and growing into a sense of identity that fits for them as whole people. Each of those factors takes time to identify and work through, and each area affects the whole. When traumatized people are dissociative, there's another level of complexity. Often, people with DID have parts/people inside who experience themselves as a different sex than the person's actual biological body. They may have both males and females inside, and a variety of expressions of gender roles, some that conform to their culture, and some that don't.

Sometimes dissociative people identify as being transgender, and may begin to seek help to physically transition. Clinicians working with dissociative clients have generally been told transitioning is not a good idea unless the person is 100% sure, throughout their system, that this is what is needed. The reasoning behind this is helpful. People who are dissociative need to take time to know their internal system, to have the ability to communicate with other self-states, and to be able to find consensus around this issue before proceeding. The need for the decision to be at 100%, however, is actually an unrealistic expectation. It is not at all uncommon for people choosing elective medical treatments and surgeries to have some trepidation or questions about their decision. Setting a different standard and demanding the decision be totally and completely without question, stops people from lifting and addressing concerns, and may result in their getting the treatment by denying any concerns they may have, or failing to get the treatment because they can't deny that they have concerns.

In addition, some people may transition, and over time, decide to detransition. Julie Graham, MFT, Director of Gender Health in San Francisco, notes that people who have transitioned, and then, at a later time, felt it right to detransition are often criticized and told they are harming others who have transitioned or are considering it by detransitioning. Julie points out that this kind of reversal is not judged in other elective surgeries, such as having one's tubes tied, having breast implants, etc. People who choose to reverse other elective surgeries are not judged for doing so. People who detransition, by contrast, are often harshly judged, making their personal challenges far more difficult than they need to be.

This is a very complicated area for people to navigate, and they need helping professionals to be able to hear their concerns and sort through the issues involved, taking the time to help them find the path that will be the best fit for them moving forward. Professionals working with dissociative people with sex or gender role issues need to know clients' systems well, help people with healthy internal communication, and work on the impact of trauma on the person's sexual and gender role issues. It is also critical that any medical professional working with dissociative people who are considering transitioning, (or detransitioning) work collaboratively with both clients and their therapists. Sometimes, different parts/people in a dissociative system attend therapy sessions or medical appointments, so both professionals only get to know a fraction of the person's system, making potential decisions at risk of creating more internal conflict rather than less.

Finally, there is the issue of pronouns—how to know which ones to use. The names, pronouns, and self-descriptions given by people reflect how they experience themselves. Being seen accurately, as people experience themselves, plays a major role in the development of a healthy relationship. Therefore, names, descriptions, and pronouns matter both for the people coming in for therapy and for professionals working with them. To refuse to use the names or pronouns given by people can easily feel like not being seen, or like being judged or rejected. So, whenever possible, use the names and pronouns people provide for themselves. If a clinician has an issue with a name or pronoun, that can be raised, respectfully, in session. This most commonly comes up when people have taken on names that have negative connotations. It helps clinicians to understand why the person is using names like that, and what it might mean to choose another name. The name is most likely there for a reason that was, at least initially, helpful, and it may still be helpful for some reason.

New Developments

In addition, people have varying ways of identifying their internal experience. Some refer to parts of themselves, others to self-states, or alters inside, while some talk about their inside people. Some people also refer to their system as being "plural", instead of referring to themselves through the diagnosis of DID. Others prefer saying they're DID. It varies, and it's important to be able to hear and see how people experience themselves. As much as possible, at least start from where they are and create a process in which any change that may need to happen can do so naturally in a way that fits for that particular person.

With the explosion of information and interactions through the internet, the diagnosis of Dissociative Identity Disorder has become more well-known. Information about the diagnosis may be shared in a highly professional manner, with care taken to be as accurate a portrayal as possible of the diagnosis and people's experiences of being dissociative. That has been helpful for many people, increasing knowledge and reducing shame. At the same time, the popularization of the language of dissociation has resulted in people using that language for similar, or sometimes very different, experiences. Clients may appear in therapy, stating they have DID, and it becomes very important to take some time and learn what that person means when they refer to that diagnosis. Also, how did they learn that they had DID? For some, they have been diagnosed previously by a clinician skilled in being able to diagnose the condition accurately. At the other end of this spectrum, the person may have seen a simple chart on social media, felt that the description matched their experience, and claimed the diagnosis. The evolution of online communities is having an impact on individuals, and the therapist who may treat them. If a client is connected to online communities, it is very helpful for the clinician to learn about those communities and how they are perceiving and defining themselves, (Christensen, 2022). It is also important to treat all clients with dignity, however they came to the diagnosis of DID, and help them identify and work with the issues that motivated them to seek therapy.

Bullying

Therapists may also be subjected to bullying by the client. While anger may be present, bullying behavior is often an attempt to lift oneself up by putting another person down, more about control and dominance than anger. In these cases, the client may or may not be aware of using intimidation to pursue his or her own agenda. The first step in dealing with any bully is to say the person's name and, gently but firmly, let him or her know that you will not be talked to in that manner (Horn, 2003). In other words, stop the behavior immediately. Let the person know that there are other, and far better, ways to engage with someone to see if getting their needs met is possible. It's helpful at some point to get a sense of where this behavior was learned, how people react to it, and what effect that has on the person. In most cases, bullying may succeed in having the person get his or her way in the moment, but it harms or destroys the relationship. The therapist can model different ways to state one's needs that would not be perceived as bullying and may be more successful in both getting needs met and preserving relationships.

In a dissociative system, there may be a part that is bullying because it's the part that represents the abuser and keeps the system in line with that abuser's expectations. That is a protective function that works in the abusive situation, but not in the rest of life.

It's also important to note that clients may have no other examples of how to get their needs met, so they're using what they know, and often that doesn't work very well. It can be frustrating to not be able to communicate in a way that others can hear, and bullying is an ineffective way to communicate. The therapist will also be likely to pick up on how the client was treated, the feeling of being bullied. That is also something that can be discussed. "It must be frustrating to try to get what you want or need and have people back away or be upset with you. On the other side, it's clear how being bullied would make you want to back away, physically and emotionally. Is that a familiar experience for you? Do you know the experience of being bullied?"

Having dealt with the inappropriate bullying behavior, take the time to look at the underlying need and see if that can be addressed appropriately. Clear feedback is helpful, "When you ask in that manner, I back away and don't want to give you anything; but when you ask in this new manner, I find myself considering how I can help you." This approach helps clients differentiate between what they are needing and how that need can be expressed, in a way that will sabotage the request or one that will help it be heard.

Consistently set limits along with the reassurance that the limits will be helpful. Over time, things do get better when intimidation and bullying stops. Whenever there is a better outcome because the interaction did not include any kind of threat, point that out. Notice improvement and success whenever you can, by stating it, talking about it, or even making a brief acknowledgment, like a nod or smile. People need feedback, clear feedback, to help them notice and hold on to their progress. A lot of people coming out of traumatic situations feel demoralized, powerless, and easily shamed. To have people see their struggle and affirm their progress builds a sense of accomplishment and pride. They need that, and they deserve it. It may also make them very uncomfortable—another thing to notice with grace.

Threats

Occasionally, a client may become threatening, verbally, or even physically abusive in some way. Sometimes, the client may threaten the therapeutic relationship emotionally. For example, a client once said something deliberately cruel to her therapist. The therapist teared up, hurt, then stood up and left the room. Outside the office, she took several deep breaths, composed herself and returned to the room. She told the client, "If you want to know if you can hurt me, you can. If you want to know if you can destroy this relationship, you can. It's your choice."

In this example, hurtful behavior like that can sabotage the therapeutic relationship, and that needs to be clear. If something that is frightening or hurtful occurs, it needs to be addressed immediately. In this example, the therapist felt safe enough to return to the room and confront the client. With that, the two of them talked about the relationship and how it required both of them to be respectful of the other. That therapy continued, with the client choosing not to deliberately hurt the therapist again. For the therapist, it was a view into the client's experience with a sadistic parent, the person in the client's life who deliberately hurt her, and she used that to inform how she worked with the client around the client's issues with her mother.

There are cases, however, when it does not feel safe enough to continue in the session, or to continue at all. For instance, a client came into therapy and sat far away from the therapist, farther than normal. He then pulled out a knife and said he was going to kill the therapist and then himself. The therapist told him to put the knife away, letting him know what would happen if he didn't do that immediately. He didn't, so the therapist left the room and called the police.

In the case of the client with the knife, there was a long-term relationship with no previous threats made. The therapist chose to talk with the client and see if continuing might be possible. The client apologized, was upset at what he had done, and agreed to have pockets and backpack checked before entering the office until it could be determined that he would no longer threaten the therapist. That worked for that client and therapist, and they jointly worked on the meaning of the threat that had been made.

Had that client and therapist not had a long history and strong relationship, that therapy would have been over. Therapy cannot continue when there is insufficient safety for either therapist or client. In that example, the therapist could have talked with the police when they arrived, and with the client, and had the police take the client to a safe inpatient facility where he could be evaluated and helped to get appropriate treatment elsewhere.

After any threatening incident, the therapist needs to assess whether therapy can continue. The safe container of the therapy has been damaged or destroyed. The therapist is under no obligation to work with a person who is dangerous. The nature of the threat, and the nature of the relationship are both important in making this decision. If it's no longer possible to continue with therapy, the dangerous client should be referred for help that can be given in a secure environment. For example, a therapist in the first few sessions of working with a new client was shocked when the client stood up, picked up a chair and lifted it over his head as if to throw it at her. She stood and told him forcefully to "Put that down!", and he did, fortunately. She then talked with him, and the result was to refer him to an inpatient treatment program. He had too much going on to manage it once a week in outpatient therapy. He was relieved by the referral and went to the inpatient facility. While that threat was not as potentially lethal as the one mentioned previously, there was no way for this therapist to know what was happening to provoke this behavior, and no way to engage with this client to have any confidence that this threat would not be repeated, or escalate.

In both these cases, the key was the strength and quality of the therapeutic relationship. That allowed the therapist a referential framework by which to evaluate the potential for future threats and the probability of threats being acted out. The bond between therapist and client provided a counterbalance to the fears and other emotions driving the client's behavior.

Another kind of threat comes from the client who presents as potentially litigious. Engaging in therapy under the threat of a potential lawsuit is extremely difficult, if not impossible. The client is essentially holding the therapist hostage, inhibiting the process and creating a power dynamic that is counter-productive to healing. That dynamic may be a living example of what the client endured. If that can be discussed and used therapeutically, it may be possible to work with someone like this. However, in these cases, it is advisable to have consultation, supervision, excellent notes, and legal counsel appropriate for mental health workers. Even with all of that, if the therapist does not feel secure enough to provide appropriate counseling services in that environment, it is best to refer the person elsewhere, where there may be a better chance for that person to be helped.

Occasionally, a client will believe that their therapist may be threatened by their abuser. In most cases, this is a fear and not a reality. However, every potential threat to a therapist needs to be taken seriously. Check in with clients to determine what makes them believe there is an actual threat. In some cases, the client's exploring what's behind the feeling of threat to the therapist will result in the perceived threat dissipating. In those cases, it's usually an old belief that has never been examined, and not realistic. In other cases, the abuser may actually be telling the client that they will hurt the therapist if the client continues to go to therapy. How realistic is that claim? If the abuser is elderly and disabled, it's not very realistic. If the abuser is relatively healthy, local, and has a history of aggression, the threat is much higher. If details are unknown, always err on the side of caution.

With people who are dissociative, the threat may come from a self-state within the person. When that's the case, it's helpful to attempt to communicate with the part that appears threatening. One way to do this is to "talk through" to that part of the system, which means talking to the client assuming the threatening part can hear and understand.

A statement opening such a dialogue might sound something like; "If the part or parts of you that wants to hurt me are listening, I hope they will consider coming out to talk with me. Something is obviously not ok for some reason, and it would help to know what that is. If I know, I can work to help make therapy more helpful to you as a whole person."

Sometimes, when the client is approached in that manner, the part that is angry and upset will come out. The therapist needs to be prepared to work with an intense part of the person's system in a non-judgmental way, and try to learn from that part what is triggering that defensive reaction. As mentioned previously, therapy threatening and self-harming behaviors frequently serve an important protective purpose. Reframing the unacceptable behavior as an attempt to create safety in a world where everything is threatening, and normal means are believed to be ineffective, helps reduce the tension and conflict and strengthens the therapeutic relationship as a collaborative endeavor to construct a safe haven where the work can be done.

One of the dynamics that may be going on with threatening behavior is an unconscious need to have the therapist know the client's experience. The client who purposely said something extremely hurtful had been raised by a sadistic mother. After that incident in therapy, the therapist had a greater awareness of the cruelty that saturated the client's home, a constant source of deep pain for the client. Whether the therapist shared that directly or not, it informed her and had an influence on the work that came after that event. The client with the knife had been threatened like that in his life, and a part of him had identified with his aggressor. Perhaps the man with the almost-thrown chair had been frightened in the past by a big person coming at him, or someone with sudden, surprising bursts of violence. Or, maybe there was so much within him that he simply couldn't contain it. There are reasons for threatening or scary behavior. Whenever it is safe to explore this, it can be very helpful. When the therapy needs to end, it can be helpful to relay that information to the next person or institution working with the person so that there may be a growing sense of what is fueling the behavior that hurts the person's chances of being helped.

There are also stories from therapists about clients deliberately breaking the therapist's rules, virtually demanding to be terminated. Different things may prompt that kind of behavior. Therapy may be working well, and the person's awareness of their life and emotions may be overwhelming, so the client desperately needs to leave. Sometimes, the client fears that remaining may harm the therapist, fearing that hearing what happened may be painful to the therapist or even 'contaminate' them, so the client attempts to protect the therapist by leaving. There are also times when the client is still in contact with abusive people, and those people threaten to harm the therapist if the client continues to go for help. That is typically an attempt to intimidate a client into leaving therapy, and seldom an actual threat to the therapist.

When any kind of harmful behavior or threat takes place, the first thing to do is to insure the safety of the therapist and the client as much as possible. If given the choice between caution and risk, choose caution.

Suggestions

Assess the level of threat immediately. With serious threats, take action to protect both therapist and client. Err on the side of caution - it is better to have to deal with people being embarrassed than harmed.

Have emergency procedures in place. These may include:

- "Panic button" placed within easy reach that will automatically call for help
- Exits available to both client and therapist - neither one blocked from leaving the room
- Staff or colleagues available to intervene
- In shared offices or clinics, establish a regular practice of emergency procedures
- In private offices, panic buttons, speed dial, and any other quick connections make it possible to call in help when necessary. (Check with local law enforcement and mental health resources to make sure the latest information regarding emergency procedures is in place.)

Early in therapy, discuss the need for the therapy to be a safe place for both client and therapist and how any threat to that will need to be addressed as soon as possible. Let the client know that any fears he or she may have regarding any kind of threat should be discussed.

Let the client know that anything that happens in therapy that feels threatening to either the client or the therapist will be talked about immediately to make sure that both people are safe and that the therapy may proceed.

In private counseling offices, it is best to meet with new clients while other people are in the building and available for help if help is needed. If the office stands alone, and there are no people nearby who could step in and assist the therapist, it is best not to see clients who could be seen as possibly threatening. These would include people with a history of violence or those needing help because they are currently in a violent relationship. They should be seen in offices where there is backup available in case it is needed to keep the client, and therapist, safe.

10 Difficult Emotions

Anger

One of the most difficult emotions to work with is anger. Many people shy away from an angry, aggressive client, or dissociative client's angry self-states. The work can be frightening, and in some cases, dangerous. Anger is a very powerful emotion, and it's often the reaction to the person being hurt, shamed, or frightened. It's defensive and protective. Learning how to manage anger is an essential part of a person's healing journey. Anger itself is not bad. In many cases, it's helpful. It can be protective, stop a person from being manipulated or abused. Or anger can be destructive, keeping helpful people at a distance resulting in isolation, or harming people or property, resulting in ruined relationships and incarceration.

> It is important to note that clients, especially in the beginning of treatment, may appear to be hostile, rejecting, or fearful of treatment or the therapist. The therapist's ability to respond with acceptance and an openness to discuss these challenges is an important asset in establishing the alliance.
>
> (Norcross, 2011)

People learn how to express anger from their caregivers and the environment in which they grow. Abusive people teach their victims that anger is destructive and used to gain power and control. People who have been victimized may grow up with only violent expressions of anger and have no experience of anger being dealt with in a manageable, constructive manner. In therapy, anger can feel out of control and scary, something to be avoided or something that evokes shame.

Identifying anger and addressing it quickly can prevent escalation. Normally, if frustration or anger are seen, and people are asked about it, they will share what they're upset about, sometimes with great intensity, and the wave of upset will pass. Some people, however, have so much rage inside, that to talk about a little will release too much. Some clients may share that fear, and if they do, it's wise to ask them about it. For some, their fear of anger comes

DOI: 10.4324/9781003217541-12

from fear of reprisals, and for others, the fear comes from the sense that once released, the anger will not be able to be contained. For both groups of people, and for those who have both fears, learning pacing skills is essential. To learn to stop oneself, calm down, and then re-engage in sorting out the anger, stopping again, and as many times as necessary, to never go "above the line" can be a very difficult but immensely satisfying experience.

Learning harm-reduction skills can also help. People can learn how to mitigate the effects of their anger on others and themselves, taking steps to change the harmful behavior while they learn more effective communication skills.

For example, a family struggling with the father's domestic violence came in for their session, and the father admitted that he had gotten angry and hit the wall. Up until then, the father had hit the people in his family. Hitting the wall was different—he had managed to have some influence on how his anger came out. In the midst of his rage, he had turned away from his family and hit the wall instead, hurting only himself. The therapist noticed the shift, and could see the strength it had taken this man in that moment of anger to stop himself from hitting anyone. She reflected that strength back to him, and he broke down and cried. He was learning to control himself, and protect his family. Continuing in this direction, he would learn to stop hitting anything and begin to be able to talk about how he felt, even when angry.

The same dynamic can happen within dissociative people, with anger being acted out either on other people or on the self. Angry parts of the self can move past the person's conscious control and hurt the self or others. Noticing when the person manages to curtail the anger in any way, stopping or limiting the harm can help the person identify the growing strength of self-control, making them safer. It does not feel good to most people to be out of control. For most, it evokes shame. Self-control and being able to deal with intense feelings appropriately builds self-esteem and a good sense of pride.

Sometimes anger may be directed at the therapist for something said or done, or not said or not done. When the anger is at the therapist, it's helpful to be able to hear it. It's common in these situations for the therapist to become defensive, feeling judged or attacked, a very upsetting experience. It's a natural reaction. When that happens, if the therapist can hear the anger and respond rather than react, things go better. Even if that's challenging, the therapist can respond and acknowledge what's going on, "This is very difficult, and very important. I need to understand what has made you so upset, and that may take some time." Saying something like that can give the therapist a bit of time in which to settle, preventing an automatic reaction that would not be helpful. Then, the therapist needs to listen, with the awareness that the client may not have the skill to be appropriate in how the message is delivered.

For instance, there are likely to be a lot of "you" messages rather than "I" messages, such as "You always...", "You never...", the kind of communication that generally leads to defensiveness, argument, and upset. Clients have seldom had the time and training to be able to express themselves in nonviolent language, such as "I feel hurt when you...", or "I feel upset/angry when you..." That relationship-supporting kind of language may be completely unknown, and the language that was learned by the client may be highly provoking of the therapist.

Often, the anger being expressed signals a rupture in the relationship, and the manner in which it's expressed makes that rupture more extreme. If the therapist can hear the genuine distress of the client and work on repairing the rupture, there will be a time at which the therapist can teach the client more effective ways of expressing anger. For example, the therapist may reframe the client's complaint by saying, "So you're saying that when I ..., you feel...". That puts the communication in a healthy form, and may make it easier for the therapist to respond. It's not reasonable to expect clients to express their anger well and constructively when they've never had the experience of seeing or hearing anger being managed in that manner.

A Few Common Messages Addressed to Therapists

"You Just Don't Get It"

Maybe you do, and maybe you don't. However, when someone says that, it's clear that something is missing, so simply ask, "What am I missing?" The answer will be helpful, whether it's something that was not seen and understood, or whether the sense of knowing what's going on just didn't get communicated well enough to be heard by the other.

"You Don't Understand"

Evidently, you don't, or you're not succeeding in letting the person know you do. Ask what it would take for the person to know you understand. At times, it may be a more complete verbal acknowledgment, and learning to give that to the client can help the process. Responding not only with the words said by the client, but also with the emotional impact of what's been shared, for the client, and the therapist can result in a feeling of being seen and heard well.

Sometimes, however, the client is asking for some kind of behavioral response that is not possible or not therapeutic. The client may be needing more than is available or reasonable, such as excessive amounts of time, whether that's in extra sessions or through phone contact or online interactions outside the office. Severely traumatized people often have boundary issues and will push to have needs met in ways that don't fit the therapeutic relationship. Responding to these needs takes sensitivity and a strong message of respect for the client. Finding out that requests are inappropriate often triggers shame, so setting limits needs to be done with great care. Acknowledging the reality of the need helps, along with the regret that those needs were not met or cannot be met. The client can then feel the loss while hopefully still feeling the connection to the therapist.

Actually talking about the unique nature of the therapeutic relationship is beneficial. Unfortunately, this is something rarely done. Relational issues unique to therapy are too often assumed but not articulated. Worse, they are put forth in simplistic, rigid rules without the openness to discuss the nuances of each particular relationship. This failure to speak about the nature of the therapeutic relationship directly with the client underlies many painful ruptures and therapeutic failures (Dalenberg, 2013).

"This is not Working"

A statement like this is an invitation to ask about expectations and to examine what is and is not working in the therapy. Sometimes the source of the frustration is the client's inability to meet their own expectations about themselves. Sometimes the source is in unmet needs in regards to the therapist, or the difficulty of the process. The work is sometimes very difficult and no one wants to have to endure emotional pain any longer than necessary. When techniques prove inadequate, or reveal more work to be done, clients become understandably upset.

Sometimes, as was stated above, the problem is an unspoken or unresolved difficulty in the therapeutic relationship. Therapist and client may have very different expectations of the relationship and the process. Asking what's not working for the client begins a dialogue about the client's expectations and where they are not being met. Those expectations may or may not be realistic, but in either case, they need to be recognized and addressed.

One client would frequently rail about the failure of the therapist, of therapy, of the inadequacy of the field of psychotherapy to address the trauma of his profound childhood abuse, and of the failings of the entire medical realm. In listening to his condemnations, the failures of his parents to adequately protect him from his childhood abusers and to respond to his abuse became clear. His difficulty expressing that intense resentment directly was transferred on to others he perceived as caregivers. Exploring the transference dynamic, the roles and responsibilities of treatment, apparently improved the quality of the therapeutic relationship and the efficacy of psychotherapy in general - until the therapist failed to appreciate other elements of the client's experience based on his gender identity and sexuality. When the next charges of "this isn't working" and "you don't get it" were leveled, a roadblock and significant rupture occurred until the therapist could accept and acknowledge that he indeed had missed the point.

In the expression of anger, even when expressed in less than optimal ways, the ground rules of therapy remain in place—do no harm, no physical or deliberate emotional damage to people or property. Even with the very best intentions, clients may say hurtful things, expressing themselves in less than optimal ways. There needs to be some grace given in these situations, based on the awareness that the client is in therapy to learn how to deal with feelings, especially these intense ones, and having the opportunity to work with intense, interpersonal issues in a safe, therapeutic situation can be potentially life-changing. The client who is angry at the therapist and is heard respectfully, not punished for the anger, guided in how better to express it, and has the experience of the anger being acknowledged and resolved is given a template to use for any time in the future when angry with someone close.

Working With Anger and Angry Alters in a Dissociative System

In a dissociative system, the angry parts of the person are usually there for their protection. They are often as critical and mean as the people who abused them, because that's what they needed to be in order to keep the person safe. To have an internal reminder of what can and can't be said or done may make life difficult, but it also reminds the person to keep the rules established by the perpetrator, and as long as the perpetrator is in contact with the person, that constant reminder may help. The goal of working with angry parts is not to get rid of them. The goal is to help them learn to protect the person in ways that are not retraumatizing. Another goal is to help the rest of the person accept the angry part or parts, acknowledge their contribution to survival and work with them to find ways to keep their strength and power while learning to not scare, intimidate, or harm others. It may take a lot of time working with the person to help their whole system see angry, abusive, persecutory alters in an accepting way. These alters are there to protect the person, by constantly remembering the abuser and how the abuser might react. They are frequently pushed away, as if they were the abusers. However, they are more like the person's Special Forces, their frontline defense against the abusers. It may take a lot of time to help the person see how important their work was in helping the person survive, and even manage to retain innocent places/alters inside. So, the person needs to find a way to "invite those parts to the table", to value their contribution and involve them in the healing of the whole person.

In therapy, angry alters may emerge to slow down or stop the therapy when it's progressing too rapidly, when intolerable material is about to emerge, or when the person isn't safe enough to become vulnerable. Angry alters in this situation act like brakes on the system when it's going too fast. The therapist and client may be surprised or frustrated, feeling that progress is being blocked, and it may be, but for a reason. If at all possible, talk to the angry part and ask about what that part is doing for the person, what's the function of the anger?

For example, a therapist may be doing trauma work with parts of the client's internal system and be suddenly confronted by an angry part who is scary and completely derails the process. That is not uncommon. The angry alter is reminiscent of the abuser, replaying the consequences of being real, speaking the truth, sharing the secret. It's an extreme form of the feeling people get when they say something that they were taught not to say; a combination of guilt and fear of reprisals. In the case of the survivor, the consequences of doing the forbidden, talking about what happened, would be severe. There're reasons why the survivor developed a strong internal abuser/ protector.

The angry/protector part of the person keeps other parts of the self-system away from harm by scaring them into silence, making them duck and run for cover—which may replicate what happened in the trauma. The abuser/pro- tector alter also shows what their perpetrator was like and the energy that came from the abuser. That angry/protector part is indeed scary; capable of scaring the therapist in the same manner the whole system was originally ter- rified by the perpetrator. In session, it may ease the communication to com- ment on that—that the angry/protector part learned well how to say the things the abuser said and that the angry behaviors help the other parts of self to hide and not be surprised by an imminent attack.

For the therapist, it helps to examine how it felt to be in the angry alter's presence. Did it cause a feeling of being vulnerable, smaller than usual, and apprehensive? Did it cause worry about being hurt? All of those experiences may be very familiar to the experiences of the client, and feeling the threat may help the therapist understand why the client is split and how hard it may be to trust anyone and remain engaged in the process.

Also, consider that the angry alter is relating in the only way they know how to relate. Their socialization was impacted by the relationship with a perpetrator. The fact that the client has shown up in the office and talked, knowing the goal is to change how things are with them and the whole system says a lot about the potential for cooperation and growth.

In people with dissociative issues, anger is often compartmentalized, apparently absent or blatantly present in high intensity. In therapy, the therapist gets a sense of the client's abuser and their style of abuse through listening to the angry alters within the dissociative system. While some thera- pists find this experience frightening and attempt to avoid dealing with the angry alters, it's actually very helpful to engage them as soon as feasible and make them an integral part of the person's healing journey. Often, they're the parts who took the worst abuse, and aligned themselves with the abuser in order to live. Because they did that, the person may have been able to keep their softer emotions and more hopeful perceptions of life alive. The angry alters are often thought of as "not Mes" in the system, and too frequently left out of therapy. It's similar to sending troops off to war and not wanting anything to do with them when they return.

Suggestions

First, teach people how to calm themselves; to gain control over their behavior. Learning and experiencing that first-hand can be inspiring and empowering.

One of the fastest ways to do that is to teach them how to gain control over their physiological reactions by controlling their breath. They can't control their heartbeat or other physiological reactions, but they can control their breath. To calm the body, fill the lungs with air and then blow it out as slowly and for as long a time as possible. Repeat that, filling the lungs and exhaling slowly, controlling the exhale, blowing out as long as possible. This activates the parasympathetic nervous system. With enough repetitions, the body starts to relax, and the person is better able to think and act rationally.

With some people, the use of slow exhaling to calm the nervous system can be taught with the image of blowing soap bubbles slowly. It's the same process, but the image may be more soothing and acceptable for some people, especially those who view control as something harmful.

These two approaches to the same exercise illustrate how techniques can be adjusted to fit the client. A person who is incarcerated would most likely connect with the idea of being able to control him or herself. Someone who is currently able to access safe places may prefer the softer image of blowing bubbles to help become calmer. If the client comes up with another image that works with this exercise, use that one.

Teach people about anger, the levels of intensity of different kinds of anger, how it can be expressed safely, and how it can be helpful in protecting a person and addressing things that are wrong. Anger accesses energy, from the small amount found in being miffed or annoyed, to the overwhelming power of rage. There are gradations of anger, and it's helpful to be aware of discrepancies between triggering events and the level of the angry response. In a lot of survivors, their reactions do not match the events; alternating between being overly suppressed or dissociated or larger and more vehement than the event warrants. Having the reaction match the situation allows the person to choose behavior that can be helpful.

Create a worksheet with words for anger from mild to extreme and behavior that would be appropriate at each level. Along with that, add notes on how the person may be handling each level in the present, and whether that behavior is acceptable or needs to be changed. It's reassuring to people to discover that they do some things well enough or even very well.

In sessions, have the client practice expressing varying levels of anger, using the words that fit. When the client appears to have some degree of anger and there doesn't seem to be any connection to that, practice stating the feeling at different levels, from mild to severe and see if the person can identify what level they are experiencing. Oftentimes, a person will say, "I don't know." When that happens, explore that with the person, saying something like, "If you did know, what feeling do you think you would be having?" It's possible to continue with that line of conversation, and that would sound like this, "I know you don't know, but given what you know about yourself, how do you imagine you might feel?" Then, "Go ahead and guess what the feeling might be. It's just a guess. Play with that thought and see what comes to mind."

When the person does say something, just notice it as interesting. When a person guesses, the guess comes from somewhere inside, so it is a bit of information. It may indicate how the person does feel, or it may indicate what the person thinks the therapist wants to hear. Either way, it has given the client a little more time to explore their internal reality.

Explore how other people handled anger in the person's home. Who did what? What worked and what didn't? Did any of those strategies improve relationships?

Has the client ever experienced anger being expressed in a way that did improve the relationship? What was that like? Has the client ever done that with success? Describe that in detail and notice whatever allowed the person to succeed in that manner.

Shame

"I'm a worthless piece of sh!t, and I don't deserve the air that I breathe."

What do you say or do when someone says that? Arguing won't help. Telling the person this isn't the truth seldom makes a difference. This is Shame talking. Shame and powerlessness underlie most interpersonal traumas. The inability to stop something shameful from happening crushes the feelings of self-worth and personal power. The experience is so devastating that years may go by without the person being able to acknowledge this level of anguish.

So, what is shame? Shame is a physiological state. In this state there is an inherent sense of being flawed, fundamentally bad. It's not the same as guilt. Guilt is about behavior, the reaction to things the person has done which feel wrong, but it's not about the self. People can feel guilty about wrong behavior and still know they are fundamentally good people—someone who has done something bad, not someone who is bad (Lewis, 1971).

MRI studies show shame differs from guilt neurobiologically. When a person is experiencing shame, they show increased activation of the dorsolateral prefrontal cortex, the insula, the dorsal anterior cingulate cortex, and the posterior cingulate cortex along with corresponding increased activity in subcortical regions (Michl et al., 2014).

Shame, complex trauma, PTSD, and dissociation are closely interrelated. Dorahy and colleagues (2013) found dissociation and shame predicted complex PTSD. In turn, complex PTSD predicts relationship anxiety and depression. Combining all three, complex PTSD, dissociation, and avoidance in response to shame predicts fear in relationships. Similarly, Platt and Freyd (2015) found that high betrayal trauma predicts shame and dissociation. They speculate that when the relationship is important (a condition necessary for betrayal), a person will seek to preserve the relationship via dissociating or detaching from awareness of the abuse. However, given the abuse is perpetrated by someone close to the victim, the victim may internalize a perceived and imagined motive for the abuse by believing in a supposed inherent flaw.

When a person is shamed, the message is that the person IS bad, and that shame creates a basis for defense mechanisms (Wurmser, 1981). Shame, felt directly, causes a collapse, physically and mentally. People caught up in shame lower their heads, and their bodies deflate. They are rendered powerless. Also, "Shame signals a threat to the social bond, and is therefore vital in establishing where one stands in a relationship." (Galaway & Hudson, 1996). The experience is so overwhelming that people will do just about anything to avoid it, and when it's felt, they may do anything to escape it, including suicide. The psyche does what it needs to do to protect the person from connecting with the experience of shame. The usual reactions to shame are all geared to protect the person from the overwhelming feeling of shame. Donald Nathanson described the "Compass of Shame", with defensive tactics taking four potential tracks - withdrawal, avoidance, attack other, and attack self (Nathanson, 1992).

For survivors, shame can be painfully reinforcing. They feel shamed during the abuse, then shamed again when attempting to talk about the abuse, or acting out the abuse, either as victim or abuser. They end up feeling trapped and disempowered by the shame, which also adds to it.

The difficulty is in feeling the shame and allowing it to move, not blocking it and keeping it stuck, but letting it be there in the presence of a non-shaming person, someone who sees it and still sees the value of the person. That's what helps the shame diminish. The obvious problem is that people find shame intolerable, so it takes a lot of knowledge, willingness, and support to allow shame to be felt in a way that helps it subside.

One of the fundamental needs of a human being is to be seen by another, truly seen in an accepting way. When a person has been traumatized, however, that being seen may evoke fear, fear of the traumatic experience being recognized, or the feelings evoked by it being seen and not accepted, especially the feeling of shame. There is a fear of disclosure. Survivors often have

Figure 10.1 Compass of Shame: Avoidant Behaviors and Masking Emotions

negative experiences when they try to talk about their trauma. They may not be heard, or they may be blamed or shamed for the trauma (too typical in rape cases), or have their trauma dismissed in some way, such as being told to get over it, or to pray and ask forgiveness. Seldom do people find others who have the ability to listen deeply to the survivor's experience, allowing themselves to feel the impact of the trauma even second-hand.

The denial of abuse maintains shame, and that denial may come from the perpetrators who don't want to accept responsibility for what they've done, from family or society unable to tolerate the reality of abuse in their presence, self-denial as an attempt to distance the self from one's own experience.

Therapists' denial may arise from disbelief or the inability to tolerate the intensity of the client's shame, fear of any kind of legal liability, an attempt to protect the client from feeling overwhelmed, and/or an inability to speak about shame in an effective manner.

In a recent article on the influence of shame on posttraumatic disorders, Terry Taylor notes,

> because shame is frequently considered a painful and discomforting emotion, it may fail to be addressed in the therapeutic setting by both client and therapist. Examination of potential shame-related changes in self-concept, close interpersonal relationships and social inclusion are recommended for individuals who have experienced a range of traumas to identify and address any underlying unacknowledged shame.
>
> (Taylor, 2015)

As mentioned earlier, shame is connected to feeling powerless. Eric Erickson (Erickson, 59) in discussing psychosocial stages of development posited the important developmental challenge of establishing Autonomy rather than succumbing to Shame. The dynamic may be seen as: 'If I am not able to make change, to manage my world, then I have no autonomy—I am powerless. If I am powerless to make changes (lacking autonomy), then I am shame filled'.

Nathanson noted the interplay between shame and mastery. He observed that shame inhibits experiencing the positive effects. However, he went on to say that purposeful, goal directed, intentional behavior and success leads to the effect of "enjoyment-joy", suggesting that competence and pleasure are antidotes to shame.

In working with one client, overwhelmed and mired in shame based on a history of on-going abuse by the father, the therapist was struggling to help the client re-assign the responsibility for the abuse and thus hopefully put the shame of the events onto the father. Slowly the client came closer to acknowledging her father's role and responsibility for the actions. Then in an emotionally charged moment, the client whispered, "Don't take my shame from me.".

Dumbfounded, the therapist asked why. The client, in tears replied, that if the responsibility and shame belonged to her father, then she was powerless to change his behaviors and feelings towards her. As long as she held a sense of shame, she felt she might change herself and thus win his love.

Consider then a cyclical relationship between shame and powerlessness, wherein a child is made to feel powerless and in turn feels an intense sense of shame. To avoid feeling powerless, the child then holds onto the shame. Staying stuck in a state of shame undermines the child's (client's) ability to develop mastery, increasing the perception of powerlessness, and compounding the sense of shame.

The therapeutic response is two pronged. One step involves sitting with and accepting the tragic truth that the child could not change and control the abusive parent, and that the perpetrator did not love them. In essence, accepting that at that point in time, they were indeed powerless. The second step focuses on how they have grown and can continue to grow in genuinely holding and wielding appropriate and healthy power.

Suggestions

First, teach about shame—what it is, how it impacts mind and body, and how it will emerge in some way during therapy. It is a physiological state that causes a person to collapse—the head drops down, the body caves in, and the nervous system slows down. It triggers thoughts of being worthless and fundamentally flawed, "I'm bad" messages. It may be brief and only last a short time, or it could feel huge and like something that could last forever. However it is experienced, it won't last. No emotional or physiological state lasts forever—they all shift and change over time. With that general reassurance, go over ways in which the person can stay present and help move through shame. It's different from guilt, which may also feel awful but does not collapse the person, and triggers the message, "I did something bad", allowing the person to maintain a feeling of self-worth.

Notice what triggers the shame. Knowing one's triggers can help to focus on what sets them off and what can be done to calm oneself down. For instance, there are common responses to trauma—freeze, run, fight, and collapse. The last one, the collapse, is called "tonic immobility" and is an instinctual feigned death response. In that state, the person is lucid but unable to move. That person is beyond the ability to run or fight, and there's nothing they can do about that. Their body's ancient survival mechanism had taken over. If they survive the event, they will shake for a long time, throwing off the chemistry that kept them immobile. Most people don't know this, and when they are asked "Why didn't you fight?", they think they could have and should have fought, feeling shame about not fighting back when they really had no ability to move at the time.

Saying "this is shame, it will pass". Saying that over and over until it does.

Being curious about how awful the feeling is—where is the feeling, what about it is so painful, is the pain physical, does it move or stay in place? Questions like these help the person stay present while the body moves through the experience of shame.

Notice that shame comes with a message, "You are bad!". Imagine an annoying pop up window on the computer. This one is flashing "You're bad, you're bad, you're bad…click here to find out why." It is wise to refuse to engage with this message. It's there, but the person doesn't have to "click" on it and get lost in the mind virus it will create. Instead, look for the "x" that helps shut it down—the loving and supportive messages from people who care or from spiritual resources. Even if those are not available, the awful feeling and message will eventually fade by itself. No emotion stays forever.

Sit in a chair, hold on to the sides, and breathe in and out, slowly and deeply, counting the breaths. This does several things. It gives people something to think about by focusing on counting slow breaths. Breathing slowly and deeply also quiets the nervous system. People can track how many breaths it takes to breathe through the shame attack, and will be able to notice if their shame attacks are increasing or decreasing in strength and length. Shame can cause people to feel deflated, and this exercise can help them feel a sense of agency, something they can do that helps minimize the length and impact of the shame attack.

For some people, it has helped to know that if they believe the "You are bad" message, it would make their perpetrator happy. They will have agreed to carry the shame that actually belongs to the perpetrator. For some people, that thought is so enraging, their time spent in any wave of shame is automatically shortened—their anger pushes them out.

With all of these interventions, the emotional presence of the therapist is powerful. If the therapist can sit with the client's shame and continue to be kind and compassionate, the shame will abate more quickly. If the therapist is uncomfortable with the shame, or reinforces it in any way, healing will take a lot longer. It is often very difficult for therapists to sit with the shame their clients feel. They may feel as if they are causing harm by allowing the person to feel the shame. The client's shame may trigger their own unresolved shame, and they may avoid helping the client face shame in order to keep the distance from it that they need for themselves. There may also be fears of the silence that frequently accompanies shame—there are often no words in that state, and some therapists are uncomfortable with silence. For them, silence may leave them feeling like they're not doing their job, seeing the person in such pain and saying nothing is too difficult for them. What those therapists need to learn is that their compassionate presence speaks louder and more effectively than any words they may say.

"Healing may require the therapist to be aware of the presence of shame; to bring it to mutual awareness; and to allow the victim to be with the feeling of shame in the safety of the nonjudgmental, warm and caring, therapeutic interaction to allow it to be held until it metabolizes" (Lanius, Paulson, & Corrigan, 2014).

Grief

Trauma derails a person's life. That derailment may be temporary or permanent. In either case, there is loss; loss of innocence, a worldview that sees things are fair and just, assumptions of the goodness of others, and seeing the world as a good place in which to freely roam. Trauma triggers defense mechanisms that never completely go away. Our minds and bodies are too wise for that. Once a person learns that there is danger in the world, that knowledge never leaves. It stays in order to help the person survive.

Part of spending a great deal of one's life in trauma is the loss of the life that could have been. The grief from that loss is often staggering. Knowing one's own talents, the kind of life that was desired, and seeing how trauma has made that anticipated life very difficult or impossible to achieve, confronts the client with massive loss. They need time, space, and support to deal with that realistic loss, and still be able to embrace the life they can have, and put their energy into achieving their current dreams as much as possible. The losses may include loss of physical wholeness or health, loss of family or the realization that the family they have will never become the family they need. Grieving also requires addressing the loss of opportunities for relationship or achievement, and the loss of years spent in suffering or recovery. It is helpful to talk about post-traumatic growth at some point, but not in a way that shuts down the necessary grief.

There is often also the grief of losing people—family members, friends, or any significant person. Some people have left, and some have died. Some attachments are recent, and some have lasted a lifetime. Some losses are choices, like leaving abusive people or those who will never change. Every loss is different. While there are stages of grief that have been described in the literature—denial, bargaining, anger, acceptance—these don't all show up in each person's experience, and when they do, they're not necessarily in that order. There are also times when a person loses a beloved pet, grieving as if that animal were a child or a close family member. In those cases, that animal may have provided the most trusting and loving relationship in the survivor's life, so the loss is profound.

When plunged into grief, some people go above the line of their Window of Tolerance and may keen, wail, and sob. Some people go below the line and go numb. The initial reaction is not necessarily a reflection of the depth of the person's grief. The person who keens and wails may have moments of complete lack of feeling at times. Those who are numb may periodically break down and cry.

Grief tends to come in waves, and if allowed to flow naturally, brings relief. It is not uncommon for people grieving someone who had died to go through periods of crying followed by memories of the good times. It's almost as if there's a reward for allowing the pain to be expressed. With trauma survivors, the reward may include remembering things in their lives that were good, or that reward may be the greater ability to be in the present and able to move forward. Grief releases the person from the painful past. It's still remembered, but the weight of it on one's life is lessened.

In situations of intense grief, the therapist needs to support the person's natural process as much as possible while being mindful of the person's safety and resources. Sitting with someone who is keening and wailing is very challenging, but to stop that process because of the therapist's own discomfort is not necessarily a good thing. On the other extreme, therapists may feel uncomfortable with someone who is numb with grief. In either of these extremes, support from the person's family, friends, and social groups can make a significant difference, helping accompany the grieving person through the roughest parts of the process. The therapist may also need support if the client's grief is difficult to witness for any reason.

Grief may emerge in the last stage of therapy as people heal and move out of relationships that no longer work for them. It's not uncommon for survivors to have bonded with other survivors before and during therapy. Other survivors are often the only people who understand and are able to support the person. When the person heals from the trauma, integrating it, and for dissociative people integrating the self, the connection with other survivors may no longer help either person. One person needs to move on, and the other no longer feels the same trauma-based connection, and, so, they go their separate ways. That impacts both people. For the person moving out of the trauma vortex, it's exciting and scary to begin to develop relationships with people who have not been severely traumatized. At times it can be difficult, as when the "normal" people share stories about their childhood. Traumatized people hardly ever participate in those discussions, and that can feel very lonely while in a crowd. The grief of lost relationships is part of the healing process. It doesn't mean the person no longer cares for the others, but means that the relationships no longer serve both people.

Suggestions

Rituals of remembrance when others have left or died- collecting photos and stories, and creating an album or video. Some people have also created works of art that incorporate the names of people they have lost, or images that represent them, like a painting, collage, banner, or sculpture.

Rituals of letting go of things longed for or lost - putting losses on biodegradable paper, tearing them up and throwing them into the sea. Blowing regrets and losses into bubbles that float away. The ritual developed by the client is most profound.

Writing the person's own journey as a story or myth, ending with the protagonist receiving wisdom and strength of spirit, and including the losses as some of the challenges and obstacles the hero or heroine needed to overcome.

Creating a memorial garden for personal losses or the loss of people or cherished pets, with plants that represent the losses while bringing beauty to the person's current life.

Writing a story or poem as a memorial to the loss.

Taking what has been learned from the loss and helping other people deal with similar losses. This is a wonderful thing for people to do when they are far along or finished with their own healing.

Choosing to have the legacy of what, or who, was lost can be positive. In honor of what or who was lost, the person decides to live life in a better way. That approach honors the loss within the self or of others, holding on to the value of it, and living well as a kind of commemoration.

Forgiveness vs Reconciliation

Forgiveness is one of the things that survivors are frequently told they need to do in order to heal. That's actually true, but people are often confused between forgiveness and reconciliation. Forgiveness is the process of letting go of past traumas, it's an exercise in freeing oneself. It has nothing to do with letting the perpetrator off the hook. It doesn't mean that the abuser is suddenly ok. It means the survivor is no longer controlled by the trauma. The survivor is free.

In this sense, forgiveness is a gift to the self. It's about the self and no other. It separates the person from the trauma, making a distinction between who the person is and what happened to that person. It's the shift from "I am a victim", to "I am someone who has been victimized". Feeling like "someone" is far better than feeling like "a victim". Anyone can be hurt, traumatized in many ways. For a while, the trauma may be the defining thing in their life, but that does not have to continue. Forgiveness is the process of moving out from under the trauma and no longer identifying with it. The trauma is part of that person's life experience, and is past.

Forgiveness, fortunately, does not require the abuser to heal and show up for the victim. It means working through the trauma so that it no longer has a serious impact on the survivor's life. One survivor summarized the process by saying, "My past is finally past". It's still there, but it's no longer intruding in the person's everyday life. It's lost its power. The survivor is free of the burden of the abuse. They still carry the knowledge and all that was learned, but it becomes a choice to tap into that, or not.

When Nelson Mandela was released after 27 years in prison, he said, "As I walked out the door toward my freedom, I knew that if I did not leave all the anger, hatred, and bitterness behind, that I would still be in prison."

People are frequently uncomfortable with unresolved issues. When those people think of forgiveness, they assume the problem is supposed to be over, and all the people involved have moved beyond the trauma and are moving forward with a healthy relationship. In the best scenarios, that is true. However, that is an example of both forgiveness and reconciliation, when both the abuser and victim have worked through the trauma, and healed to the point of being able to relate in a healthy manner. That is, unfortunately, unusual. it is more often the case that the abuser is still dangerous, or unrepentant, or not acknowledging the abuse. This means that reconciliation is not appropriate.

While there is a difference between forgiveness and reconciliation, often the two are seen as one, and the person who has been hurt is encouraged to "forgive" their abuser. They're told to forgive and forget. That's not a good idea, especially if the abuser is still abusive. In that case, it's potentially dangerous. Reconciliation can occur when the person who has been hurt has done their work, the abuser has also done their work, and the person who was hurt chooses to reconcile. Forgiveness is a part of healing, reconciliation is optional. George Rhoades described the difference in these two processes as "forgiveness in, and forgiveness out" (personal communication, 2015, ISSTD conference). The inner process is critical, the outer process is not, it's dependent on the people involved and the choice of the survivor.

Part of the process of forgiveness may include letting go of ever having closure with the abuser. Some abusers may have died, and some are not able to heal to the point of taking responsibility for the harm they have caused. That doesn't mean the survivor can't forgive. Forgiveness is an internal thing, an inside job. It doesn't require the presence or cooperation of the abuser, and that's good because a lot of abusers never show up for healing.

Suggestions

Writing exercise: write down the name of the abusive person, what that person did, how it felt, and the feelings and beliefs it left behind that are still being carried.

Notice how those beliefs and feelings are maintaining a connection with the abuser.

Notice how that feels.

Imagine those beliefs and feelings like a rope attaching you to the abuser. You are holding it in your hand. What might happen if you let it go? Spend time with that because it matters.

Some people fear that letting go is the same as saying it didn't matter. Not true.

Find the place inside where the truth of how much it matters can be found. It may help to create an image or find a token of some kind to represent the reality of the trauma, like a painting, a poem, or a tree planted in memory of what happened.

Sometimes letting go brings a fear of forgetting and finding oneself in another abusive relationship. There are other ways to remember and those need to be identified clearly. If the abuser was a parent or family member, would letting go of the trauma result in not being able to resist returning to the family? In this case, it usually helps to enlist the help of friends or partners who will help prevent an inappropriate return, or will accompany the person if they need to return for some reason.

Check to see if holding on to the trauma is a way to avoid feeling the loss it created, like loss of innocence, connection, or opportunities. Anger and defenses may feel better than the loss, and that can keep a person stuck.

Evaluate the possibility of reconciliation. What evidence is there to support the idea that the abuser is no longer dangerous physically or emotionally? Has the abuser taken responsibility for their behavior that harmed the person? How well did they do that? Was there any offer from the abuser to help the person harmed to hear - an offer to listen to the person, pay for therapy or attend joint sessions? And finally, does the person harmed actually want to reconcile? It can be very healing to be able to do this, and when it happens, it tends to be an organic process, with both the abuser and person who was victimized gradually healing and becoming able to reconnect in a healthy manner. Forcing either forgiveness or reconciliation seldom works, and may backfire, causing the process to take longer.

Spirituality:

Psychology literally means "study of the soul", but over time, it has evolved into a study of the brain and behavior. Spirituality is often intentionally left out of psychological treatments, with the belief that it is a separate discipline, and not appropriately part of therapy. Human beings, however, don't tend to separate their spiritual beliefs from their lives in such a complete way. Spiritual beliefs and experiences can have a profound effect on a person's emotional health and behavior. With trauma survivors, their connection to genuine, healthy spirituality may provide them with a secure attachment not found from the other people in their lives. For example, there have been many clients who have felt the presence of God in their lives as the main source of their continuing ability to live, love, and grow. Other clients, especially those who have been abused with rituals or by religious leaders, have turned away from their spiritual roots, losing that resource and community.

While it is inappropriate for secular therapists to give spiritual counsel to clients, it is appropriate to ask about the person's spiritual life and how it may be helping or hurting their healing process.

For people with attachment issues, those same issues are likely to show up in the person's experience with spirituality. People with secure attachments have the easiest time connecting positively with spiritual resources. Those with insecure attachments may join organizations where they become overly dependent. Those with avoidant attachments may not feel a genuine spiritual connection even if they are involved in a spiritual community. People with disorganized attachment issues may have tumultuous or unintegrated experiences in community, or may compartmentalize their spiritual life so that it has little or nothing to do with how they live the rest of their lives.

A good, solid spiritual connection provides the person with many of the benefits of a secure attachment, a consistent, reliable source of love, support, and guidance. At its best, spirituality provides non-shaming ways to examine the self, see where attitudes or behaviors are harmful, and graceful ways to engage more positive behavior. A healthy community can also give people the kind of interpersonal connections that were absent in abusive or neglectful homes. At its worst, spirituality can be expressed negatively, a form of control over people, stifling their growth, shaming, blaming, and disempowering.

There are also sayings or beliefs attributed to religions that are often used to justify abuse. For instance, people who have been beaten may have been told it was for their own good, and had that supported by the saying, "spare the rod and spoil the child". It may be helpful to know that a rod is a long stick used by shepherds to guide their sheep away from danger, fast rivers, or toxic plants. It was not used to hit the sheep, but to aid in protecting them. It was for guidance, not punishment. Another saying, "honor thy father and thy mother" (Ephesians 6:2) is widely known, but there's another passage nearby, (Ephesians 6:4) that cautions parents, "do not provoke your child to anger", which many people have never noticed or connected to the first saying. It is extremely difficult for a child to honor a parent who is being abusive - the abuse creates distance, automatically. It's the parents' responsibility to relate to the child in a way that creates an environment in which the child can honor the parent.

In addition, all major religions teach what is generally known as the "Golden Rule". Judaism and Christianity teach, "You will love your neighbor as yourself" (Leviticus 19:18). Islam teaches, "Not one of you is a believer until he loves for his brother what he loves for himself" (Forty Hadith of an-Nawawi 13). In Confucian texts, it reads, "Try your best to treat others as you would wish to be treated yourself, and you will find that this is the shortest way to benevolence" (Mencius VII.A.4). The Hindu version is, "One should not behave towards others in a way which is disagreeable to oneself. This is the essence of morality. All other activities are due to selfish desire" (Mahabharata, Anusasana Parva 113.8). The list of similar sayings could go on, but the point being made is that all major religions teach respect and consideration for others.

If the client comes with a belief system that is supporting destructive attitudes and behavior to self or other, it would be helpful to refer that person to the appropriate expert for help understanding their religion in a more beneficial manner. It is advisable that the therapist knows the person whom the client will be referred to well enough to know that they will be supportive of the therapy, helping in their own area in a way that facilitates the client's overall growth.

Assessing the client's spiritual life should be a natural part of taking that person's history. Asking about the nature and place of spirituality for the person opens the door to an entire area of that person's life that may have a great deal of power to help, or block, their healing. It's information that will help to understand the whole person, and what resources in that area may be available to help in the therapeutic process.

With clients with DID, there may be several approaches to spirituality and religion. Sometimes there are parts of the person who present as spiritual beings, positive or negative. Knowing that can help the therapist see the person's spiritual resources and struggles. It can also help the therapist know what internal struggles may be going on. While some clients may have helpful spiritual assistance from inside, others may have negative spiritual introjects that reinforce shame inside. In some cases, clients may feel possessed, and the therapist will need to discover what that means to the person. Is it a cultural experience, or does it come from an experience of being forced to experience something horrendous? Is it an intrusion from the outside, or a manifestation of feelings or dynamics on the inside, or both? It may take a great deal of time to sort out what is going on inside, and what may originally appear negative may turn out to be positive, and vice versa.

Suggestions

Include questions about the person's religious upbringing and spiritual life in the initial interview. That can be done very simply, as part of exploring things that impacted their early life and may be affecting them in the present. "Were you raised in any particular religion, and if so, which one? What was that experience like for you?" Then go on to ask what place, if any, religion or spirituality plays in their life currently.

When a client presents with abuse in a spiritual setting, such as clergy abuse, or an experience in a dangerous cult, the impact on the person's spiritual life may be profound. When working with the trauma, invite the person to share the spiritual effect of the trauma. That may be something the person will need to have additional support to process, from the appropriate religiously trained person, but the questions about the impact of the abuse on all areas of life, including the spiritual, can be asked in therapy.

Seek out people in the community who can assist clients with spiritual issues outside the scope of therapy.

11 Endings—The Good, The Bad, and The Ugly

Termination; Suicide; Influence vs Control

The Good

Therapy may end well, because the person has worked through their trauma, integrated their consciousness as much as they need, and is ready and able to move on with their life. For some, this means they have fully integrated and are no longer dissociative, no longer experiencing themselves as having more than one consciousness inside. For others, they have achieved a level of co-consciousness and internal cooperation that allows them to live life in a way that feels good and satisfying to them. These people have dealt with therapy through Stage 3 to their satisfaction, and it is clear that they have become capable of managing and enjoying their own lives without needing to continue to come for therapy.

People who end therapy well, may grieve the loss of their connection with the therapist, but they also celebrate their achievement in being able to leave and manage life on their own.

The Bad

Sometimes therapy does not end well. Clients may lose their insurance, need to move, have health problems or other things that make continuing with therapy to be impossible at that time. For them, leaving is challenging.

It can help in those situations to provide the client with as many local and online resources as possible. It can also help to review their therapy and chart out where they were when they started and how much growth they have achieved. With that, add a "road map" for their next steps in healing. A good map for healing will give them the sense of what to focus on, what resources are most important, and where they can trust what they have within them.

Another "bad" ending may happen when the therapist needs to leave—to move, retire, or step back for health or any other reasons. This is particularly

DOI: 10.4324/9781003217541-13

hard on both people. The therapist is now in the position of being the source of the client's pain. There are three major aspects to manage, relating to the client, the process of transferring or ending therapy, and the experience of the therapist who is in a life-transition.

Clinically, how does a person help soothe another when they are causing the pain by leaving? For therapists, this is a time when outside support— supervision, consultation, therapy—is extremely helpful. The therapist will need to be able to hear as much of the impact on the client of their leaving as possible, and provide as many resources as they can before they leave. Acknowledging the difficulty and pain of this situation is essential, as well as recalling and reinforcing the importance of the relationship and the gains that have been made.

The process of transferring a client can be equally challenging. It's difficult to find therapists who work with complex PTSD and dissociative disorders. Finding one in the right geographical area, with the necessary insurance coverage, and with openings in their practice can be daunting.

As the practice winds down, the therapist is faced with the loss of their work—the loss of the kind of deep, meaningful connection with other people that comes from working in this field. Even when retirement is something chosen and longed for, there is likely to be some feeling of loss in the process.

The Ugly

Sometimes things don't turn out well. Sometimes the client cannot manage to leave when it feels that therapy has done what it can and it's time to step out into the world. For some, the attachment to the therapist may be one of the few, or only, genuine connections to other human beings that they have felt. That makes it extremely hard to leave. For them, spacing out sessions, and allowing them to move away slowly, may help. This replicates a "rapprochement" developmental stage, where the young child leaves the care-giver and goes and moves away, interacting with others, and then comes back to touch base, reconnecting and feeling the attachment to the care-giver. That reassures the child and allows the child to move away again. Eventually, the child takes the feeling of attachment along, inside. For clients, this becomes an "earned secure attachment".

Another way things can end awfully is if the therapist unexpectedly dies. That's a shock to everyone, and can leave the client out in the air with no support at all. Having a Therapeutic Will is one way to deal with that possibility. When therapists have that in place, they can notify the client, even as a part of the initial intake, and the client will know that someone will be there in that worst case scenario. The Therapist Will designates who will tell the clients, and gives directions about who to refer people to in the event that the therapist becomes disabled or dies.

The Most Traumatic Termination

When a Client Commits Suicide—What Happens to the Therapist?

> For one therapist, it came out of the blue, the phone ringing late on a Friday evening, and then two police officers at his door, asking him to identify a battered body. For another, it began with an empty chair in a quiet consulting room, the clock ticking past the hour of appointment, foreboding turning to dread and later to certainty. Still another found out almost by accident. Arriving at the hospital where he worked as a psychiatry resident, he overheard a group of colleagues talking about a suicide. "Who was it?"' he asked. The answer, he remembered, doubled him over, "like I had been punched in the stomach.'"
>
> (Goode, 2001)

In her book, *Terminating Therapy*, Denise Davis (2008) does mention the impact of the suicide of a client on the clinician, but only briefly, calling the termination of therapy through suicide to be "the most traumatic termination of all". The advice given is to seek support "in the context of a legally protected discussion with an attorney or personal therapist". That advice is followed by cautions to therapists and colleagues offering support to each other to avoid discussing any questions that might be self-incriminating if the case resulted in a legal action. Common questions such as "What do you think happened", therefore, are out of bounds.

While such advice is important, the result of all the cautions around talking about such a trauma can leave the therapist with few, if any, safe ways to process the shock, grief, and complicated feelings following a client suicide. Not all therapists have their own therapists. Not all therapists have their own legal counsel. Some can't afford either, or they are simply not readily available in whatever area the clinician practices.

In addition, the therapist may be called upon to submit clinical progress notes to a review team or jury, adding to the stress of an already seriously stressful situation (Davis, 2008). That said, make sure to document how to address suicidal ideation, assessments, and steps taken to intervene.

Immediate Responsibilities—If The Worst Happens

- Access immediate support from a colleague or supervisor
- Contact malpractice carrier and/or legal counsel for administrative support
- Cancel or re-schedule appointments to allow time to complete immediate tasks
- Understand and respect client confidentiality. Prior to contacting surviving family: Clarify with legal counsel state law regarding who hold the privilege, and have a list of resources for suicide survivors.

- Contact surviving family when appropriate
- Complete the written clinical record
- Notify other patients if needed (i.e. group members, patients on the same unit, etc.)
- Address unpaid bills

What Happens After: Legal issues—Confidentiality

> Generally, confidentiality survives the death of the patient. In other words, the deceased patient continues to be entitled to confidentiality, and the practitioner is under a continuing duty to protect the confidentiality of the records and information pertaining to the deceased patient. Similarly, the psychotherapist-patient privilege, which "belongs" to the patient, survives the death of the patient.
>
> (Leslie, 2008)

Even though the client is deceased, maintaining confidentiality in dealing with family and friends is still important, and having a release is still necessary before sharing records. Leslie (2008) goes on to state, "…first instinct after the patient dies and upon receiving a request for information about the deceased patient should be to resist disclosure." Legal issues usually include examining records and may involve potential investigations, highlighting the need to contact the insurance company in a timely manner.

If the patient is deceased, their authorized representative would have to authorize the disclosure. The state could amend these statutes to modify the circumstances under which the person's authorized representative could assert the privilege after the person's death. Any such amendments would have to comply with HIPAA.

In general, HIPAA preempts contrary state laws that provide less protection for individual health information. The HHS website has more information on when HIPAA pre-empts state law: http://www.hhs.gov/hipaafaq/state/399.html.

Reality Check

There is no need to assume there will be legal consequences. In a study Ruskin and colleagues (2004) found that out of 120 psychiatrists and trainees who experienced a patient's suicide, 9% reported being sued, and only two of those actually went to trial. Case law in the US has established that suicide cannot be reliably predicted. The main vulnerability clinicians face would come from negligence—failure to assess risk or act on the basis of that assessment (Ellis & Patel, 2012)

Impact on Professional Life

When facing family and friends of the deceased, it is considered ethical to express sympathy. "Expressing sympathy or a general sense of benevolence relating to the pain, suffering or death of a person involved in an accident and made to that person or the family of that person" are statements protected under California law (Frankel & Alban, 2013). Check the laws in your own state or country.

Attending the funeral or memorial service is optional, neither required nor forbidden. It depends on the circumstances of each individual case.

Help for the Therapist

Too often, therapists are left to deal with their own reactions to suicide on their own. It is highly recommended that anyone who has lost someone to suicide, including the therapist, talk to someone who can help - supervisors, mentors and others. It's also wise to avoid acting on extreme reactions, which could lead to isolating or behaving like a "super therapist". Therapists need time to grieve, just like all the other people who are experiencing the loss of the person. Becoming familiar with the research on suicide can help the therapist gain some perspective on what happened, and not feel so alone with the consequences (DeAngelis, 2008).

Jeffrey Sung (2016) offers similar advice, directing therapist survivors to look for both support from peers and from supervision, to manage both the personal and professional aspects of this experience. He also advises looking into the literature written on this subject and, if possible, have one's own personal therapy. Being able to recognize what is personally helpful, including whether or not to engage in funerals, memorials, or any other kind of ritual around the person's passing, can make the healing go more smoothly.

Common reactions to client suicide are an initial shock, denial and numbness, sadness, anxiety, anger, intense distress, PTSD, existential questioning, and sometimes a feeling of relief.

The therapist should notice their own reactions. These may include counter transferential issues. If the therapist feels a little bit relieved, might the wish for relief have been one of the elements behind the client's suicide? How about anger, sadness, anxiety, intense stress, PTSD, confusion and existential questioning? Was the client struggling with these issues? If so, the counter-transference can help the therapist learn, first hand, more about how difficult life was for this person, and that may allow for a little more grace for the therapist, and more understanding of other survivors.

When a client commits suicide, the therapist is both personally and professionally impacted. It becomes a kind of twin bereavement, felt in both areas of their life. Therapists also often confront a professional void—with little or no recognition of their loss and all that they go through after losing a client. This is even more so for the therapists who work with complex PTSD and Dissociative Disorders, areas in which there is often already a kind of professional void, with therapists having few, or no, colleagues working with people with these diagnoses.

The result of all of this can be a disruption of the therapist's professional sense of self. Many therapists also struggle with self-doubt, self-blame, and fear of blame by others. Since many people become therapists with the desire to help others, losing a client to suicide can strike at the core of the person's sense of identity and purpose.

The trauma hits the therapist emotionally related to the client, their treatment of the client, their interactions with colleagues, their professional philosophy, and their concerns about potential liability (Tillman, 2006). In addition, there is often a stigma around suicide, making necessary conversations about it more challenging, and adding to the impact of a suicide on others.

It can be helpful for the therapist to notice their own trauma response as a familiar process. While therapists seldom actually run, fight, and literally collapse, that trauma pattern is still evident in the experiences of being stunned (freeze), in immediate denial/disbelief (run), upset with self, client, situation, etc. (fight), and capitulating to the truth of what's happened (collapse/acceptance).

Similar to the trauma work with clients, therapists who have suffered the trauma of losing a client to suicide will also need to take time to stabilize, process the trauma and grieve, and integrate the experience and grow from it.

One common response is, "I should have known". In the beginning of the process of confronting a client's suicide, this can be temporarily helpful, a chance to look for clues that only appear in hindsight. However, no one can expect to know what they have not been told or taught. That's an assumption of omniscience. When a therapist persists in thinking "I should have known", at some point, this becomes a kind of wish - a wish to have known what needed to be known in order to prevent death. "I wish I had known" is more accurate. Notice the difference in feeling between saying "should" and "wish".

Meanwhile, the therapist faces the questions and reflections that virtually all people ask when a person they know commits suicide.

After "I should have known" comes the assumption that if you had known, you would have been able to do exactly the right thing to bring about the result that you wanted. That's an assumption of omnipotence.

In reality, if things had been different, they would be different, and either the same, better, or worse.

The basic problem is the reality of lack of control and power over what happens to others. People have influence, but not control, and sometimes they're actually powerless.

Wishes to have known and been able to prevent a suicide are normal for a while. If they persist, it may be because they bring the power/responsibility back to the therapist. At times, that feeling of there being something that could have been said or done is easier than facing the powerlessness and finality of the loss of the person.

Death is so final. Staying with the agonizing self-questioning may actually feel better than facing the finality, and helplessness, of loss.

What can be helpful when processing what happened is to learn all that's possible about clues that may have been missed, and any resources that weren't known.

It's also possible that clues may have been missed because the client chose to hide them. A client once told her therapist that if she was going to suicide, she'd make sure the therapist didn't know—so that she wouldn't stop her, and also, to protect the therapist from feeling responsible.

Influence vs Control

Therapists have influence over how their clients think, feel, and behave, but they do not have control. Consider that there are 168 hours in a week. Notice the difference between the hours clients are in therapy and the hours in which they are not. Those few hours have a very real impact on the person's life. However, for all those other hours, the person is out in the world, and facing struggles that come both from internal and external sources. Professionals who work a lot with suicidal clients know that suicide is inherently unpredictable and there is no level of vigilance that will be enough in some cases.

Did Therapy Fail?

People automatically equate suicide with therapeutic failure. Question that assumption. Therapy may have been the only experience of being seen and treated with dignity in that person's life. The therapist may be the only one who truly understood and empathized with that person's life experience, one of the few, or only, kind and caring witnesses to that person's life. The person may have lived longer because of having the refuge and support of therapy. They may have had a better quality of life for a while. That's a powerful thing. The presence of a caring person matters.

Transforming the Loss—Post-Traumatic Growth

Post-traumatic Growth is associated with psychological-mindedness, the belief in discussing one's problems, openness to change, and perceived social support. It often results in a desire to use what was learned and give back (Jordan & McIntosh, 2014).

Traumatic experiences change people. The therapists' power lies in giving people some choice in how that trauma changes them. They have the ability to direct that change by being conscious of their own processes, and mindfully doing what they can to aim themselves towards growth. It doesn't have to be a straight path, or a smooth one—it usually isn't—but the goal needs to be as clear as possible and kept in view as much as possible. Each person gets to choose the legacy that will evolve from this trauma.

Transforming the Loss—The Legacy

While death ends the possibilities of that person's life, it does not end the therapist's ability to honor that person through an intentional legacy. Sharing wisdom gained in the journey with them, in memory of them, is one thing a therapist can do for the clients who are no longer here. Some therapists create a memorial of some kind for them (while maintaining appropriate confidentiality) through writing, drawing, music, art, or dance. Some people plant flowers or trees. Others take lessons from the experiences with the client and use those to help others—both therapists and clients – through teaching, writing, consultation, or supervision. There are pictures, plants, and other items in many therapists' offices that are there in honor of people lost.

Most of all, the greatest legacy to give a client lost is to live more fully, more deeply, in honor of their life.

Final Thought

Suicide impacts us because life matters, and we know that, even when that life is painfully challenging. Therapists see the client's struggle to live, and witness their courage in seeking truth, growth, and health.

Losing a client is a loss that stays with the survivors, and it's up to them to honor that client (and themselves) by learning from their life, and becoming a better person/therapist because they have seen them, known them, and walked a while beside them.

Endings Where Everyone Continues to Live

When therapy ends, usually both people are still alive. They may even still live in the same area. While the professional relationship may be officially over, the feeling of connection doesn't automatically go away. Clients miss their therapists, and therapists often miss their clients. Sometimes, clients ask for contact after the therapy is over. What should a therapist do with that?

In this situation, the professional relationship remains. So, if contact does occur, it needs to maintain the relationship. So, if both past therapist and previous client live in the same area, they may see each other after therapy has ended. How might they best handle that situation? Talking this out prior to the end of therapy is helpful. They can both collaborate on how to manage contact, if it does occur, so that it feels appropriate to both people. They may agree to smile and say "hello", or just nod to each other. The therapist may take their cue from the client, or vice versa. Each relationship is different, and each social environment is different, so these things need to be considered on an individual basis.

12 Maintaining the Balance

The PIESS Chart

One of the challenges of working with trauma and dissociation is to maintain balance in how the client is perceived, how the work with the client progresses, and how therapists maintain themselves through the process. The PIESS Chart is a simple way to remember and assess the balance in all areas of the person's life, to notice where things are in place and strong, and where there are weaknesses that need to be strengthened, so the "wheel" will roll.

The PIESS chart represents the areas in the client's life that need to be addressed in therapy, sometimes directly in the therapy, or through adjunct work with other professionals. In therapy, the emotional domain is usually the main focus, with the intellectual and relational areas integrated into emotional knowledge and growth. A person is much more complex than that, and other areas of life impact growth and healing. Physical difficulties may be part of the expression of trauma, somatic expressions, or separate issues that need the attention of a physician. Social issues impact the amount of support the client experiences in life outside therapy, something that can help or hinder growth. The spiritual, a part that is often left out of therapy, can have a major impact on the survivor's healing. A secure attachment to a transcendent source of love and support and connection to a loving community can sometimes make the difference in a person's ability to move through the dark and difficult time in their process.

In using the chart, the client and therapist can determine what percentage of each section is full, and which sections are in need of attention. It's common for people with difficulties in one area to neglect the others. If people learn that struggles in one area can be helped by maintaining as much health as possible in all areas, they develop their own sense of being able to help themselves, and they receive more of the support they need. For instance, a client devastated by the impact of remembering abuse, finally acknowledging what he had always known, withdraws into his apartment, just wanting to be alone. His friend stops by, sees his distress, and brings him over to stay the night with him. The client is no longer alone, someone kind and caring is by

DOI: 10.4324/9781003217541-14

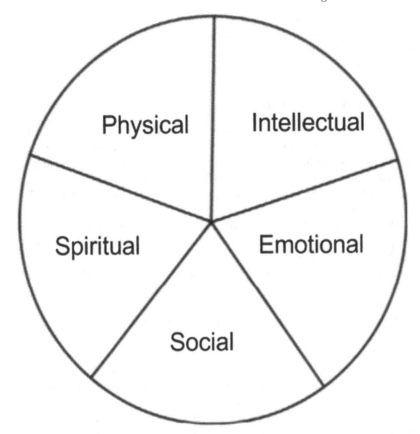

Figure 12.1 PIESS Chart (Physical, Intellectual, Emotional, Social, Spiritual)

his side, checking on him, he gets fed dinner, goes to a meeting and has contact with other people who are struggling and healing, sleeps better than he would have at home, and begins to recover. In the chart, his emotional section started out as empty, but with the support through the social and physical sections, and maybe even the spiritual, his emotional section begins to fill a little, and his life begins to return to a better sense of balance.

When all sections of the PIESS chart are full, the person is in excellent health. Normally, there are variations, sometimes daily or within a day, in each of these sections, so people seldom have all areas covered completely. Noticing the areas, however, helps people have a sense of the balance or lack of balance in their life, and where they need to invest their time and energy.

Using this chart, have the client fill in or list things and people that help in each section. Just noticing that may be helpful. Having the chart up somewhere, on a bulletin board, desk, or refrigerator door, may help the person remember to seek wholeness and involve all areas in their healing.

It is also helpful for therapists to use this image to notice if their own lives are well balanced or have areas that need attention. Being mindful of this for themselves will make it easier and more natural to notice the areas in and out of balance in the clients' lives.

The Five Aspects of Health

The goal is to integrate all of these into a whole life, keeping them in balance. Start with becoming aware of each of these aspects, including developing the ability to "self-witness", to notice how you're feeling and thinking, to be able to reflect on yourself with kindness, stop what you may be saying or doing when it doesn't serve you or others, and be able to "course correct".

Physical health refers not only to a healthy body, but also to an awareness of the body and how it communicates to self and others. Emotional health includes how we feel, and how to manage our own emotions so that we communicate effectively while treating others with dignity. Affect regulation skills should be taught throughout the lifespan. Intellectual health is the ability to think clearly, to think critically, and to integrate ideas with the rest of our reality. Social health involves developing strong, safe, respectful connections with other people, and being able to be vulnerable, present, and kind with ourselves and those with whom we work, play, and live. Spiritual health refers to being connected to life energy, "spirit", in a way that enlivens our being and connects us with all of life. This may come from being connected with an organized religion, but not necessarily. Sometimes, not always, organized religion actually gets in the way of spiritual development. When our spirit is healthy, we have depth and meaning in our lives, light in our eyes, and a felt sense of connection with all.

The Trauma Therapist

There is a lot to learn to become a competent trauma therapist. The areas that need study are the dynamics of trauma, the impact on the body, brain, emotions, and relationships, techniques that are useful in the healing process, the dynamics of the therapist-client relationship, and how to include that relationship in the therapeutic process. Of all of these, the last one is the one that is most often neglected. It is also the area in which the therapist has the most power. In meta-studies of the outcome of therapy, 50% of outcome is dependent on the client, 40% is the result of the therapist-client relationship, and the remaining 10% contains all the other factors, including techniques (Duncan, et. al., 2009).

While techniques are very helpful and should be learned, they actually contribute only a fraction to the outcome. In the training of trauma therapists, however, it is common to see techniques highlighted and the relationship of the therapist and client virtually ignored. What would happen if both were taught in the proportions to the effect they seem to have on outcomes? Why isn't that happening? First, teaching people how to be in intense personal relationships involves the person becoming very self-aware, which means deep self-reflection and interactions with others who can provide feedback and guidance. This is usually done through personal therapy. Ideally, the person who wants to become a trauma therapist, or who is one, should have a personal therapist or the equivalent of that in their life. The purpose of that would be to learn about oneself and continue to pay attention and tend to one's own psyche while working in this field. Second, working with the therapist to become more fully self-aware and develop the skills to continue to be self-reflexive in the midst of working with trauma survivors takes a lot of time. It's not something that fits in a semester or two of instruction. It becomes a part of the therapist's way of life, using therapy, journaling, workshops, yoga, meditation, and other on-going avenues to self-awareness and health.

When working with traumatized clients, therapists need to include their heart. That's another part that doesn't get trained well in graduate schools. It involves being a loving, caring person in the midst of confronting the effects of the worst kinds of human behavior. When the therapist can see the person struggling to heal, see beyond the trauma story to the person caught up in it, it frees the client from that story. People are not their trauma, they are people who have experienced that trauma, and now want to be free of it so they can live their lives. When the therapist sees that, and can keep that connection, it helps the client see it, too. It gives them a whole new way of perceiving their experience, a perspective that shows them a way out from under the burden of what happened to them.

Working with people who have been traumatized means witnessing the effect of trauma, and that has an impact on the therapist. For many people who become therapists, the goal is to help people have fuller and healthier lives. Part of working with complex trauma and dissociative issues is to confront overwhelming events, and deal with the survivor's experience of being helpless, powerless, and deeply wounded. One therapist described working with survivors of severe trauma as like walking into hell, taking the person's hand, and walking back out together. The truth of that statement is that the therapist needs to be able to meet the client where he, she, or they are, and that is often in their own personal hell. It's not uncommon for therapists to be apprehensive about connecting that deeply with the client. That may come from a fear that acknowledging the depth of the woundedness might cause it to become worse, as if seeing it would reinforce it. Actually, what usually happens is the opposite. When people are truly seen and met where they are, it allows them to move. It's almost as if they need to be seen in that awful place before they can leave it. Leaving without connection is a kind of dissociation, a moving away from something that can't be faced, and thus remains.

Another fear that arises in working with traumatized people is the limit to what the therapist will be able to provide. There may be limits to the number of sessions the client is allowed, or to the length of time given for each session. There may be other factors that lead the therapist to think that the time available to work with the client will be clearly insufficient to take many steps on the healing path.

How much can a therapist do? What are the limits of caring and helping that can be provided, both because of the nature of the therapy, and the resources brought to therapy by client and therapist? At the beginning of therapy, it is helpful to be as clear as possible about what treatment does and does not offer. This helps both people set realistic goals.

When the therapy will be limited, it can help to let the client know what is seen, even if that can't be addressed in therapy. Saying something like, "You only have a few sessions here, and I can tell from what you've already shared that we will not have time to address what's happened to you at the depth that you need and deserve. I am not happy about that, so I want to make sure we make the best of the time we have, and see if we can lay out a path for you to continue your work when we're done here," acknowledges the situation and still holds hope for what happens after this therapy ends.

Another difficulty therapists face is discerning the amount of pain or upset the client can manage within their Window of Tolerance. Sometimes the client holds back, fearful of being overwhelmed, and sometimes the client jumps in far too deeply. There are also times when the therapist prevents the client from dealing with difficult feelings because the therapist is uncomfortable with them. In other words, therapists may put the brakes on the process because they can't tolerate as much as the client can. That limits the client's ability to move forward. It's the therapist's responsibility to manage their own emotions well enough to allow the client to be as emotionally authentic and healthy as possible.

Therapists may put on the brakes for a number of reasons. They may not know how much the client can safely tolerate, or may have other concerns about the client's situation that are cause for caution. There are also times, however, when it's the therapist who cannot tolerate what the client is facing. That's when the therapist needs to take a step back and do some self-reflection, preferably with the assistance of a therapist or colleague. Perhaps the client's trauma is triggering the therapist's past. Or, maybe the therapist has rules about how much emotion is appropriate and the client is breaking those rules. In that case, consultation and/or supervision would be helpful to determine whether the client is pushing the emotional boundaries of therapy or whether the therapist has their own personal work to do in order to be available to the client.

Working with trauma survivors almost always triggers the therapist at some point. For some therapists those moments are rare. For others, they may be common. Knowing one's own history and emotional vulnerabilities is essential for staying in this field in a way that supports the health of both therapist and client.

There are also times when the client is having such a difficult time that nothing seems to help. The therapist will see the client suffer, and can't stop or mediate that suffering. Therapists can't always stop clients from hurting themselves or feeling awful. At these times, there may be a pull from the clients to make them feel better, which the therapist can't do. However, the therapist can support the client moving through their misery. They can be supported but not rescued. For therapists, that can be a very hard place to stand, wanting to help the person feel better and knowing the only thing to do is stay close and accompany the person through that period of misery. While doing that, the therapist will be likely to pick up on the client's feelings of powerlessness in the face of the trauma. That is useful information, something that can help the therapists know more about the client's experience and help develop more compassion for the client.

One analogy that is useful for both the client and the therapist is to compare psychotherapy with physical therapy. It is well known that a person in physical therapy will need to practice, and need to address the issue over and over. Recovery is slow when damage is great. There is no shame in that. When doing physical therapy, people can only do so much or they will re-injure themselves. In therapy, the client needs to stay within limits emotionally in the same manner, and the therapist needs to have the patience to help the client do the 'exercises' repeatedly, knowing they will help over time.

Psychotherapy, just like physical therapy, can be painful at times, and that pain needs to be endured within limits. In psychotherapy, both the client and the therapist are likely to experience some pain in the process. The therapist needs to know that and have a sense of how much pain needs to be tolerated in order to heal, and also needs to be able to remain emotionally present with the client through painful times. That means the therapist has to have the ability to tolerate being in the presence of someone in deep emotional pain and continue to be supportive and compassionate. That takes time to develop, and comes most quickly to people who are also doing their own psychological work.

How available are you, in terms of time, energy, and emotional availability? These clients need more, and tend to receive more, appropriately, but there's a fine line between supporting them to that extent and encouraging dependency. Offering more reassurance can be helpful, and the ability to tolerate emotional stress, engage as much as appropriate and still set necessary limits becomes easier with the experience of how much that actually helps the person.

Therapist Defense System—The Light and the Shadow

Most therapists can and do learn to work with emotional intensity and stay present. In doing so, they become stronger people. If they are not able to learn that set of skills, they may automatically use defense mechanisms to protect themselves that will hinder or harm the progress of the therapy. Part of the process of learning to stay present and helpful when emotions and behaviors are challenging is the repeated experiences of not being able to do this well. We learn the deepest lessons from experience.

Most trauma survivors want and need to share what has happened to them. Being able to talk about it with another person present, listening, and being compassionate can have a major impact, providing healing in relationships for harm that was caused in a relationship. Trauma can be intensely lonely. Often no one sees their fear, pain, and upset, or they see it and fail to respond. That failure to respond is a form of betrayal and exacerbates the trauma (Chefetz, 2015).

Trauma therapists are in the unusual position of having to be personally present while protecting themselves from being overwhelmed. As part of that, they need to know their own personal defense mechanisms, how they react when scared, angry, disgusted, horrified, or grief stricken. Knowing that, they can become aware of their automatic response and, over time, become able to allow it to happen if appropriate to the situation, or curb it when it would be harmful to the therapeutic process. Curbing it and being capable of responding in another way, is a learned skill, one that will keep the connection with the client and help the therapy progress.

For example, remember the story of the client who said something deliberately cruel. The therapist was instantly hurt, stood up, and walked out of the room. So far, that was the therapist displaying her normal defensive style—when hurt by abusive people, she leaves. However, leaving would not help the therapeutic process, so this therapist stood outside the door of her office, took ten slow, deep breaths, calmed herself and returned to the room. She told the client, "If you want to know if you can hurt me, you can. If you want to know if you can sabotage this therapy, you can. It's your choice." Now what has happened in the relationship is on the table, ready for discussion.

The Therapist Defense System, when used well, is a combination of self-awareness and boundaries, necessary for the therapeutic relationship to thrive. When used poorly, it's defensive and offensive, damaging to that relationship.

The Light Side

Good defenses protect the person. In order for them to work well, the person needs to be able to use them consciously so that they facilitate the therapy and don't impede it. Boundaries are part of every person's defense system and can be physical, or emotional in nature. Boundaries determine how close people can be to each other, physically and emotionally to ensure connection and safety They create safety, both for the therapist and the client. Boundaries are part of the structure of the therapy, and they are also part of each therapist's personal emotional defense system. There is a healthy need for emotional protection, boundaries, that allows the therapist to engage authentically, stay present in the room, but not be overwhelmed. Having good boundaries also lets the client know that he or she can truly share feelings, memories, and all that is necessary for the work to continue and not have to worry about taking care of the therapist.

Good Fences Make Good Neighbors

Learning to listen without becoming lost or overwhelmed is something that comes with time and practice. The therapist needs to be emotionally close enough to feel connected to the client, but not so close that the client's emotional difficulties overwhelm the therapist.

One way to look at it is to imagine seeing the client through the lens of a camera. A wide-angle lens view may take in more than is useful and overwhelm the therapist. An example of that is the therapist who listened to the client's description of a traumatic experience that included a number of people, with several of them being abused. The therapist automatically visualized the whole scene and all the traumatized people in it. That night she dreamt of that scene. That was too much. In the next session, she imagined seeing the client through a narrower lens, like a close-up, focusing only on the client and not allowing herself to visualize the other people in the scene. The client was the only one she could help, and focusing on her stopped the therapist's overwhelm.

Other therapists may have the opposite problem, automatically distancing themselves from the client in order to stay away from disturbing images or emotions. In those cases, the client is left out with too little connection with the therapist. That therapist will need to learn to come close enough to be with the client while maintaining enough emotional distance to remain present and helpful.

A good defense system, like the city gates of old, is open for business, but closed to invasion. The example given above about the therapist who temporarily left her office when she was emotionally attacked by the client demonstrates how the gate closed when the therapy became unsafe, but could open again if safety could be restored. In that case, the client was told the effects of her behavior and the potential consequences. The trust between therapist and client was temporarily broken, but the therapist came back, opening that door again to let the client know what the boundaries were if she wanted to continue. The therapist took care of herself, and because she did, by leaving and then by calming herself, she was able to return and let the client know what could happen next.

For the therapist, closing the gate may be necessary but need not be hostile. Closing the gate with conscious and therapeutic intention advances the therapy—and that's the difference between a defense system that works and one that doesn't.

People who have been severely traumatized have had too much experience with hurtful people. Unfortunately, that means they've learned hurtful behavior, whether they act that out or not, so there is the possibility that the therapist will encounter hurtful behavior and will need to know how to handle that.

Being real, authentic, without sharing personal history or personal aspects of life is a positive defense. It allows the therapist a way to be completely present with the feeling that the relationship with the client is held in a place close, but not the same as a friend or family member. Sometimes clients will ask for personal information. Usually, what they want and need is the sense of knowing the therapist as a real person. It's not the external things that really matter, the marital status, whether the therapist has children or not, what they do outside the office, it's the reality of the person that matters. Is the therapist present and real in relationship to the client? Is the therapist a genuine person, with the ability to communicate that to the client in sessions? Being present and real is very powerful, and often very difficult. It requires some vulner-ability on the part of the therapist, which can only happen if there has been sufficient trust established between therapist and client. If enough safety has been created, the ability of the therapist to be real and fairly transparent models that emotional courage to the client.

For many clients, relationships involve either hiding behind strong defenses or letting the other person know everything about them - which usually results in a feeling of shame after the over-sharing. To experience a relationship in which the other person is appropriately real, with clear boundaries and the ability to genuinely connect gives the client a new experience.

The therapist being real and present involves being empathically attuned with the client enough to get an internal sense of the client's experience and being able to speak and behave in a way that communicates that connection to the client. For instance, in hearing that a client had received a serious medical diagnosis, the therapist teared up and expressed genuine concern for the client. When another client expressed being angry about an abusive situation, the therapist nodded and said he could thoroughly understand why that was so upsetting—it felt upsetting just to hear it. In each case, the thera-pist was touched by the experience of the client, but not overwhelmed or derailed from the ability to help the client. The focus did not shift to the therapist. The focus remained on the client.

Part of this healthy limit setting, and appropriate defense, is the ability to share the unique nature of the therapeutic relationship. Talking about it openly is empowering for the client. There's a reason why therapists don't share much personal information. It's to ensure that the time and focus is on the client. The therapeutic relationship is not reciprocal like relationships with friends and family. It's heavily one-sided, in favor of the client, and it's that way for a reason. The client needs the therapist's full attention without having to return that attention in a like manner. The relationship exists for the ben-efit of the client. The fact that the therapist also benefits is a consequence of knowing, working with and helping another human being.

The Shadow Side—Therapists' Defenses that Don't Work

When things are challenging in therapy, therapists will often feel defensive, as most humans do, and will often bring that defensiveness into the therapy. When the therapist's own defense system takes over, when the role of therapist is abandoned, therapy is endangered. The rupture can be repaired, and that often strengthens the therapy. However, if the rupture solidifies, the therapy slows, stalls, and is frequently over.

Common Therapist Defense System Stances that are not Helpful

I'm ok, you're not. There's a judgmental edge to this when it's used as a defense. It's not a statement that reflects the therapist doing well and the client having trouble. When this emerges as a defense, it's being used to distance from the client, and to assume a higher status. When the therapist is using this defense, it's judgmental, and that is not helpful to anyone. It's not unusual for the client to be struggling with feeling ok, and when the therapist has this attitude, it not only distances the therapist from the client, it also reinforces negative self-perceptions in the client. The client is ok as a human being, even if he or she is struggling with difficult emotions and behaviors.

The first person to feel the effects of things not working well is the client. The therapist is there to recognize the problem and work with the client to overcome it. When the therapist pulls away with the attitude of being better than the client, the relationship suffers, and progress stalls or moves backwards.

If the therapist feels this distance, it's more helpful to name it. "I'm feeling myself pulling away from you. Something is happening here that I need some time to process. I don't want to say or do anything that will make your path or our relationship any more difficult, and I'm not quite sure how to do that right now." That's honest. When the therapist distances, the client almost always notices it, and the tendency for clients is to take it personally. They need to hear that what they are experiencing in the room with the therapist is real, and that there will be a way to talk it through. It's also very helpful for the client to hear the therapist taking responsibility for their own reactions. It may be the first time another person has considered the relationship important enough to want to preserve it.

Intellectualization can be used as a defense when it results in retreating into analysis as a way to avoid the emotional reality in the room, as opposed to using the mind to help move the process forward. When things become uncomfortable, people often step away from the feelings by thinking about things, asking "why", and moving into an intellectual discussion that ignores the emotional reality in the room. Or, the therapist may become intrigued with the client's diagnosis, or even begin to lecture the client. Psycho-education is very helpful, but not if it's used to stop the process so that the therapist can remove themselves from a difficult emotional reality.

Relying on techniques to hide from the relationship is another defense the therapist may use. Techniques are very helpful as a part of the therapy. However, there are times when the techniques are center stage, and the client becomes peripheral, like an extra in a movie, lost in the midst of the action. In these cases, the therapist may be using techniques like a barrier between therapist and client rather than something integrated into the relationship to facilitate healing.

Over-diagnosing can be like a shield for the therapist, used by the therapist to hide behind the role of diagnostician, distancing from the human being present in the room, and adding diagnoses to explain the difficulty in the therapy rather than addressing behavioral or relational problems.

There are times when the therapist may be engaged in diagnosing the client as part of the original assessment or treatment and that's appropriate. When used as a defense, the therapist will seek other diagnostic labels to put on the client instead of working with whatever is uncomfortable in the room. The classic example of this is the therapist over diagnosing the client as a sex addict just because the client has behaved in a seductive manner.

Shaming the client by saying or inferring that the client is "bad" can be another way for the therapist to defend him or herself. The area where this often emerges is with hostile alters in a dissociative system. Rather than deal with that aspect of the person, their function in the system, strengths and weaknesses, alliances, etc., the therapist will label some parts "bad" and attempt to get rid of them. That is shaming the whole person, because dissociative aspects of the person are parts of a whole person, and they are there for a reason. Shaming them distances them from both the therapist and the client, making it far harder for the client to heal.

Blaming the client can be a defensive strategy when the therapist attributes a disruption in the relationship to the client, giving a "this is your fault" message, when it's not solely the client's problem. It's a defense when the therapist knows at some level that they did or said something to contribute to the problem and is not willing to own it. One way this may happen is for the therapist to deny what they did or said, and blame the client for misinterpreting, thereby denying the client's reality of what was real in order to preserve the therapist's ego.

Denying resentments, saying "of course I'm not angry" with hostility and a grimace is a defensive posture. It isn't real, and because it's a denial of reality, it is not helpful to the therapy. It's also a missed opportunity to deal with anger in the relationship in a positive manner. If the therapist is angry, they need to be able to claim that anger and deal with it constructively. Maybe the anger comes from something in the relationship with the client, and maybe it's from somewhere else, but clients very seldom have the experience of being able to address anger and not have someone be hurt by it. It's actually not that hard for a therapist to say, "yes, I am angry, and it's not about you...", or "yes, I am angry. When you said (or did) that, I felt attacked (disrespected, hurt, upset, etc.), and that's not ok with me. We need to talk about this. Whatever you were trying to tell me got lost in the anger. Let's try again." When a therapist acknowledges the reality in the room, it helps clients know when their perceptions are correct, which helps them differentiate between current issues and triggers from their past.

Putting responsibility onto the client inappropriately, as in playing the victim, making the client feel like they have abused the therapist when that has not happened can be a way for the therapist to back away when upset. One time this defensive strategy may come up is when the client needs to talk about disturbing things that happened, and the therapist is unable to hear what is being said. If the therapist is aware of feeling victimized by the client's narrative, they could say, "what happened to you is so upsetting, I'm having a hard time even listening to it at the moment. Let's take a breather. I want to be able to hear what you say, and I'm aware of how hard it is for you to speak. Looks like it's hard for both of us. I can understand why it's taken so long for you to share, and I want you to keep going. What's this like for you?" Normally, that will open the discussion about the difficulty of speaking and seeing the other person's reaction. Sometimes, however, it will become apparent that what's being shared is intentionally disturbing, putting the therapist in the position of witnessing something intolerable. That's another dynamic, and it may be a way the client shares an experience through transferring it onto the therapist rather than speaking about it. It could also be evidence of a thread of sadism in the client, or in the client's experience.

Occasionally, a therapist may feel threatened by the client's talent or intelligence, and seek to maintain a feeling of authority over the client, keeping the client in a one-down position, the equivalent of a therapy "glass ceiling". This is a kind of power-over dynamic and may emerge when the therapist is feeling vulnerable or dealing with personal issues that affect their own self esteem. There are times when the client is equally intelligent or more intelligent than the therapist, and that can become something the therapist recognizes and applauds in the client. Most therapists are happy to do that, a dynamic that can be the countertransference of a parent/authority being proud of the client, encouraging the person to succeed in a way similar to that of a parent or teacher.

Pushing at a client's vulnerabilities in order to keep him or her destabilized and dependent is another way in which a therapist may try to take care of his/her own needs at the expense of the client. If the therapist emphasizes issues that still remain unresolved while ignoring those that have progressed in such a way that the client feels they will never heal enough to please the therapist, that's a problem. Pleasing the therapist is not the goal—or shouldn't be—because that would be fostering the reliance on an external locus of control, and keeping the client in a one-down position in order to take care of the therapist.

A more typical defense is to block any feedback from the client about the therapist's behavior in relation to the client, acting as if that were out of bounds of the therapy. Being able to address issues in the relationship between therapist and client enables the client to learn interpersonal skills that are very helpful in life. This is a rich area for growth, and if the therapist resists or prevents feedback, very helpful interactions may never happen, and old inhibiting rules may be reinforced. Further, in avoiding client feedback, the therapist misses out on rich and robust opportunities for their own growth, personally and professionally.

At times, a therapist will threaten to terminate or refer a client because of feeling uncomfortable (not endangered) and doesn't want to deal with that discomfort directly. It's perfectly acceptable to refer or terminate a client who is threatening the therapist, or whose issues are beyond the therapist's scope of practice. There needs to be a solid base of safety for both therapist and client in order to work in therapy, and the therapist needs to have enough knowledge and competence to genuinely assist the client. However, threatening to terminate or refer in order to silence the client, or to avoid a situation/feeling/pattern of behavior that needs to be addressed in the therapy is not acceptable. For example, one therapist terminated with a client who was in the hospital because of a suicide attempt. The therapist couldn't handle the situation, and refused to continue to work with the client, leaving her in the hospital with no therapist to work with when she was discharged. That is an example of client abandonment, especially egregious because of the obvious fragility of the client.

Other types of defenses therapists may find themselves using are numbing, becoming aggressive, becoming co-dependent, having their boundaries slip so that they become either enmeshed or disconnected, or physically leaving and staying gone by failing to return or by forcing a termination.

Not returning phone calls in a timely manner or repeatedly canceling appointments may be a kind of avoidance, or the result of being too busy or too tired. The clients need the therapists to be clear about what they do and don't do, and be reliable with scheduling, return calls, and other aspects of the therapeutic relationship.

Therapists need to know their own defensive style, and that of the client, so that defensive interactions can be minimized.

Suggestions

Write a list of your own defense strategies. For example, what comes first—anger, avoidance, denial, distraction, or other? The therapist who left the room when hurt knew that was what she did, and that knowledge helped her be able to choose to return and engage in a more helpful manner. If that first defensive reaction doesn't work, what's the next likely reaction? And after that, what would come third? If the therapist is aware of his/her/their own defensive line-up, it will be easier to identify what's going on and take conscious control of the situation.

Next, take a moment after each interaction with a client and check in to see if there's any sense of pulling out defenses. Listen to your own internal dialogue about the client or session. Catching it early helps defuse it more quickly.

Finally, step back emotionally and consider the client. What has life been like for this person? What's the current issues being dealt with in and out of therapy? What is the client needing from therapy and the therapist at this time?

Asking these questions can help the therapist gain valuable perspective on the client's process and the reasons for behavior that may be upsetting to the therapist. Often when the therapist goes through this process, it will become clear that therapist and client are in the midst of a transference/counter-transference re-enactment, and the therapist may be experiencing what the client experienced in the past - frustration, desperation, and loss of hope. If so, that's a glimpse into the life of the client that is valuable for the therapy. Reflecting that back to the client is one way to use this information. For example, saying something along the lines of, "Upset, angry, frantic, trying everything you know and having none of it work, becoming desperate and wanting to give up—does any of that feel familiar to you?" In many cases, it does, and the client only learned that through having the experience of things not working in therapy and choosing to be open to what's happening rather than defending against it.

Listen to feedback from your clients. Is there something in what they say that rings true inside of you? Look for that, even if it feels trivial to you. It's not possible or important to be perfect, in fact, if it were possible to be perfect, a lot of powerful therapeutic experiences would be missed. Noticing your own ways of reacting and responding, and how that can affect the clients, will enhance your effectiveness. It will allow you to be more honest, and give you the opportunity to demonstrate how to face your own imperfections, learn, grow, and move on with grace. For the clients, it's a model of how a mature person takes responsibility for their own behavior. That is something many clients have never witnessed.

Self-Management

There's a saying in this field that trauma therapists last about two years, or 20+. What makes the difference in those extremes? Virtually everyone who enters this field does so with a sincere desire to help. Most of those therapists burn out and leave. What does it take to stay?

Working with severe trauma produces secondary PTSD, vicarious traumatization, and burn out. It's not easy to sit with horror every working day, to try not to take it home, but to find it invading thoughts and dreams. Most therapists in the 20+ category know the experience of being overwhelmed and questioning whether to continue in this field or leave.

Those therapists who have stayed have found ways to deal with the trauma that work for them. Those who have left, have left because their psyches and life situations did not make working with this population possible, and for those who leave, that is most likely a good decision.

What does it take to stay? Tolerance for ambiguity, for emotional intensity, for holding onto the reality that life includes both good and evil, often in the same person—all of those qualities help the therapist to be able to stay.

It also takes a willingness to feel inadequate, on a fairly regular basis. The enormity of trauma renders virtually everyone powerless at times. Feeling deskilled is a familiar feeling to someone working with severe trauma and dissociation. It mimics the experiences of the clients, and once that is known, it can become something that's helpful.

When to Stop

Sometimes it's appropriate, and necessary, to stop therapy before the client has completed his or her process. The well-known situations where this happens are terminations because of the therapist or client moving away, retirement, and loss of insurance. Situations that are less frequently discussed are those where the therapist feels inadequately trained to deal with the client's issues, where the client may have threatened the therapist, where the client is not adequately engaged in therapy to be able to make any progress, and where the therapist becomes aware that the situation is not therapeutic and can't be made to be so. In all of those situations, the therapist needs to do what they can to transfer the client to a therapeutic place more appropriate to their needs, whether that be inpatient or a referral to another therapist or clinic. The client should be told clearly, in a non-rejecting or shaming way, the reasons for the termination and/or referral.

In these situations, it is best if the therapist has consultation, and if possible, supervision prior to and during any termination. Terminations can be very upsetting, triggering abandonment issues among other things. Both people need as much support as possible to make the best transition to a new, and hopefully more productive, setting.

A fairly common situation is for a therapist, having worked with a client for a while begins to see how much the client has suffered, and may begin to see signs of dissociation. By that time, the therapist and client may have established a connection that feels good to both of them. The therapist is then confronted with the reality of working with a client whose diagnosis has shifted to something more complicated than first believed. Should the client be transferred to a therapist who has more experience with the more difficult diagnosis, or should the therapist try to continue with the client because of the strength of the relationship? It is very important in this situation to seek consultation.

It may be possible to continue to work with the client if there is sufficient consultation and/or supervision possible. If there is neither, then the therapist will need to talk with the client about the situation. For some clients, the attachment to the therapist is the most significant part of their process. For others, while the attachment may be there, they are aware of the need to work with therapists who are trained to deal with the complexity of their symptoms. Being able to talk about the situation, including the feelings involved, will make whatever decision is reached feel more collaborative, and that will help with the future of the therapy.

Sometimes therapy ends because the therapist becomes incapacitated, or dies. While no one wants to think about that, it is helpful to consider that possibility and plan for it, just in case. As was mentioned earlier, it is now recommended that therapists have a professional will, with instructions on where clients can be referred, and how records are to be handled. This should be part of the information given at the beginning of therapy, along with the office procedures, and policies around confidentiality. When this is included from the start, the client knows that there is a plan for them to be transferred if anything happens to the therapist. It's reassuring to know that, and it also is a reality check, making it clear that there is no guarantee that the therapist will be available forever. When this is done well, there is a person designated to contact the clients and transfer their records to a therapist recommended for that client by the current therapist. The client then knows that the referral was made with him/her in mind which can make the situation a little bit smoother. The person helping with the transition should be a therapist trained to facilitate this process (Frankel, 2015).

13 Conclusion

Difficult therapeutic situations challenge both the client and the therapist. When therapy becomes difficult, it is often because the client comes with multiple experiences of trauma. Because the trauma has focused so much of clients' time and energy on survival, they have not had the opportunity to develop in many areas of life, and will have perceptions and reactions from a traumatic past that interfere with the ability to be present. The repercussions of the trauma reverberate through the therapy forcing both client and therapist to strengthen their relationship to hold against the storm of affect and devastation of loss. What is lost—time, health, opportunities, relationships, etc. —cannot be restored without conscious thought and work. The greatest gains are made when the client is motivated and capable of change, and the therapist is knowledgeable about trauma and available to connect with the client in a genuine, healing relationship designed to empower the client to grow.

The work is collaborative, and both people will grow and change in the process. The therapist is challenged to remain grounded and kind, reliable and consistent in the face of the client's emotional turmoil, giving the client the experience of relating to a healthy, emotionally attuned person. That ability to attune, regulate self and others, and maintain progress on the road to recovery takes a great deal of strength and courage, heart energy and wisdom. The benefit is to see clients free themselves from the harm done by others and have as much of their lives as possible. The clients leave, and both clients and therapists benefit from their time together.

When an abuser hurts someone, they steal from the abused something fundamental and essential to being a person. When the abuse is chronic and on-going, the developing child's ability to grow into their authentic self is stolen. Instead the child learns to assume myriad roles seeking safety and shelter. The legacy of trauma is confusion and chaos. The client arrives with a host of defenses, fears, and profound mistrust. In spite of this, they risk and hope.

To respond empathically and effectively the therapist must go beyond the dissociative defenses, the post traumatic turmoil, to sit with the painful feelings, the profound losses, the bitter betrayals, reaching out and responding to the authentic self-developing and emerging from within.

DOI: 10.4324/9781003217541-15

Complex trauma occurs within the context of a close interpersonal relationship and can only be treated within the context of a close interpersonal relationship. Our 'voice' goes with them, and theirs remains with us, and each in our own way benefits from knowing one another.

From the Center Out

In therapy, there are two major approaches—bottom up, and top down. The bottom up is somatic, paying attention to the body and all the information we get from it. Top down is focusing on how we think, our beliefs, our self-talk, etc. No one seems to notice that when those two are integrated, we're heart-centered, present in our bodies and present in our minds and connected to ourselves and others through our hearts. It's our heart that defines what means most to us in our lives—and everyone already knows that. We just seldom talk about it.

Trauma treatment involves working from the top down, using all the things we've learned to work with the mind, brain, beliefs and feelings. It also involves working from the bottom up, accessing somatic resources, and learning to live a fully embodied life.

The therapist needs to know and use both, and more. The therapist needs to integrate mind and body, and come from the center, from the heart. From the center out is a model that combines intellect, emotion, sensory input, intuition, and genuine caring connection. With this, we also center the importance of the relationship in the healing process. This is how we establish and connect with the power relationship has to heal—from the center out.

Links

Intersectionality

- Crenshaw, Kimberley: https://time.com/5786710/kimberle-crenshaw-intersectionality/
- Maladaptive Daydreaming: https://daydreamresearch.wixsite.com/md-research/measures
- Sexual Arousal Non-concordance: https://www.ted.com/talks/emily_nagoski_the_truth_about_unwanted_arousal?language=en

Suicide

Confidentiality/Privilege: Death of the Patient, Legal Issues

- CPH & Associates: https://www.cphins.com/confidentialityprivilege-death-of-the-patient/
- HHS website has more information on when HIPAA pre-empts state law: http://www.hhs.gov/hipaafaq/state/399.html.
- DeAngelis, Tori, article dealing with suicide: https://www.apa.org/gradpsych/2008/11/suicide
- Grief, family, friends: https://www.compassionatefriends.org/http://www.suicidology.org/suicide-survivors/suicide-loss-survivors
- Ken Pope, webpage, resources: http://www.kspope.com/suicide/
- Suicide, warning signs: http://www.suicidology.org/resources/warning-signs
- Suicide resource for clinicians: http://www.suicidology.org/suicide-survivors/clinician-survivors
- Sung, Jeffrey, help for clinicians: http://www.cliniciansurvivor.org/
- ISSTD: www.isst-d.org

Yoga

- Grounding yoga videos: https://www.youtube.com/watch?v=CfJEmuNVNm8 https://www.youtube.com/watch?v=d3dE8qsC6UM

DOI: 10.4324/9781003217541-16

References

Ainsworth, M., Blehar, M., Waters, E., & Wall, S. (1978). *Patterns of Attachment: A Psychological Study of the Strange Situation*. Psychology Press.

American Psychiatric Association. (2013). Diagnostic and statistical manual of mental disorders, *DSM-5*, 5(5). American Psychiatric Association.

American Psychiatric Association. (2022). *Diagnostic and Statistical Manual of Mental Disorders*, 5th Ed. American Psychiatric Association.

Andrewes, D. G., & Jenkins, L. M. (2019). The role of the amygdala and the ventromedial prefrontal cortex in emotional regulation: Implications for post-traumatic stress disorder. *Neuropsychology Review*, 29(2), 220–243. doi:10.1007/s11065-019-09398-4.

Atwood, G. E., & Stolorow, R. D. (2016). Walking the Tightrope of Emotional Dwelling. *Psychoanalytic Dialogues*, 26(1), 103–108. doi:10.1080/10481885.2016.1123525.

Arnold, M. E. (2017) Supporting adolescent exploration and commitment: Identity formation, thriving, and positive youth development. *Journal of Youth Develeopment*, 12 (4),1–15.

Bandler, R. (1985) *Using your Brain – for a Change*. Real People Press.

Barrett, M. J. & Fish, L.S. (2014) *Treating Complex Trauma: A Relational Blueprint for Collaboration and Change*. Routledge.

Bateson, G., Jackson, D. D., Haley, J., & Weakland, J. (1956). Toward a theory of schizophrenia. *Klassiekers van de kinder-en jeugdpsychiatrie* II, 303.

Bateson, G., Jackson, D. D., Haley, J., & Weakland, J. H. (1963). A note on the double bind – 1962. *Family process*, 2(1), 154–161.

Beere, D. B. (2009). The self-system as mechanism for the dissociative disorders: An extension of the perceptual theory of dissociation. In P. F. Dell & J. A. O'Neill (Eds.), *Dissociation and Dissociative Disorders: DSM-V and Beyond* (pp. 277–285). Routledge.

Benishek, D., & Wichowski, H. (2003). Dissociation in Adults With a Diagnosis of Substance Abuse. *Nursing Times*, 99(20), 34–36.

Bowlby, J. (1988). *A Secure Base: Clinical Applications of Attachment Theory*. Routledge.

Brand, B. L., Myrick, A. C., Loewenstein, R. J., Classen, C. C., Lanius, R., McNary, S. W., & Putnam, F. W. (2012). A survey of practices and recommended treatment interventions among expert therapists treating patients with dissociative identity disorder and dissociative disorder not otherwise specified. *Psychological Trauma: Theory, Research, Practice, and Policy*, 4(5), 490.

Brand, B. L., Schielke, H. J., Putnam, K. T., Putnam, F. W., Loewenstein, R. J., Myrick, A., Jepsen, E. K. K., Langeland, W., Steele, K., Classen, C. C. and Lanius, R.A. (2019). An Online Educational Program for Individuals With Dissociative

Disorders and Their Clinicians: 1-Year and 2-Year Follow-Up. *Journal of Traumatic Stress*, 32: 156–166. doi:10.1002/jts.22370.

Brand, B. L., Schielke, H. J., Schiavone, F., & Lanius, R.A. (2022). *Finding Solid Ground: Overcoming Obstacles in Trauma Treatment*. Oxford University Press.

Braun, B. G. (1988). The BASK model of dissociation. *Dissociation*, 1(1), 4–23.

Brewerton, T. D. (2019) An Overview of Trauma-Informed Care and Practice for Eating Disorders, *Journal of Aggression, Maltreatment & Trauma*, 28(4), 445–462, doi:10.1080/10926771.2018.1532940.

Burger, J. M. (1984), Desire for control, locus of control, and proneness to depression. *Journal of Personality*, 52(1) 71–89. doi:10.1111/j.1467-6494.1984.tb00551.x.

Carey, B. (2008). H.M., an Unforgettable Amnesiac, Dies at 82. http://www.nytimes.com/2008/12/05/us/05hm.html?pagewanted=all&_r=0.

Carlat, D. (2012). *The Psychiatric Interview, A Practical Guide*, 3rd ed, Lippicott, Williams, & Wilkins.

Caul, D. (1978, May). Hypnotherapy in the treatment of multiple personalities. In Workshop on multiple personality at the American Psychiatric Association annual convention, Atlanta.

Center for Disease Control and Prevention. Injury Prevention & Control: Division of Violence Prevention (2014). http://www.cdc.gov/violenceprevention/acestudy/.

Chandler, D. G. (2009). *The Campaigns of Napoleon*. Scribner.

Christensen, E. M. (2022). The online community: DID and plurality. *European Journal of Trauma & Dissociation*, 6(2), 100257.

Chefetz, R. (2015). *Intensive Psychotherapy for Persistent Dissociative Processes: The Fear of Being Real*. W.W. Norton & Co.

Chefetz, R. A. (1997). Special case transferences countertransferences in the treatment of dissociative disorders. *Dissociation*, 10(4), 255–265.

Chu, J. (2011). *Rebuilding Shattered Lives*, 2nd ed. Wiley & Sons, Inc.

Ciszkowski, G. (In press). *Saving Grace*.

Clayton, K (2004) The interrelatedness of disconnection; The relationship between dissociative tendencies and alexithymia, *Journal of Trauma and Dissociation*, 5(1), 77–101.

Coker, A. L., Weston, R., Creson, D. L., Justice, B., & Blakeney, P. (2005). PTSD symptoms among men and women survivors of intimate partner violence: The role of risk and protective factors. *Violence and Victims*, 20(6), 625–643. doi:10.1891/088667005780927421.

Connors, K. J., Kemper, E. J., Hamel, J., & Ensign, C. (2008). Dissociation among domestic violence clients. Presentation at the 25th International Conference of the International Society for the Study of Trauma and Dissociation, Chicago, IL.

Connors, K. J., & Mayhew, C. W. (2006). The "Difficult" Client: Complex inter-relationships among dissociative identity disorder, complex post–traumatic stress disorder, borderline personality disorder and disorganized attachment. Presentation at the 23rd International Conference of the International Society for the Study of Trauma and Dissociation, Los Angeles, CA.

Courtois, C., & Ford, J. (2013). *Treating Complex Trauma: A Sequenced, Relationship-Based Approach*. Guilford.

Courtois, C. A., & Ford, J. D. (Eds.). (2020). *Treating complex traumatic stress disorders in: scientific foundations and therapeutic models*. Guilford Press.

Crenshaw, K. (2018). She Coined the Term "Intersectionality" over 30 Years Ago. Here's What it Means Today. *Time Magazine*. https://time.com/5786710/kimberle-crenshaw-intersectionality/.

Dalai Lama, & Cutler, H. (1998). *The Art of Happiness: A Handbook for Living*. Riverhead Books.

Dalenberg, C., (2013). Countertransference and Transference Crises in Working with Traumatized Patients, Plenary. ISSTD Annual Conference, October 23–27, Long Beach, California.

Dalenberg, C. J., Brand, B. L., Gleaves, D. H., Dorahy, M. J., Loewenstein, R. J., Cardena, E. …Spiegel, D. (2012). Evaluation of the evidence for the trauma and fantasy models of dissociation. *Psychological bulletin*, 138(3), 550.

Dallam, S. J. (2001). The Long-term Medical Consequences of Childhood Maltreatment. In Franey, K., Geffner, R., & Falconer, R. (Eds.), *The cost of child maltreatment: Who pays? We all do*. Family Violence & Sexual Assault Institute.

Dallam, S. J. (2012). *A Model of the Retraumatization Process: A Meta-Synthesis of Childhood Sexual Abuse Survivors' Experiences in Healthcare*. Dissertation, University of Kansas.

Daniels, J. K., Frewen, P., Theberge, J., & Lanius, R. A. (2016). Structural brain aberrations associated with the dissociative subtype of post-traumatic stress disorder. *Acta Psychiatrica Scandinavica*, 133(3), 232–240.

Danylchuk, L. (2015). *Counseling Adolescents: Trauma and group process*. Harvard Graduate School of Education.

Davis, Denise E. (2008) *Terminating Therapy: A Professional Guide to Ending on a Positive Note*. Wiley & Sons.

DeAngelis, T. (2008). Coping with a client's suicide. *GradPSYCH Magazine*, 11.

Dell, P. (2006). The Multidimensional Inventory of Dissociation: (MID): A Comprehensive Measure of Pathological Dissociation. *Journal of Trauma and Dissociation*, 7(2), 77–106.

Dell, P., & O'Neill, J. (Eds) (2009). *Dissociation and the Dissociative Disorders: DSM-V and Beyond*. Routledge.

Deng, H., Xiao, X., & Wang, Z. (2016). Periaqueductal Gray Neuronal Activities Underlie Different Aspects of Defensive Behaviors. *The Journal of Neuroscience: The official journal of the Society for Neuroscience*, 36(29), 7580–7588. doi:10.1523/JNEUROSCI.4425-15.2016.

Derogatis, L. R., Lipman, R. S., Rickels, K., Uhlenhuth, E. H., & Covi, L. (1974). The Hopkins Symptom Checklist (HSCL): A self-report symptom inventory. *Behavioral science*, 19(1), 1–15.

Derogatis, L. R., & Savitz, K. L. (1999). The SCL-90-R, Brief Symptom Inventory, and Matching Clinical Rating Scales. In M. E. Maruish (Ed.), *The use of psychological testing for treatment planning and outcomes assessment* (pp. 679–724). Lawrence Erlbaum Associates Publishers.

Derogatis, L. R., & Unger, R. 2010. Symptom Checklist-90-Revised. *Corsini Encyclopedia of Psychology*. Sheppard Pratt Hospital and Johns Hopkins University School of Medicine & Towson University. http://psycnet.apa.org/index.cfm?fa=search.display Record&uid=1999-02767-022#.

Dorahy, M. J., Corry, M., Shannon, M., Webb, K., McDermott, B., Ryan, M., & Dyer, K. F. (2013). Complex trauma and intimate relationships: The impact of shame, guilt and dissociation. *Journal of affective disorders*, 147(1–3),72–79.

Duncan, B., Miller, S., Wampold, B., & Hubble, M. (Eds) (2009). *The Heart and Soul of Change: Delivering What Works in Therapy*, 2nd Ed. American Psychological Association.

Edwards, K. M., Kamat, R., Tomfohr, L. M., Ancoli-Israel, S., & Dimsdale, J. E. (2014). Obstructive sleep apnea and neurocognitive performance: The role of cortisol. *Sleep Medicine*, 15(1), 27–32. doi:10.1016/j.sleep.2013.08.789.

Eells, T. D. (2015). *Psychotherapy case formulation*. American Psychological Association.

Ellis, Thomas E., Patel, Amee B., (2012) Client Suicide: What Now?*Cognitive and Behavioral Practice*, 19, 277–287.

Erikson, E. H. (1994). *Identity and the life cycle*. WW Norton & Company.

Erikson, E. H. (1950). *Childhood and Society*. W. W. Norton & Company.

Felitti, V. J., Anda, R. F., Nordenberg, D., Williamson, D. F., Spitz, A. M., Edwards, V., Koss, M. P., & Marks, J. S. (1998). Relationship of childhood abuse and household dysfunction to many of the leading causes of death in adults. The Adverse Childhood Experiences (ACE) Study. *American Journal of Preventive Medicine*, 14(4), 245–258.

Fine, C., & Berkowitz, A. (2001). The Wreathing Protocol: The Imbrication of Hypnosis and EMDR in the Treatment of Dissociative Identity Disorder and other Dissociative Responses. *American Journal of Clinical Hypnosis*, 43(3–4), 275–290.

Fink, A. M. (2020). Sleep neurobiology and the critical care environment. *Critical Care Nurse*, 40(4), e1–e6.

First, M. B., Williams, J. B., Karg, R. S., & Spitzer, R. L. (2015). *User's guide for the structured clinical interview for DSM-5 disorders, research version (SCID-5-RV)*. American Psychiatric Association.

Foote, B., Smolin, M,. Kaplan, M., Legatt, M., & Lipshitz, D. (2006). Prevalence of Dissociative Disorders in Psychiatric Outpatients. *The American Journal of Psychiatry*, 163(4), 623–629.

Ford, Julian D., & Gomez, Jennifer M. (2015). The Relationship of Psychological Trauma and Dissociative and Posttraumatic Stress Disorders to Nonsuicidal Self-Injury and Suicidality: A Review. *Journal of Trauma and Dissociation*, 16, 232–271.

Ford, J., & Smith, S. (2008). Complex posttraumatic stress disorder in trauma-exposed adults receiving public sector outpatient substance abuse disorder treatment, *Addiction Research & Theory*, 16(2), 193.

Ford, J. D., & Courtois C. (2020) *Treating Complex Traumatic Stress Disorders in Adults*, 2nd ed. Guilford.

Ford, J. D., & Smith, S. F. (2008). Complex posttraumatic stress disorder in trauma-exposed adults receiving public sector outpatient substance abuse disorder treatment. *Addiction Research & Theory*, 16(2), 193–203.

Forner, C. (2015). Depersonalization disorder after intense meditation. Dissociative-Disorders@Listserv.Icors.Org.

Frankel. A. S. (2015). *Beyond the professional will: Three things they didn't teach us in graduate school*. San Francisco Psychological Association.

Frankel, S., & Alban, A. (2013). Suicide: Risk Management Considerations. *The California Psychologist*, 46(3).https://www.cpapsych.org/page/423.

Freud, S. (1953). Introductory lectures on psycho-analysis (1916–17). In J. Strachey (Trans and Ed) *The standard edition of the complete psychological works of Sigmund Freud*, Vol. 16. The Hogarth Press, and Institute of Psychoanalysis.

Freyd, J. J., Klest, B., & Allard, C. B. (2005). Betrayal trauma: Relationship to physical health, psychological distress, and a written disclosure intervention. *Journal of trauma & dissociation*, 6(3), 83–104.

Fromm, E. (1988). *To Have or To Be*. Open Road.

Galaway, B., & Hudson, J. (1996). *Restorative justice: international perspectives*. Criminal Justice Press.

Gerson, M. J. (2014). Clinical Implications for the Expressions of Self and Identity in Adolescent Psychotherapy: Case Studies of a Vampiress and a Gangster. *Psychoanalytic Dialogues*, 24(6), 718–732.

Gielen, N., Havermans, R.C., Tekelenburg, M. & Jansen, A., (2012) Prevalence of post-traumatic stress disorder among patients with substance use disorder: It is higher than clinicians think it is, *European Journal of Psychotraumatology*, 3(1), doi:10.3402/ejpt.v3i0.17734.

Giordano, A. L., Prosek, E. A., Stamman, J., Callahan, M. M., Loseu, S., Bevly, C. M., Cross, K., Woehler, E. S., Calzada, R.-M. R., & Chadwell, K. (2016). Addressing trauma in substance abuse treatment. *Journal of Alcohol and Drug Education*, 60(2), 55–71. https://www.jstor.org/stable/48514566.

Gomez, F., Kilpela, L. S., Middlemass, K. M., & Becker, C. B. (2021). Sexual trauma uniquely associated with eating disorders: A replication study. *Psychological Trauma: Theory, Research, Practice, and Policy*, 13(2), 202–205.

Gonzalez, A., Mosquera, D., & Morrison, M. R. (2012). *EMDR and dissociation: The progressive approach*. AI.

Goode, E., (2001). Patient Suicide Brings Therapists Lasting Pain. *NY Times*, January 16, 2001, Section F, p.1.

Guze, B., Richeimer, S., & Siegel, D. (1990). *The Handbook of Psychiatry: Residents of the UCLA Department of Psychiatry*. Year Book Medical Publishers, Inc..

Hassan, S. (1988). *Combating Cult Mind Control*. Park Press.

Henning, J. A., Brand, B., & Courtois, C. A. (2021). Graduate training and certification in trauma treatment for clinical practitioners. *Training and Education in Professional Psychology*. doi:10.1037/tep0000326.

Herman, J. (1997). *Trauma and Recovery: The Aftermath of violence – From Domestic Abuse to Political Terror*. Basic Books.

Horn, S. (2003). *Take the Bully by the Horns: Stop Unethical, Uncooperative, or Unpleasant People from Running and Ruining Your Life*. St. Martin's Press.

Howard, B. J. (1991). Discipline in early childhood. *Pediatric Clinics of North America*, 38 (6), 1351–1369.

Howard, H. A. (2017). Promoting safety in hypnosis: A clinical instrument for the assessment of alertness. *American Journal of Clinical Hypnosis*, 59(4), 344–362.

Howell, E. F. (2011). *Understanding and treating dissociative identity disorder: A relational approach*. Routledge.

Hubel, D. H., Wiesel, T. N., (1970), *The period of susceptibility to the physiological effects of unilateral eye closure in kittens*. The Journal of Physiology, 206 doi:10.1113/jphysiol.1970.sp009022..

International Society for the Study of Trauma and Dissociation. (2011). Guidelines for Treating Dissociative Identity Disorder in Adults, Third Revision, *Journal of Trauma and Dissociation.12*(2), 115–187.

Iverson, K. M., Gradus, J. L., Resick, P. A., Suvak, M. K., Smith, K. F., & Monson, C. M. (2011). Cognitive-behavioral therapy for PTSD and depression symptoms reduces risk for future intimate partner violence among interpersonal trauma survivors. *Journal of consulting and clinical psychology*, 79(2), 193–202. doi:10.1037/a0022512.

Iverson, K. M., Litwack, S. D., Pineles, S. L., Suvak, M. K., Vaughn, R. A., & Resick, P. A. (2013). Predictors of intimate partner violence revictimization: The relative impact of distinct PTSD symptoms, dissociation, and coping strategies. *Journal of traumatic stress*, 26(1), 102–110.

Ivey-Stephenson, A. Z., Demissie, Z., Crosby, A. E., et al. (2019). Suicidal Ideation and Behaviors Among High School Students—Youth Risk Behavior Survey, United States. *MMWR Suppl 2020*, 69(Suppl. 1), 47–55. doi:10.15585/mmwr.su6901a6.

Janet, P. (1907) *The Major Symptoms of Hysteria*. Macmillan.

Jordan, J. R., & McIntosh, J. L. (Eds.) (2014). *Grief After Suicide. Understanding the Consequences and Caring for the Survivors.* Routledge.

Karadag, F., Sar, V., Tamar-Gurol, D., Evren, C., Karagoz, M., & Erkiran, M. (2005). Disorders among inpatients with drug or alcohol dependency. *Journal of Clinical Psychiatry*, 66(10), 1247–1253.

Karpman, S. (1968). Fairy Tales and Script Drama Analysis. *Transactional Analysis Bulletin*, 7(26), 39–42. http://www.karpmandramatriangle.com/index.html.

Kincheski, G. C., Mota-Ortiz, S. R., Pavesi, E., Canteras, N. S., & Carobrez, A. P. (2012). The dorsolateral periaqueductal gray and its role in mediating fear learning to life threatening events. *PloS one*, 7(11), e50361. https://doi.org/10.1371/journal.pone.0050361.

King, Lynda A., King, Daniel W., Leskin, Gregory Alan, & Foy, David W. (1995). The Los Angeles Symptom Checklist: a self-report measure of posttraumatic stress disorder. *Assessment*, 2, 1–17. http://www.ptsd.va.gov/professional/assessment/adult-sr/lasc.asp.

Kinsler, Philip J. (2018). *Complex Psychological Trauma: The Centrality of Relationship.* Routledge.

Kluft, R. (1993). The Initial Stages of Psychotherapy in the Treatment of Multiple Personality Disorder Patients. *Dissociation*, 1(2/3), 145.

Kluft, R. & Fine, C. (Eds.) (1993). *Clinical Perspectives on Multiple Personality Disorder.* American Psychiatric Press.

Kluft, R. (2012). Issues in the Detection of Those Suffering Adverse Effects in Hypnosis Training Workshops. *American Journal of Clinical Hypnosis*, 54: 213–232.

Kluft, R. P. (2013). *Shelter from the storm: Processing the traumatic memories of DID/DDNOS patients with the fractionated abreaction technique.* CreatSpace Independent Publishing Platform.

Kuo, J. R., Kaloupek, D. G., & Woodward, S. H. (2012). Amygdala volume in combat-exposed veterans with and without posttraumatic stress disorder: a cross-sectional study. *Archives of general psychiatry*, 69(10), 1080–1086.

Kulkarni, M., Porter, K. E., & Rauch, S. A. (2012). Anger, dissociation, and PTSD among male veterans entering into PTSD treatment. *Journal of Anxiety Disorders*, 26 (2), 271–278.

Lanius, R., Brand, B., Vermetten, E., Freewin, P. A., & Spiegel, D. (2012). The dissociative subtype of posttraumatic stress disorder: Rationale, clinical and neurobiological evidence, and implications. *Depression and Anxiety*, 29, 701–708.

Lanius, U, Paulsen, S., & Corrigan, F. (2014). *Neurobiology and the Treatment of Traumatic Dissociation: Towards an Embodied Self.* Springer Press.

Lanius, R. A., Wolf, E. J., Miller, M. W., Frewen, P. A., Vermetten, E., Brand, B., & Spiegel, D. (2014). The dissociative subtype of PTSD. *Handbook of PTSD: Science and Practice* (pp. 234–250), Routledge.

LeDoux, J. (1996). Emotional networks and motor control: a fearful view. *Progress in Brain Research*, 107, 437.

Leslie, R. (2008). Confidentiality/Privilege, Death of a Client. CPH & Associates – Avoiding Liability. *Bulletin*, November.

Lewis, H.B. (1971). *Shame and Guilt in Neurosis.* International Universities Press.

Lilly, M. M., & Graham-Bermann, S. A. (2010). Intimate partner violence and PTSD: The moderating role of emotion-focused coping. *Violence and victims*, 25(5), 604–616.

Liotti, G. (1984). Cognitive therapy, attachment theory, and psychiatric nosology: A clinical and theoretical inquiry into their interdependence. In *Cognitive psychotherapies: Recent development in theory, research and practice.* Ballinger.

Liotti, G. (1992) Disorganized/disoriented attachment in the etiology of the dissociative disorders. *Dissociation*, 5(4), 196–204.

Madden, N. (2004). *Psychologists' Skepticism and Knowledge About Dissociative Identity Disorder in Adolescents*. Doctoral Dissertation. Philadelphia College of Osteopathic Medicine, Department of Psychology.

Maier, S. F., & Seligman, M. E. P. (2016). Learned helplessness at fifty: Insights from neuroscience. *Psychological Review*, 123(4), 349–367.

Malik F, & Marwaha R. (2022). *Developmental Stages of Social Emotional Development In Children*. https://www.ncbi.nlm.nih.gov/books/NBK534819/.

Mantakos, S. M. (2008) *Psychometric Properties of the Dissociative Partner Violence Scale*, Unpublished Masters' Thesis.

Menninger, K. (1945). *The Human Mind*. Knopf.

Michl P, Meindl T, Meister F, Born C, Engel RR, Reiser M, Hennig-Fast K (2014). Neurobiological underpinnings of shame and guilt: A pilot fMRI study. *Soc Cogn Affect Neurosci*, 9, 150–157.

Middleton, W. (2013). Ongoing Incestuous Abuse During Adulthood. *Journal of Trauma and Dissociation*. 14(3), 251.

Mushtaq, R., Shoib, S., Shah, T., & Mushtaq, S. (2014). Relationship between loneliness, psychiatric disorders and physical health? A review on the psychological aspects of loneliness. *Journal of clinical and diagnostic research: JCDR*, 8(9), WE01.

Mychailyszyn, M. P., Brand, B. L., Webermann, A. R.Şar, V. & Draijer, N. (2021). Differentiating dissociative from non-dissociative disorders: A meta-analysis of the Structured Clinical Interview for DSM Dissociative Disorders (SCID-D). *Journal of Trauma & Dissociation*. doi:10.1080/15299732.2020.1760169.

Myers, C. S. (1940). *Shell Shock in France 1914–1918*. Cambridge University Press.

Nagoski, E.. (2018). The Truth About Unwanted Arousal. Ted Talks, https://www.ted.com/talks/emily_nagoski_the_truth_about_unwanted_arousal.

Najt, P., Fusar-Poli, P., & Brambilla, P. (2011). Co-occurring mental and substance abuse disorders: A review on the potential predictors and clinical outcomes. *Psychiatry Research*, 186(2–3), 159–164.

Nathanson, D. (1992). *Shame and Pride: Affect, Sex, and the Birth of Self*. W. W. Norton & Co.

Nester, S. M., Brand, B. L., Schielke, H. J., & Kumar, S., (2022). An examination of the relations between emotion dysregulation, dissociation, and self-injury among dissociative disorder patients. *European Journal of Psychotraumatology*, 13(1). doi:10.1080/20008198.2022.2031592.

Nester, S., Boi, C., Brand, B., & Schielke H., (2022). The reasons dissociative disorder patients self-injure. *European Journal of Psychotraumatology*, 13(1). doi:10.1080/20008198.2022.2026738.

Newton, N. J., Chauhan, P. K., & Pates, J. L. (2020). Facing the future: Generativity, stagnation, intended legacies, and well-being in later life. *Journal of Adult Development*, 27(1), 70–80.

Nijenhuis, E. R., Spinhoven, P., Dyck, R. V., Hart, O. V. D., & Vanderlinden, J. (1997). The development of the somatoform dissociation questionnaire (SDQ-5) as a screening instrument for dissociative disorders. *Acta Psychiatrica Scandinavica*, 96(5), 311–318.

Nijenhuis, E. & Van der Hart, O. (2011) Dissociation in Trauma: A New Definition and Comparison with Previous Formulations. *Journal of Trauma and Dissociation*, 12, 417.

Nilsson, D., Lejonclou, A., & Holmqvist, R. (2020). Psychoform and somatoform dissociation among individuals with eating disorders. *Nordic Journal of Psychiatry*, 74(1), 1–8.

Norcross, J. (2011). *Psychotherapy Relationships That Work: Evidence-Based Responsiveness.* Oxford University Press.

Norcross, J. C., & Lambert, M. J. (2014). Relationship science and practice in psychotherapy: closing commentary. *Psychotherapy*, 51(3), 398.

Ogden, P., Minton, K., & Pain, C. (2006). *Trauma and the Body: A Sensorimotor Approach to Psychotherapy.* W. W. Norton.

Orenstein, G. A., & Lewis, L. (2021). Erikson's Stages of Psychosocial Development. https://www.ncbi.nlm.nih.gov/books/NBK556096/.

Ounes, S., & Popp, J., (2019). High Cortisol and the Risk of Dementia and Alzheimer's Disease: A Review of the Literature. *Frontiers in Aging Neuroscience* 11. https://www.frontiersin.org/article/10.3389/fnagi.2019. doi:10.3389/fnagi.2019.000431.

Parish-Plass, N. (2021). Animal-assisted psychotherapy for developmental trauma through the lens of interpersonal neurobiology of trauma: Creating connection with self and others. *Journal of Psychotherapy Integration*, 31(3), 302.

Perez, S., Johnson, D. M., & Wright, C. V. (2012). The attenuating effect of empowerment on IPV-related PTSD symptoms in battered women living in domestic violence shelters. *Violence against women*, 18(1), 102–117.

Perls, F., Hefferline, G., & Goodman, P. (1951). *Gestalt therapy: Excitement and Growth in the Human Personality.* Blackwells.

Perry, B. D. (2001). The neurodevelopmental impact of violence in childhood. In D. Schetky & E. P. Benedek (Eds), *Textbook of Child and Adolescent Forensic Psychiatry* (pp. 221–238), American Psychiatric Press, Inc.

Peters, S. K., Dunlop K., & Downar, J. (2016). Cortico-striatal-thalamic loop circuits of the salience network: A central pathway in psychiatric disease and treatment. *Frontiers in Systems Neuroscience*, 10. doi:10.3389/fnsys.2016.00104.

Piaget, J. (1952). *The origins of intelligence in children.* International Universities Press.

Pisani, A. R., Murrie, D. C. & Silverman, M. M. (2016), Reformulating Suicide Risk Formulation: From Prediction to Prevention. *Acad Psychiatry*, 40, 623–629 doi:10.1007/s40596-015-0434-6.

Platt, M. G., & Freyd, J. J. (2015). Betray my trust, shame on me: Shame, dissociation, fear, and betrayal trauma. *Psychological Trauma: Theory, Research, Practice, and Policy*, 7 (4), 398.

Porges, Stephen W. (2021). *Polyvagal Safety.* W. W. Norton, New York.

Putnam, W., Guroff, J. J., Silberman, E. K., Barban, L., & Post, R.M. (1986) The clinical phenomenology of multiple personality disorder: review of 100 recent cases. *Journal of Clinical Psychiatry*, 47, 285–293.

Putnam, F. W. (1990). *Child Dissociative Checklist (CDC)* [Database record]. APA PsycTests. doi:10.1037/t02069-000.

Reinders, A. A. T. S., Willemsen, A. T., Vos, H. P., den Boer, J. A., & Nijenhuis, E. R. (2012). Fact or factitious? A psychobiological study of authentic and simulated dissociative identity states. *PloS one*, 7(6), e39279.

Reinders, A. A. T. S., Chalavi, S., Schlumpf, Y. R., Vissia, E. M., Nijenhuis, E. R. S., Jäncke, L., Veltman, D. J., & Ecker, C. (2018). Neurodevelopmental origins of abnormal cortical morphology in dissociative identity disorder. *Acta Psychiatrica Scandinavica*, 137(2), 157–170.

Reinders, A., & Veltman, D. (2021). Dissociative identity disorder: Out of the shadows at last? *The British Journal of Psychiatry*, 219(2), 413–414. doi:10.1192/bjp.2020.168.

Rosen, S. (Ed.) (1982). *My Voice Will Go With You: The teaching tales of Milton H. Erickson.* W. W. Norton.

Ross, C. (1996–2007). Dissociative Disorders Interview Schedule. http://www.rossinst.com/ddis.html.

Ross, C. (2007). *The Trauma Model: A solution to the problem of comorbidity in psychiatry.* Manitou Communications, Inc.

Ross, C. A., & Halpern, N. (2009). *Trauma Model Therapy: A Treatment Approach for Trauma Dissociation & Complex Comorbidity.* Manitou Communications, Inc.

Runyan, D. K., Dunne, M. P., Zolotor, A. J., Madrid, B., Jain, D., Gerbaka, B., ... & Youssef, R. M. (2009). The development and piloting of the ISPCAN Child Abuse Screening Tool—Parent version (ICAST-P). *Child abuse & neglect*, 33(11), 826–832.

Ruskin, R., Sakinofsky, I., Bagby, R. M., Dickens, S., & Sousa, G. (2004). Impact of patient suicide on psychiatrists and psychiatric trainees. *Academic Psychiatry*, 28(2), 104–110.

Sachs, A. (2013). Boundary modifications in the treatment of people with dissociative disorders: A pilot study. *Journal of Trauma & Dissociation*, 14 (2), 159. doi:10.1080/15299732.2012.714677.

Sanders, S., Jacobson, J. M., & Ting, L. (2008). Preparing for the inevitable: Training social workers to cope with client suicide. *Journal of Teaching in Social Work*, 28(1–2), 1–18.

Sar, V., & Öztürk, E. (2007) Functional Dissociation of the Self: A Sociocognitive Approach to Trauma and Dissociation, *Journal of Trauma & Dissociation*, 8(4). doi:10.1300/J229v08n04_05.

Seeley, W. W., Menon, V., Schatzberg, A. F., Keller, J., Glover, G. H., Kenna, H., Reiss, A. L., & Greicius, M. D., (2007) Dissociable intrinsic connectivity networks for salience processing and executive control. *Journal of Neuroscience.* 27(9) 2349–2356; doi:10.1523/JNEUROSCI.5587-06.2007.

Seeley, W. W. (2019). The Salience Network: A Neural System for Perceiving and Responding to Homeostatic Demands. *Journal of Neuroscience.* 39(50) 9878–9882. doi:10.1523/JNEUROSCI.1138-17.2019.

Sege, R. D., & Harper Browne, C. (2017). Responding to ACEs with HOPE: Health outcomes from positive experiences. *Academic Pediatrics*, 17(7S), S79–S85.

Siegel, D. J. (2012). *The Developing Mind: How Relationships and the Brain Interact to Shape Who We Are*, 2nd ed. Guilford Press.

Siegel, D. J. (2020). *The Developing Mind: How Relationships and the Brain Interact to Shape Who We Are*, 3rd ed. Guilford Press.

Silverman, A. B., Reinherz, H. Z., & Giaconia, R. M. (1996). The Long-term Sequelae of Child and Adolescent Abuse: A Longitudinal Community Study. *Child Abuse and Neglect*, 20(8), 709–723.

Soral, W., Kofta, M., & Bukowski, M. (2021). Helplessness experience and intentional (un-) binding: Control deprivation disrupts the implicit sense of agency. *Journal of Experimental Psychology: General*, 150(2), 289–305.

Steinberg, M. (1993). *Structured Clinical Interview for DSM-IV Dissociative Disorders (SCID-D).* American Psychiatric Press.

Stolorow, (2015). A phenomenological-contextual, existential, and ethical perspective on emotional trauma. *Psychoanalytic Review*, 102(1), 124.

Sung, J. (2016). Sample individual practitioner practices for responding to client suicide. www.cliniciansurvivor.org.

Svrakic, D. M., & Zorumski, C. F. (2021). Neuroscience of Object Relations in Health and Disorder: A Proposal for an Integrative Model. *Frontiers in psychology*, 12, 583743.

Tagay, S., Schlottbohm, E., Reyes-Rodriguez, M. L., Repic, N. & Senf, W. (2014) Eating Disorders, Trauma, PTSD, *and Psychosocial Resources, Eating Disorders, The Journal of Treatment & Prevention* 22(1), 33–49. doi:10.1080/10640266.2014.857517.

Tatomir, A., Micu, C., & Crivii, C. (2014). The impact of stress and glucocorticoids on memory. *Clujul medical*, 87(1), 3–6. doi:10.15386/cjm.2014.8872.871.at1cm2.

Taylor, T. (2015). The Influence of Shame on Posttrauma disorders: Have We Failed to See the Obvious? *European Journal of Psychotraumatology*, 6.

Teicher, M. H., Andersen, S. L., Polcari, A., Anderson, C. M., Navalta, C. P., & Kim, D. M. (2003). The neurobiological consequences of early stress and childhood maltreatment. *Neuroscience & Biobehavioral Reviews*, 27(1), 36.

Teicher, M. H., & Samson, J. A. (2016). Annual Research Review: Enduring neurobiological effects of childhood abuse and neglect. *Journal of Child Psychology & Psychiatry*, 57(3), 241–266.

Teicher, M. (2008). Abuse and Sensitive Periods. https://drteicher.wordpress.com/2008/12/14/hello-world/.

Terr, L. (1991). Childhood Traumas: An Outline and Overview. *American Journal of Psychiatry*, 148(1), 12–16.

Tillman, J. G. (2006). When a patient commits suicide: An empirical study of psychoanalytic clinicians. *The International Journal of Psycho-Analysis*, 87, 159–177.

Van Derbur, M. (2003). Miss America By Day. Oak Hill Ridge Press.

Van der Hart, O., Nijenhuis, E., & Steele, K. (2006). *The Haunted Self: Structural Dissociation and the Treatment of Chronic Traumatization*. W. W. Norton & Co.

Van der Kolk, B.A., & Greenburg, M. S. (1987) The Psychobiology of the Trauma Response: Hyperarousal, Constriction, and Addiction to Traumatic Exposure. In B.A. van der Kolk (Ed.), *Psychological Trauma* (pp. 63–88). American Psychiatric Press.

Vissia, E. M., Giesen, M. E., Chalavi, S., Nijenhuis, E. RS., Draijer, N., Brand, B., & Reinders, A. A. T. S. (2016). Is it Trauma- or Fantasy-based? Comparing dissociative identity disorder, post-traumatic stress disorder, simulators, and controls. *Acta Psychiatrica Scandinavica*. doi:10.1111/acps.12590.

Weathers, F. W., Litz, B. T., Keane, T. M., Palmieri, P. A., Marx, B. P., & Schnurr, P. P. (2013). The PTSD Checklist for DSM-5 (PCL-5). http://www.ptsd.va.gov/professional/assessment/adult-sr/ptsd-checklist.asp.

Webb, T. (2010). Compass of shame-avoidant behaviours and masking emotions. Developed from Nathanson, D. L. (1992) *Shame and pride*. Norton. http://www.ejpt.net/index.php/ejpt/article/view/28847.

Webermann, A., Myrich, A., Taylor, C., Chasson, G, & Brand, B. (2016). Dissociative, depressive, and PTSD symptom severity as correlates of nonsuicidal self-injury and suicidality in dissociative disorder patients, *Journal of Trauma & Dissociation*, 17(1), 67–80, doi:10.1080/15299732.2015.1067941.

Webermann, A. R., Brand, B. L., & Chasson, G. S. (2014). Childhood maltreatment and intimate partner violence in dissociative disorder patients. *European Journal of Psychotraumatology*, 5(1), 24568.

Weems, C. F., Russell, J. D., Herringa, R. J., & Carrion, V. G. (2021). Translating the neuroscience of adverse childhood experiences to inform policy and foster population-level resilience. *American Psychologist*, 76(2), 188.

Westerhof, G. J., Bohlmeijer, E. T., & McAdams, D. P. (2017) The Relation of Ego Integrity and Despair to Personality Traits and Mental Health, *The Journals of Gerontology: Series B*, 72(3), 400–407. doi:10.1093/geronb/gbv062.

Widom, C., Marmorstein, N., & White, H. (2006). Childhood victimization and illicit drug use in middle adulthood. *Psychology of Addictive Behaviors*. 20(4), 394–403.

Wurmser, L. (1981). *The Mask of Shame*. Johns Hopkins University Press.

Zerubavel, N., Messman-Moore, T. L., DiLillo, D., & Gratz, K. L. (2018). Childhood sexual abuse and fear of abandonment moderate the relation of intimate partner violence to severity of dissociation. *Journal of Trauma & Dissociation*, 19(1), 9–24.

Zoroglu, S. S., Tuzun, U., Sar, V., Tutkun, H., Savaş, H. A., Ozturk, M., Alyanak, B. & Kora, M. E. (2003). Suicide attempt and self-mutilation among Turkish high school students in relation with abuse, neglect and dissociation. *Psychiatry and Clinical Neurosciences*, 57, 119–126. doi:10.1046/j.1440–1819.2003.01088.x.

Index

clients 65; with alexithymia 129–130;
behavior 4; with complex trauma
66; with dissociative issues 65–66;
emotional space 119; personality
styles 65–67; personal resources 71;
phenomenological experience of 34;
phenomenological presentation 7;
self-reflection 125
co-consciousness 70
cognitive development of child 9
cognitive distortions 55
cognitive maps 11
cognitive schema 10, 140
collaborative/collaboration 74–77, 127;
goal setting 124–128; inquiry 60;
modeling of rational authority
117–119; process 124
comforting 74–75, 79–80
communication 74–77, 127; internal
methods of 80; methods of 161
comorbidity 53–54
compartmentalization 23
complex post-traumatic stress disorder
(c-PTSD) 7–9, 39, 49, 56, 63, 75–77,
171, 186, 202
complex trauma 8, 18–36, 47–48, 72, 90,
91, 93, 239; BASK model 28–30; and
dissociation 20–26; Ego State model
27–28; etiology 34–35; Sequential
Model 30–31; Trauma Model
31–33
Complex Trauma Disorder 94
complex traumatic experiences 87
conditioned paranoia 169
conditioning 114–115, 162, 164,
168, 170
confidentiality 217
conflict, overwhelming 22
confucian 212
confusion 64, 115
Connors, K. J. 50
consciousness 109, 167–168
constant hypervigilance 38
containment 74–75, 80; strategies 80
control behavior (EN) 105
control network (EN) 41
control problem, locus of 32
coping skills 103
corpus callosum 37, 45
countertransference 109, 131–132
creating safety 73–74
creating stability 74–75
Crenshaw, K. 4
critical thinking skills 127

cultural traditions 58
cumulative trauma 31

Dalenberg, C. J. 101
Dallam, S. 150
Dalle Grave, R. 51
Davis, D. 216
DD *see* dissociative disorders (DD)
DDNOS category 47–48
dealing with anger 199–202
declarative memory 38
decompensating, risk of 87
Dell, P. 24, 56
dependency *vs.* support 103–105
depersonalization 5, 23, 47, 56, 57, 80
derealization 5, 23, 26, 41, 47, 56, 57,
65, 80
DES-Taxon 50–51
developmental/developments 189;
critical stages of 20; dynamics 10;
trauma 9–11 *see also* complex trauma;
etiology 34–35
diagnosis 47; prevalence 48–52; tools and
structural interviews 56–58
diagnostic tools and structural interviews
56–58; informal assessment 63–67;
initial psychiatric assessment 59;
screening and diagnostic tests 59
Dickinson, E. 20
DID *see* dissociative identity disorder
(DID)
difficult emotions, 195
discipline, forms of 61
discordant emotions 8
discrimination, process of 44
disorganized attachment 96
dissociative amnesia 5
dissociative clients 25, 26, 75, 104,
160–161
dissociative defenses 25, 90, 238
dissociative disorders (DD) 23, 47, 73,
84–85, 172, 218; diagnosis and
treatment of 54, 55
Dissociative Disorders Interview Schedule
(DDIS) 57; interview schedule:
Dissociative Experiences Scale (DES)
56; Structured Interview for DSM-IV
Dissociative Disorder 54
dissociative/dissociation 6, 11, 20–26,
187–189, 202; comorbidity 53–54;
conceptual models of: BASK model
28–30; Ego State Model 27–28;
Sequential Model 30–31; structural
model 33; definition of 24; description